'This long-overdue study by the Winston father and son duo finally elevates the fake news debate to a completely new, high level, taking in its historical, philosophical, legalistic, scientific and ethical dimensions – and much more. Writing with panache and wit, the authors create a text for all teachers, students and members of the public seeking a reliable – and still challenging – guide through the fake news jungle.'

Richard Lance Keeble, Professor of Journalism,
University of Lincoln

'This book comes at an optimal time, providing the kind of cultural and contextual history missing from a lot of the debates around fake news. Offering countervailing perspectives, *The Roots of Fake News* allows the audience to see how what is taken for granted about journalistic practice and epistemology invites bad actors to exploit often ignored vulnerabilities.'

Brian Creech, Associate Professor of Journalism at the
School of Media and Communication at Temple University

THE ROOTS OF FAKE NEWS

The Roots of Fake News argues that 'fake news' is not a problem caused by the power of the internet, or by the failure of good journalism to assert itself. Rather, it is within the news's ideological foundations – professionalism, neutrality, and most especially objectivity – that the true roots of the current 'crisis' are to be found.

Placing the concept of media objectivity in a fuller historical context, this book examines how current perceptions of a crisis in journalism actually fit within a long history of the ways news media have avoided, obscured, or simply ignored the difficulties involved in promising objectivity, let alone 'truth'. The book examines journalism's relationships with other spheres of human endeavour (science, law, philosophy) concerned with the pursuit of objective truth, to argue that the rising tide of 'fake news' is not an attack on the traditional ideologies which have supported journalism. Rather, it is an inevitable result of their inherent flaws and vulnerabilities.

This is a valuable resource for students and scholars of journalism and history alike who are interested in understanding the historical roots, and philosophical context of a fiercely contemporary issue.

Brian Winston is the Lincoln Professor at the University of Lincoln (UK). He is the author of *A Right to Offend, The Rushdie Fatwa and After* and also writes on documentary film and media technology. He was the founding director of the Glasgow University Media Group.

Matthew Winston is the author of *Gonzo Text: Disentangling Meaning in Hunter S. Thompson's Journalism*. He teaches in the School of Media, Communication and Sociology at the University of Leicester.

THE ROOTS OF FAKE NEWS

Objecting to Objective Journalism

Brian Winston and Matthew Winston

LONDON AND NEW YORK

First published 2021
by Routledge
2 Park Square, Milton Park, Abingdon, Oxon OX14 4RN

and by Routledge
52 Vanderbilt Avenue, New York, NY 10017

Routledge is an imprint of the Taylor & Francis Group, an informa business

© 2021 Brian Winston and Matthew Winston

The right of Brian Winston and Matthew Winston to be identified as authors of this work has been asserted by them in accordance with sections 77 and 78 of the Copyright, Designs and Patents Act 1988.

All rights reserved. No part of this book may be reprinted or reproduced or utilised in any form or by any electronic, mechanical, or other means, now known or hereafter invented, including photocopying and recording, or in any information storage or retrieval system, without permission in writing from the publishers.

Trademark notice: Product or corporate names may be trademarks or registered trademarks, and are used only for identification and explanation without intent to infringe.

British Library Cataloguing-in-Publication Data
A catalogue record for this book is available from the British Library

Library of Congress Cataloging-in-Publication Data
A catalog record has been requested for this book

ISBN: 9780367145453 (hbk)
ISBN: 9780367145460 (pbk)
ISBN: 9780429032264 (ebk)

Typeset in Bembo
by Newgen Publishing UK

in memoriam
**THE VICTIMS
OF
THE BOWLING GREEN MASSACRE
2017**

CONTENTS

Acknowledgements   *xii*

Crisis?   1

Foreword: Roots, fakery, and objectivity   3
'[L]et us count our spoons'

Roots   15

1   'Strange newes': Printed news 1485—   17
'The Frightening and Truly Extraordinary Story'

2   'Newes': The coming of the newspaper 1600—   33
'For the better information of the people'

3   'Booming a newspaper': Newspapers and news-media 1800—   50
'Many a good newspaper story has been ruined by over-verification'

4   'Oh, the humanity!': Legacy news media 1900—   69
'The public interest, convenience, or necessity'

5   Online: Digital news 1980—   84
'I come from Cyberspace, the new home of Mind'

6 'Info wars': News platforms 2000— 97
'But journalism is like the most honoured professions in other ways'

Objecting to objectivity 107

7 Fact: 'Hard' science 109
'What is behind a scientific text? ... Inscriptions'

8 Fact: 'Thick' descriptions 119
'Cultural analysis is intrinsically incomplete'

9 Judgement: The legal mindset 132
'To collect all the proofs on both sides; to compare them'

10 Judgement: The fine print 145
'No provider ... shall be treated as the publisher'

11 Truth: The philosophical approach 155
'Journalism by nature is reactive and practical'

12 Truth: Moral philosophy 166
'Clear and verifiable links between cause and effect are still lacking'

The fourth estate 177

13 Shouting fire on a crowded website 179
'Don't confuse me with the facts. I've got a closed mind'

14 Speaking truth to power 193
'[M]ore important far than they all'

Index *203*

'Pamphlets of news, set out every Saturday, but made all at home, no syllable of truth in them; than which there cannot be a greater disease in nature, nor a fouler scorn put upon the times.'

Ben Jonson, 1625

ACKNOWLEDGEMENTS

This book is a response to the fake news moral panic but it is grounded in a sense that such 21st century brouhahas reflect a deeper malaise in the journalism project. Since the assumption here is an unashamed agreement with the Enlightenment insistence on the critical importance of a free press to democracy, to examine the matter of the deeper ills weakening the press at this time becomes urgent.

Such a task cannot be undertaken but by standing on others' shoulders and we are obviously indebted to all the scholars and reflective journalists cited in the pages that follow. But we also owe a special debt of thanks to Bob Franklin and Paul Bowman, for their support and guidance during Matthew Winston's doctoral study of Hunter S. Thompson's Gonzo journalism, a project from which much of this volume's theoretical framework ultimately derives.

Thanks also to Gail Vanstone, Stephen Knowlton, and Karen Freeman for their insights, and especially to Richard Keeble for a constant stream of illuminating conversation over the years.

Matthew Winston
Brian Winston
Leicester & Lincoln, UK
February 2020

Crisis?

FOREWORD: ROOTS, FAKERY, AND OBJECTIVITY

'[L]et us count our spoons'
    Samuel Johnson, 1709–1784
        Writer

This book is neither a defense of, nor an attack on, journalism, but it is unashamedly anchored in the traditional western belief that independent media are essential to any free and just society. We do not believe that it is outdated or ironic to see the press as an essential part of a functioning democracy, a guard over the guardians, a speaker of truth to power, a comforter of the afflicted and an afflicter of the comfortable. On the contrary, we believe that, without a free press, both public discourse and maybe even democracy itself cannot exist except as ugly caricatures of what they should be. Moreover, we fear that the press's ability to perform its essential functions is increasingly imperiled as it seems to be subject to attack and distrust at historically high levels. Its role as an agent in the social order – however defined – appears threatened. But whether this might or might not amount to a crisis cannot be addressed without a consideration of context; and that is our purpose here.

The press has all too often behaved like Samuel Johnson's amoral writer: 'when he leaves our houses', Dr Johnson advised, 'let us count our spoons'.[1] It is because of journalism's perceived shortcomings and failures to live up to its own lofty ideals, that we distrust it. And such problems are not new. Journalism's fundamental difficulties are in fact far, far older than current panics about supposedly recent plagues of fakery, alt facts and post-truths. They run far, far deeper than the surface upheavals occasioned by 21st-century communication technologies. The crux of the matter is, we contend, the vulnerability to attack which journalism creates through its own claims of virtue – of neutrality and objectivity and truthfulness. Repeated and repeated and repeated is that 'journalism's first obligation is to the truth'.[2] However, in practice, the press leaves aside the challenge of defining truth itself (a question which has been vexing humanity for millennia) and its practice is, and always has been, quite cavalier with the 'truth' – however defined. When it comes to this 'first obligation' the press behaves like 'jesting Pilate'; it does 'not stay for an answer'.[3]

Instantly though, the archives and the daily flood of what we call the news reveal that 'truth' is a rather flexible obligation. The demonstrable historical fact is that, from its 15th-century origins onwards, for the press, 'truth' has in effect always been more of a brand than a promise – more of a sales pitch and marketing slogan than any sort of reliable descriptor of product. If truth is the obligation, then journalism's own standard sets the enterprise up to fail, not just in the sense of striving for an impossible goal – which would not necessarily be a bad thing – but in the sense of rendering ever more visible to the public the fact that the product does not entirely correspond to the manufacturer's claims.

Journalism's subject is the world of externally verifiable 'facts'. The fundamental problem with that is, in whatever the medium, it cannot but present us with signs of these facts – indicators, material reflecting or symbolising this referent; and in the process there is, unavoidably and inevitably, slippage, as there must be between any referent and its sign. (There is a reason an item on a news platform is called a 'story'.) Like any other cultural text, in any medium/form, the news is a representation of reality, not reality itself. Applying a distinction between factual and fictional texts made by documentary film scholar Bill Nichols,[4] what is in play here are the difficulties of any representation ever being **the** story about **the** world. There is no difficulty with fiction – **a** story about **a** world, but journalism's ideal is this impossibility: **the** story about **the** world. In practice, even producing **a** story about **the** world is problematic. A 'true representation' is actually a very complicated concept. As Walter Lippmann, the 20th century journalist as much as any responsible for the rhetorical pretensions of the American press, famously declared: 'News and truth are not the same thing, and must be clearly distinguished'.[5] News/Truth? Defining the news is easier than grappling with the idea of truth.

All journalism is information, but not all information is journalism. There is, for example, gossip. A friend may tell us of a mutual acquaintance leaving their spouse to run away with their personal trainer. Gossip such as this brings interesting new information, but it is not intrinsically any part of 'the news', and the friend is not thought to be acting as a journalist. This remains the case until – if the mutual acquaintance happened to be famous enough – later on the story might show up in the papers, or in any other news medium. Similarly, while there are public statements from authority, whether they are a tweet from a president or a pronouncement from a king, promulgations and official communications of all kinds, are not in themselves 'news' either, though again they may be the subject matter of news. The 'news' is defined not by being, of itself, information, but by being published as such. This is meant in the sense that an earthquake itself is not 'the news'. It is an event. The news report about it is what makes it part of 'the news'. In that sense, we take journalism to be what happens between the earthquake itself and the audience receiving that news report.

In speaking of journalism, we are thus speaking of the processes which relay such information, normally regarding recent events grounded in the actual world – observed and/or independently witnessed – and, supposedly, out of the ordinary ('man bites dog' not 'dog bites man'[6]). These reports and accounts in whatever form are collected into publications generally addressed to the public and disseminated via any media platform. Given the vexations of defining truth, making a value judgement of the processes in terms of 'truthful' journalism being 'good' journalism is of no help. 'Good journalism' is, of course, culturally constructed, like what is meant by having good manners or being a good friend.

And with good journalism (that is, the idea of what journalism should be), as with the other two ideas, most people tend to think that their opinions on what 'good' looks like are not opinions at all. What makes a 'good' journalist is taken to be obvious, rational, natural. Except, of course, as with so many cultural constructions which are dominant (even hegemonic) in any given culture at any given time, this assumption is nonsense. What journalism should be and how it should be done are ideals (or, more properly, ideologies) which change over time and, of course, significantly vary between cultures as well. The assumption that the ideas (which became ascendant in the west only, really, over the last century – give or take – of full representative democracy) are intrinsically the most advanced, the most ethical, and/or simply the best-known way of conceiving of journalism, is, we maintain, problematic to the point of being untenable.

The ideology of good journalism prevalent in the world's secular democracies at the time of writing has become dominant to the point of being effectively all but unquestioned. As a society, we are quite ready to criticise the media for failing to reach the standards this ideology sets, but we do not tend to criticise the standards themselves, that is acknowledge and understand the inherent difficulties of meeting them. Even when we recognise that in the past, as in other countries/cultures, standards and expectations were different, there is now a clear tendency to assert, whether explicitly or implicitly, that 'professional', 'objective' journalism which we expect and demand is obviously superior to any other possible approach.

There have been contrary voices; Gaye Tuchman's, for example. She famously argued in 1972 that in journalism, objectivity may be seen as 'a strategic ritual protecting newspapermen from the risks of their trade'.[7] But today, some journalists, especially those educated in American university schools of journalism, have learned not to claim it too stridently. Outside of academic journalism and the thinking of some practitioners, though, rejection is on shaky ground. Despite these voices, we think the world at large has yet to get the message, and still generally believes that objectivity and 'good' journalism are inseparable. Wanting the following excessive hammering home of this point to be as up to date as possible, the authors will now take a moment out of final preparations of the draft manuscript of this book, ready for submission to our publishers, to type the phrase 'objective journalism' into Google's news search (on the evening of 6 February 2020), and we'll see what we see.

Top result is 'A Salute to Fair and Objective Journalism'.[8] We can't access it here – seems to be blocked in our region – but Google says it starts with the words 'Jim Lehrer died last Thursday at age 85, and with his passing another living example of civility and objectivity in the media is gone'. But it's from something called *The Coos Bay World*, which is apparently a daily paper serving the South Coast of Oregon, and you may want evidence that more prestigious and/or better known publications (no offence intended to the South Coast of Oregon) still reference the concept of objective journalism uncritically. Let us just scroll down ...

Excellent. *The New York Times*. Somebody's 'bent is for deeply immersive stories of the dispossessed in which she dispenses almost entirely with the conventions of objective journalism'.[9] (A description of someone's rejection of these 'conventions' implies that such a rejection is still noteworthy. Nobody bothers to say that a scientist dispenses with the conventions of alchemy; nobody would think of bothering to say it, because that system of thought really is dead.) Scrolling farther down, past suitable uses of the phrase in *The Seattle Times*[10] and *The Jerusalem Post*[11], looking for something perhaps a bit more recognisable ... just a second ... A *National Review* piece with the headline 'Harvard Protesters: Objective Journalism Is "Endangering Undocumented Students"', opening with the words: 'Approximately 50 Harvard University students protested outside of the building of the school's official newspaper, the Harvard Crimson, on Friday – demanding that it stop practicing objective journalism'.[12] Too conservative a publication to be persuasive here; possibly a bit old-fashioned? Hmmm ... How about *The Hill*? That's a website that was founded in the 90s. The piece is called 'Journalism industry falters when nation most needs it' and the sentence that Google noticed on our behalf is 'Producing measured and objective journalism is difficult, but it shouldn't be impossible'.[13]

To be clear, there were also critical, even oppositional mentions, but we hope the point is nonetheless made: reports of the death of objective journalism, as an ideology and as the standard people reach for when they're judging and/or criticising news content, have been greatly exaggerated. (Go ahead. Google it yourself.) Just because the idea has become in many respects untenable, and people are aware of that, does not mean that it is dead, or is even necessarily in the process of dying, in popular discourses and in the popular imagination. And that is our concern: it is possible and, given present circumstances, even necessary on these grounds to begin to object to objectivity itself as the largest worm in journalism's bud.

On first examination, this principle of objective – aka 'professional' – journalism sounds reasonable and viable. The 'good' journalist will not be at all subjective. She will leave her own opinions and convictions and biases completely out of the process as she provides a perfectly objective account of the facts of the story, whatever the story may be. In being perfectly objective, she will be fair and neutral and unbiased and impartial. It sounds great, but the most fundamental problem, the elephant in the corner of the press-room, is that this is not just difficult, but absolutely impossible, without question and without exception.

And not just practically impossible, in the sense that human beings are not in fact able to turn themselves into robots; that the idea of a human being not being subjective is a contradiction in terms. It is also theoretically impossible, in that even an imaginary journalism robot would not be able to produce this 'objective journalism'. There are other issues, most especially the inevitable constraints on what can be found out and/or confirmed, which also contribute to making objective journalism, in a fundamental sense, impossible.

Also, almost totally unexamined in the received ideal of objective journalism, is the fact that even the protocols governing, however imperfectly, the production of 'truth' in other spheres of our culture are routinely unavailable to journalists. It is overwhelmingly the usual case that, in news-gathering, they cannot replicate (as does science), cross-examine under oath (as does the law) or, readily, indulge in epistemological conjecturing (as does philosophy). Circumstances will not allow this.

And as if such problems weren't enough, conveying reports to the public involves opening a series of gates all being kept by equally subjective humans. There has been a significant academic focus on issues of editorial objectivity (i.e. the operations of the aforementioned gates) ever since the project of American media sociology began in earnest following the Second World War. Take the very concept of 'gatekeeping'. The conventional model of this process which emerged, and which endures, says that a plethora of possible stories appear, and the editors are supposed to be objective 'gatekeepers', either blocking a given story or allowing its onward passage to print or airwaves.

In the classic study of such a 'gatekeeper', carried out in 1950, a tally was made of the news agency wire-service stories run and of those spiked by the 'wire-editor' over a week's editions of a 30,000-circulation, mid-western, non-metropolitan American newspaper. This gatekeeper was in his 40s, a white (we can safely assume) male veteran journalist with 25 years or so of experience. He processed around 12,500 column inches of agencies' feeds, of which he selected about a tenth to run. The study leaves unexamined his reasoning (e.g. discards as being 'too vague', 'uninteresting'), but it does note that his bias was 'conservative', that the selection process was 'highly subjective', and, moreover, that he was dealing with material that had been equally subjectively selected by the chain of editors before him, from 'rewrite man' through bureau chief to a 'state file editor'.[14] It should also be noted that such studies, including this one, tend to consider the practical rather than the theoretical aspects of this process – how news selection is done, rather than how it can be done. The obvious implications for the ideal of objectivity, however, were, by and large, never followed up. The extensive sociological literature on newsroom operations also, perhaps not unnaturally, focuses more on what gets printed or broadcast than on what gets discarded.[15]

Such a focus, however, does not adequately address the problem of objective journalism, because it isn't enough for each story in the newspaper to be 'objective'. The newspaper itself, taken as a whole, would have to be 'objective' too. A simple thought-experiment can readily show why this is so. (To be clear, this is a *reductio ad absurdum* argument, intended only to demonstrate that a totally biased newspaper could hypothetically be produced out of totally unbiased stories.) So, imagine a newspaper that reported every story included within it in a way that was utterly factual, neutral and fair (which is not possible in reality, but is for the purposes of this scenario) – however every story was one that made one political party look bad and the other look good.

This newspaper would include only stories in which, for example, Republicans looked 'bad' and/or Democrats looked 'good'. Nothing would be inaccurate or distorted, but a Republican policy's outcomes would be covered only if they were negative. A Republican politician would be profiled only when embroiled in a scandal, saying something unpopular, losing a political scuffle, etc. For Democrats, only positive outcomes and stories would be included. If you had read only this newspaper your whole life, and it was your sole source of political knowledge, you would know of every accusation ever made against a Republican President, however minor, personal, unproven, etc., but you would never have heard of Monica Lewinsky, or Obama's expansion of the surveillance state (taking a couple of prominent Democratic downers more or less at random). Does that sound like objective journalism?

Some would argue that you can determine a theoretical set of news values through which to make your selection of which stories to tell on any given day, and then you can use these to make an objective determination, e.g. any scandal about a sitting President, whatever his or her party, should be in the paper. Once again, however, this doesn't make much sense. To illustrate why not, let's take a step back from politics for a second to talk about news more generally, and consider a different hypothetical set of circumstances. Please imagine that you run an American daily newspaper with a national readership, and then consider the list we're about to give you of ten possible news-stories. You have space in your paper to cover only five of them. (This is a spectacular oversimplification of the news-selection process, but not a radical distortion of its fundamental character.) So, on our hypothetical day, we can cover:

1. Landslide election victory in Bolivia.
2. Global oil prices drop.
3. Tornadoes in Kansas.
4. Reality TV-show finale breaks ratings record.
5. Historic governor's mansion damaged by fire.
6. Study: eating eggs lowers risk of heart disease.
7. Most Americans feel negative towards 'feminism', study shows.
8. [Named foreign billionaire] to buy NFL franchise.
9. Frank Sinatra and the Mafia: new evidence.
10. [Named A-list movie star] breaks leg filming next hotly-anticipated blockbuster.

Now, you probably know which five of those stories would be the most important to you. As a newspaper's editor you could probably guess (and/or have research on) which five might be the most important to your readers. You can even express an opinion about which five *should* be the most important to your readers, but by definition 'importance', without clear criteria, is a subjective quality. Asking which is a more important story out of tornadoes in Kansas or an election in Bolivia obviously and inevitably just prompts further questions: 'Important in what way? Important to whom?' These are and must be subjective criteria. Because of this, news-selection can never be truly objective, even if news-reporting could be, which by the way, just to say it once more, it can't.

As to just why it can't, we ask you to indulge another thought experiment. This time imagine yourself to be a reporter for a regional paper, and you have been assigned to write a story about a major new resort development on a section of undeveloped coastal wetland. Somebody is going to build a nice big hotel, some timeshare bungalows, maybe a golf course and some tennis courts. Two plausible angles are the economic, focusing on the jobs created and the flow of money into the area, or the environmental, focusing on the impact of the development on the local landscape and wildlife (perhaps some rare bird's habitat will be affected, for example).

If you write the first story and not the second, somebody might say you are biased in favour of big business. If you write the second story and not the first, somebody might say you are biased against big business. If you try to include both angles, both hypothetical critics are quite likely to say you are anyway biased against their point of view. And it is – we can't stress this hopefully self-evident point enough – not possible to present every possible viewpoint on a story (any more than it was possible to tell every news story), or to make a choice of which viewpoint(s) to include/exclude *objectively* (any more than it was possible to make objective determinations of which stories were and were not newsworthy).

The press faces other problems not of its making: externally imposed constraints on what it is told, for example, or the speed at which the marketplace demands its product. But one factor of which it is in as much control as it is of subjectivity, is its tone. This relates not just to the idea that the tone of its reporting should be impartial and unemotional, so as not to manipulate the reader, but also to the belief that its presentation – in print or in performance – should be formal, perhaps even solemn. The importance given to such aspects of tone derives from the tradition that 'good' news media are necessarily a species of serious discourse. The news is a serious matter, and so it should be presented soberly. Or at least that's the idea – it is supposedly a 'discourse of sobriety'.[16] Journalism is held to be in binary opposition to the range of frivolous public modes of communication that can be considered as entertainments. Although it can – must – be engaging, it is thought to be distinct from 'pure entertainment'.[17] By this view, journalism (apparently) unwillingly yields to the need to 'entertain', in a sense, only to ensure the audience's attention.

But any sobriety/frivolity binary is an unsustainable as the truth/fakery division. The news media, as public discourse, are not now and never have been remotely distinct from entertainment. They are entertainment, and they clothe themselves in sobriety for much the same reasons a travelling salesman might wear a suit and tie – to be taken seriously and respected, while trying to sell you something.

During the Falklands War, on 4 May 1982, 'Tony Snow aboard HMS Invincible' reported the sinking of the enemy Argentine vessel the Belgrano by the British Navy. In London, his editors on *The Sun* came up with the (in)famous page-one splash **'GOTCHA'**, which was changed in later editions as reports of the casualties came in. The paper's subordinate deck was 'Our lads sink gunboat and hole cruiser', and the article opened with the words, 'The Navy had the Argies on their knees last night after a devastating double punch.'

By contrast, on 8 September 2002, amid the tensions between Saddam Hussein and the west, *The New York Times* ever-so-soberly reported on its front page:

> Washington, Sept. 7 – …
>
> ### US SAYS HUSSEIN INTENSIFIES QUEST FOR A-BOMB PARTS
>
> New Information is Central to White House Argument for Urgent Action on Iraq
>
> **By Michael Jordan and Judith Miller**
>
> In the last 14 months, Iraq has sought to buy thousands of specially designed aluminium tubes, which American officials believe were intended as centrifuges to enrich uranium.

However, for all the sober tone of the report, unlike *The Sun* on the sinking of the Belgrano, this story was simply false. The unnamed 'sources' (e.g. an 'Iraqi opposition leader') eventually turned out to be deeply suspect, and their evidence was untriangulated by *The Times*'s reporters.

The Sun's story is presented in an explicitly partisan, vulgar, jingoistic, informal fashion, all of which are commonly thought to be markers of bad journalism. But the vulgar story was objectively factual, albeit disgusting in its presentation, while the more sober report from *The New York Times* did not have a shred of objective truth anywhere in it. Although associated in the public imagination so closely and for so long, the sober tone of a news report has no intrinsic link to the truth (or, for that matter, the social significance) of the report's content. It indicates a different kind of sales pitch, by a different kind of publication, to a different kind of audience, than that made by a less formal mode of expression; but that is not the same thing as being a sign of trustworthiness or truth. It is not even necessarily the same thing as being a sign of quality, or of (attempted) objectivity or of basic integrity. It is part of the 'branding' process.

All such confusions reflect the crux of the matter. The existential problem, and, we contend, the thickest, deepest, toughest 'root' of the fake news brouhaha is that, indeed, news is not the same as truth; it is, for unavoidable reasons both imposed and of its own making, unable, as a practice, to match its own rhetoric. The ideology of modern journalism (in the western secular democracies – mainly Anglophone – which are our focus) is built on the idea of the production of this objective journalism. But objective journalism does not, has not, cannot, and will not *ever* exist. The idea itself is impossible. The legendarily and unapologetically subjective journalist Hunter S. Thompson called the concept 'a pompous contradiction in terms'[18]. Journalistic objectivity is, we contend, a long-running swindle – a long-con, currently in the process of collapsing under the weight of its own contradictions.

There is, then, no meaningful true/false binary in journalism, and to ground a discussion of journalism's function in such terms is obfuscating. The issue of the 'truthfulness' of journalism is less a matter of black or white – honest or mendacious representation – than it is a matter of infinite shades of grey. What we think of as journalism actually comes into being in an 'interstitial position between concepts of reporting and fictional imagining' that historian Diana Purkiss noticed in the news publications of the 17th century.[19] This, we contend, is where it remains to this day, not because of avoidable practical failures, but because of its inevitable theoretical limitations. Therefore, to look for the 'roots' of fake news, as if they were part of a unique species of plant is to make a category error.[20] Fake news is not a weed with its own identifiable roots; it and *news* are both growths on the same journalistic stalk – both inhabit an interstitial position. The roots are shared.

Certainly, the term fake news can acceptably describe, on a common-sense basis, pure fiction masquerading as fact; but this has always been possible with the press. In the early centuries of the news-business, the public were sold 'NEWES' but also, alternatively as equally 'true' (or 'trewe'), actually utterly bogus and misleading reports bearing no relation to any external reality – 'STRANGE NEWES'. 'When *news* is printed', playwright Ben Jonson observed in 1625, 'though it be ne'er so false, it runs *news* still'[21][emphasis added]. The point is that distinguishing such fakery is not so much difficult as near impossible. Fake news in the pure sense of mendacity can easily display all the trappings and protocols of being the news – 'it runs *news* still'. We have to be talking of a continuum, not a binary, much less a dichotomy.

It should be noted, however, that if this is understood, then *pure* fake news – barefaced lying, at least in the mainstream news-media of the bourgeois democracies, has been pretty rare. It is at one end of the continuum and the vast majority of content lies, at one point or another, elsewhere on it. Anyway, intentional mendacity when it does appear is most commonly *impure*. To maintain the masquerade, it has to be shot through with truth. The fake news/news problem is not so much in straightforward lying as in the de facto median position which accepts the news as cultural fabrication – in its original meaning of something produced, i.e. made between 'reporting and fictional imagining'. Its legitimacy as the news is a question of the degree of accuracy with which it represents the referent involved in its presentation – how close it can get to the continuum's inaccessible truthful end.

This means that fabrication occurs at two levels: the matter to be reported can be fabricated (but isn't often), but the reporting of it must be fabricated, too – with the semiotic slippage that that inevitably involves – and that is so common as to be a given.

Hence, across the continuum the matter might be fabricated in its more modern secondary sense (OED) of being a lie, and this cannot easily be defended against. But acknowledging its fabricated nature in the original first sense is crucial to understanding the problem. The two meanings reflect, in our very language, the confusions bedeviling the news's claim on the real.

The problem, therefore, has less than nothing to do with the brouhaha created by Donald Trump. Strident Trumpian charges of 'fake news!', denying any kernel of truth in any media report which he finds to be disagreeable, are merely distracting. Such a definition of fake news is an obvious absurdity, an hysterically perverse matter of reception more reflecting the mindset of those speciously detecting its presence, and not of the practice of journalists which is our prime concern here. It is nothing but an unwarranted slur and cheap political tactic. When Trump tweeted that 'The FAKE NEWS media (failing @nytimes, @NBCnews, @ABC, @CBS, @CNN) is not my enemy, it is the enemy of the American People!'[22] in February 2017, this was not a criticism of dishonesty, but of dissent. The same was true when Hitler expressed a very similar sentiment:

> It is the press, above all, which wages a positively fanatical and slanderous struggle, tearing down everything which can be regarded as a support of national independence, cultural elevation, and the economic independence of the nation.[23]

Populism 101 holds that disagreeing with the leader is never an honest difference of opinions. To disagree with the leader, criticise the leader, be anything less than fanatically supportive of the leader, is always an attack on not just the leader, but the nation, deliberately intending it harm. Whether a private citizen, a judge, or a journalist, why else would you do it? But enough about all that. The part of this that matters the most in the context of our argument is that tackling this type of Trumpian notion of fakery (which never includes his own fabrications) with endless cross-checked rebuttals is to address the wrong issue. All the advice currently being offered in the marketplace of ideas on how to sort the *news* from the dross is never going to be foolproof. Only scepticism in the context of one's own prior knowledge, or 'collateral experience' (to use a phrase of Charles Peirce)[24] of the world, will 'protect' you from the fake, and even that is obviously far from infallible.

The rhetoric (at least) of a fake news/news dichotomy, however, must be noticed as it serves to re-enforce a vision of good and bad media which comforts 'good' (all too often simply meaning 'mainstream') media. This carries a significant cost: the current focus on the dichotomy masks the news media's deepest problems, which, as we suggest above, are located in the ideology and practice of journalism itself, rather than in the credulity of those who consume it. Trumpian attacks gain traction because journalism promises what it conspicuously fails to deliver: the more loudly it insists on its truth, the greater the threat to its credibility. Fake news flourishes not so much because of *pure* lying as because seeking to provide unassailable accounts capturing reality in its entirety, the impossible ideal of the news (as supposedly produced by objective journalism), proves indeed to be exactly that – impossible – and so every visible failure can seem like further evidence that the news is not to be trusted.

What is most concerning, then, is not fiction shot through with fact and then labelled as journalism, but the truths, such as they are, of well-intentioned journalism appearing to be tainted, whether by lies or otherwise, while claiming a high standard of objectivity, honesty, accuracy, etc. The news's truth can be undermined by mendacities but is, far more often, compromised by accidental errors of one kind or another. Moreover, it is inevitably also contaminated, at the very least, by incompleteness and subjectivity. As we have explained, hopefully persuasively, these ingredients can never be entirely excluded from the recipe. However hard it may strive to avoid such impurities, they are always present, meaning that journalism itself is *always* doomed to be impure. Noticing this cannot amount to a crisis. Nor is it valuable to postulate a straightforward dichotomy between truth and falsehood in looking for fake news's roots. Doing this only obscures the real nature of the issue which is grounded, as it has been for half a millennium, in journalism's essential challenges. Against that fake news may be presented as a matter of truth and lies, just as it is presented as being a recent and suddenly all-pervasive phenomenon, but, as we will endeavour to demonstrate, that's just wrong. Naive. Foolish. Deceptive.

Fake news.

Notes

1 Boswell, James (1768). *An Account of Corsica*. London: Edward & Charles Dilly, p. 335. Emerson is credited with the same thought: Emerson, Ralph Waldo (1888 [1844]). *The Complete Works of Ralph Waldo Emerson: The Conduct of Life, Vol. 6*. Boston: Houghton, Mifflin and Company, p. 211.
2 Kovach, Bill & Tom Rosenstiel (2001). *The Neiman Reports Special Issue*: 'The Elements of Journalism'. Cambridge, MA: The Nieman Foundation for Journalism at Harvard University, Summer.
3 Bacon, Francis (1909 [1597]). *Essays, Civil and Moral* (The Harvard Classics III:1). New York: P.F. Collier & Son, p. 1.
4 Nichols, Bill (1991). *Representing Reality: Issues and Concepts in Documentary*. Bloomington, IN: Indiana University Press, pp. 7, 109.
5 Lippman, Walter (1922). *Public Opinion*. New York: Harcourt Brace, & Company, p. 385.
6 The quote is variously attributed: Anon (n/d) '"Dog bites a man" is not news. "Man bites a dog" is news'. https://quoteinvestigator.com/2013/11/22/dog-bites/ [accessed 7 December 2019].
7 Tuchman, Gaye (1972). 'Objectivity as strategic ritual: An examination of newsmen's notions of objectivity', *American Journal of Sociology*, 77:4, p. 660.

8 'A salute to fair and objective journalism', *Coos Bay World*, 27 January 2020. https://theworldlink.com/community/reedsport/opinion/a-salute-to-fair-and-objective-journalism/article_494ed2a1-46d2-50c1-a430-b2b0816485ea.html [accessed 6 February 2020].
9 'Contemporary Brazil, captured in two novels and a journalist's collection', *The New York Times*, 24 January 2020. www.nytimes.com/2020/01/24/books/review/brazil-resistance-julian-fuks-collector-of-leftover-souls-eliane-brum.html [accessed 6 February 2020].
10 'In "Tightrope," Pulitzer-winning writers examine the woes of the U.S. working class in their hometown', *Seattle Times*, 28 January 2020. www.seattletimes.com/entertainment/books/in-tightrope-pulitzer-winning-writers-examine-the-woes-of-the-u-s-working-class-in-their-hometown/ [accessed 6 February 2020].
11 'Voices from the Arab press: Davos and underestimating climate change', *The Jerusalem Post*-29 Jan 2020. www.jpost.com/Magazine/Voices-from-the-Arab-press-Davos-and-underestimating-climate-change-615839 [accessed 6 February 2020].
12 'Harvard Protesters: Objective Journalism Is "Endangering Undocumented Students"', *National Review*, 21 November 2019. www.nationalreview.com/2019/11/harvard-protesters-objective-journalism-is-endangering-undocumented-students/ [accessed 6 February 2020].
13 'Journalism industry falters when nation most needs it', *The Hill*, 11 July 2019. https://thehill.com/opinion/technology/452382-journalism-industry-falters-when-nation-most-needs-it [accessed 6 February 2020].
14 Manning White, David (1950). 'The "Gate Keeper": A Case Study in the Selection of News', *Journaism and Mass Communications Quarterly*, 27:4.
15 e.g. Classically, Gans, Herbert (1977). *Deciding What's News: A Study of CBS Evening News, NBC Nightly News, Newsweek, and Time*; Galtung, Johan & Mari Holmboe Ruge (1965). 'The structure of foreign news: The presentation of the Congo, Cuba and Cyprus crises in four Norwegian newspapers', *Journal of Peace Research*, 2: 1. http://dx.doi.org/10.1177/002234336500200104 [accessed 20 February 2015].
16 Nichols, Bill (1991). *Representing Reality: Issues and Concepts in Documentary*. Bloomington, IN: Indiana University Press, p. 13.
17 Belsey, Andrew & Ruth Chadwick (eds) (1992). *Ethical Issues in Journalism and the Media*. London: Routledge, p. 19.
18 Thompson, Hunter S. (1983). *Fear and Loathing: On the Campaign Trail '72*. New York: Warner Books, p. 48.
19 Purkiss, Diana (2005). *Literature, Gender and Politics During the English Civil War*. Cambridge: Cambridge University Press, p. 174.
20 Ryle, Gilbert (1949). *The Concept of the Mind*. Chicago, IL: University of Chicago Press, pp 16–17.
21 Jonson, Ben (1625). *The Staple of News*. Act 1, Sc 5. http://hollowaypages.com/jonson1692news.htm [accessed 13 March 2012].
22 Trump, Donald (2017). 'Donald J. Trump✓*@realDonaldTrump*', 17 February.
23 Hitler, Adolf (1925). *Mein Kampf*, Vol. 1, Chapter 11. Munich: Eher Verlag. www.mondopolitico.com/library/meinkampf/v1c11.htm [accessed 1 January 2019].
24 Peirce, Charles S. (1931–1966). *The Collected Papers of Charles S. Peirce*, 8 vols. (C. Hartshorne, P. Weiss & A.W. Burks, eds). Cambridge: Harvard University Press, CP 8:312.

Roots

1

'STRANGE NEWES': PRINTED NEWS 1485—

'The Frightening and Truly Extraordinary Story
of a Blood-Drinking Tyrant Called Count Dracula'
Anon, 1485

Even before the moment when a pressman (perhaps it was Gutenberg himself, or perhaps it was Peter Schöffer, his earliest colleague) first[1] pulled 'the devil's tail' to screw the forme holding the inked types against a sheet of paper, what we would come to think of as the news was already a tricky business. Indeed, the 'fake news' phenomenon is not a new problem. It is not just older than Facebook et al, it is older than the newspaper itself, or the presses used to print it. To brand a broadsheet, pamphlet or bound booklet *'trewe'*, *'warrented tidings'*, *'truths'*, *'full true and particular accounts'*, *'true relations'*, *'véritable contes'* was, even with the purest intentions of offering accurate and unvarnished reports, always to give hostages to fortune. Not only could such a warrant never be totally fulfilled, but the protocols deployed to indicate, fraudulently, that truths were on offer could, and were, easily aped. It doesn't take long to set in type that you are telling the truth. And, moreover, those that were to make it their business to sell the *news* to the public were often all too ready to present grounded and ungrounded material cheek-by-jowl.

Gutenberg, his fellow metalworkers, and the burgher manuscript book-handlers who followed him into exploring print's potential, found in their buyers (churchmen, officials, scholars, aristocrats, lawyers, and fellow townsfolk) an appetite for bibles, psalters, and prayer books, reprints of Greek and Latin masterworks, chronicles, and grammars. Not all these 'vendible' *incunabula* (print in 'swaddling clothes') were received as socially positive. Pulling on the devil's tail could also produce materials to do the devil's work – playing cards, say, or frivolous fiction of only supposed moral worth (*Aesop's Fables*?), or none (*The Decameron*). Output was often neutral in the sense that it could be seen as a social good or as a social evil. Sheet music, which, from those first days, was a profitable line for the printer to exploit, could, indeed, be sacred, but also sinfully profane. The products of the printing press, like those of the wine press on which it was modelled, were not always deemed beneficial.

Despite such misgivings, however, the church, which at first flush had heralded the coming of print as 'an ascent towards God', was to be print's best customer. Apart from holy texts, indulgences, which were a prime cause of the demands for ecclesiastical reform in the century after Gutenberg, were sometimes issued one hundred thousand at a time. They were printed as a form, with a space left blank to write the name of the beneficiary who bought one. The earliest surviving example, possibly printed by Gutenberg himself, is dated 22 October 1454. A manuscript and block-printed tradition of small devotional pictures to be held as a prophylactic against plague, called *pestblätter*/plague-sheets, were also mass-produced.

The authorities, too, were among print's larger customers for ephemera. Although formal legalistic need for continued face-to-face encounters and attested, sealed written documents remained, the old regal manuscript formula – 'to all whom these presents shall come' – was soon in print. Proclamations, instructions and the like were, obviously, more efficiently printed than copied by hand. The French kings were issuing printed *occasionnels – ordonnances faict par le roi nostre signeur etc.* – from as early as 1467. By the 1480s these expanded to include reports of the king's activities – of the progress of a war in Brittany in 1488, for example. But, being official publications, they themselves do not fall within the modern western definition of journalism proper.

The voracious appetite of the printers for material to set was matched by the equally demanding public thirst for print. In addition to treasured bound books, a flood of single, largely discardable broadsheets on a wide variety of topics and other ephemera for the general market marked the first phase of print. Printers published anything they could think of: Gutenberg, for example, produced a printed calendar for 1448. Catalogues of goods, with spaces for their current prices to be inserted, speak to burgeoning commercial needs. Printed 'supplications' – single page dissertations, in effect – were required by universities awarding higher degrees. In 1517, Luther's *Disputation on the Power of Indulgences – the 95 Theses –* can be considered as following this format. The hand-written original may not have actually been nailed to the church door in Wittenberg, but it was certainly quickly printed in Basel.[2] With high demand ensuring the technology's diffusion, by the start of the 16th century more than 1,000 presses in 200 European cities and towns had produced an estimated 8 million volumes of 30,000 incunabula.[3]

In this flood of paper, there was printed news – broadsheet 'bills of news' – carrying information for the edification and entertainment of the public. From the outset, they competed in print with the more substantial newsbooks. Both were produced irregularly, usually on single topics, their titles reflecting their contents, and so are not examples of the periodical press as we are describing it. That is to say that they were not regularly issued, independently edited, unbound, numbered and dated periodicals containing, under a consistent title, a variety of news reports and other matter. Contrary to received opinion, it is rather a trick of the light to see the appearance of something recognisable as a newspaper as a direct – more or less immediate – consequence of the coming of print. Most of these individual elements did appear in print persistently, but in an ad hoc fashion. They did not appear together. Far from the proliferation of printing instantly producing *the news*, in the form of a 'newspaper', it was not until the 17th century – 150 years after Gutenberg – that printed titles displaying all the characteristics we have identified came to appear regularly in a distinct class of publications. There were many reasons for this but prime among them was the existence of rival news sources.

The Middle Ages had seen the emergence of a platform for the oral expression of news, i.e. *news* in the sense of being public, and neither gossip nor history. Minstrels were then a new class of entertainers, in effect busking across Europe performing in street, hall and court. Among the love songs and tales of chivalry which were the mainstays of their repertoires were rhymed accounts of recent events which could also be melodically recited to earn a penny from an audience.[4] From troubadours (and some female *troubairitz*) in 12th century Occitan France, a vibrant tradition, replete with guilds and rules, was sustained. Accounts that were 'trew y tolde', to use the term coined by an early 14th century English poet named Laurence Minot, were well established. Minot was writing in English, obviously from witnessed sources, rhymed reports of the military exploits of the English against the Scots and the French in the early 1330s.[5] The following century, even as Gutenberg was setting up shop, another poet, Michael Beheim, was also producing rhymed reports of current events. He was a *meistersinger*, what troubadours had become in the German lands. During the winter of 1463, he could be found in Vienna entertaining and informing the court of the Holy Roman Emperor, Frederick von Hapsburg III, of news. In a thousand-line poem, about a *wutrich* (bloodthirsty madman) called the *Trakle Waida* (devil prince) *of Wallachia*, he secured for his villain, Vlad Tepeș III, a reputation which still vibrates. His source was a hostile monk who had encountered the maniac *Trakle* (*Dracul* in Romanian), in the flesh in the Balkans.[6] Beheim is but a step away from fictional imagining, his mainstream news story being not totally mendacious, but certainly significantly distorted. The roots of fake news in the mainstream media are all to be found in this contemporary account of the historical figure who would become the fictional 'Dracula' – not a lie but, at best, a necessarily partial truth.

Constantinople had fallen to the Turks in 1453 and the 'madman' Vlad was a real, still-living person as Michael was singing about him in distant Austria. He was, in truth, the then *Voivode* of Wallachia – a pawn in the tangled, fervid politics of the Balkans at the time. But he was not necessarily a particular demonic one – only an average sort of Eastern European 15th-century tyrant. Unembellished, his (actual) everyday cruelty could be seen, in terms of the standards of the time and place, as an astute deployment of terror as a means of control in a particularly lawless historical moment. Had his informant not been a hostile Catholic cleric, Beheim could just as easily have learned of Vlad as an heroic defender of Orthodox Christianity against the threat of Islam, and a significant founding father of his country. Today, his reputation runs contentiously along these two lines, either remembered more positively, in Romania and by a number of scholars of the period, or, if remembered at all, taken as Vlad the Impaler, perpetrator of horrific atrocities, by the rest of us. It was this latter take that was to influence an Irish novelist centuries later,[7] who may or may not have also been principally inspired by a nightmare brought on by eating too much crab one night at dinner. That we are still making movies, games, books, breakfast cereal, etc. inspired by the figure of Dracula, may perhaps, in this context, be taken as a sign of some uncomfortable truths about fake news's enduring power.

Not that any positive account of Vlad would have avoided distortion, too; but, as Dr Johnson was to point out, newswriters have long believed that:

> Scarcely any thing awakens attention like a tale of cruelty. The writer of news never fails in the intermission of action to tell how the enemies murdered children and ravished virgins; and, if the scene of action be somewhat distant, scalps half the inhabitants of a province.[8]

By the 20th century this had been routinised in the unavoidable tabloid injunction that 'if it bleeds, it leads'.[9]

As far as we can tell from surviving documents, it was to be 22 years before an account of Vlad appeared in newsbook form. In 1485, the King of Hungary, who had been one of his many enemies, had printed *Dracule Wajda*, a pamphlet with a crude woodcut showing Vlad eating lunch outdoors in front of a forest of impaled bodies, while a servant chops at a pile of corpses. The tale, in German, was to be repeatedly reprinted across Europe over the next half-century, with titles such as *The Frightening and Truly Extraordinary Story of a Blood-Drinking Tyrant called Count Dracula*.[10] By that time, newsbooks were regularly appearing and they, following *Dracule Wajda*, soon came firmly to occupy journalism's 'interstitial position' – but with a significant, although not absolute, tendency to lean towards the fake/fiction side. An analysis of 500 surviving *canards* – as the French termed news broadsheets – from the period, revealed the dominance of sensationalism in general: 36% were devoted to marvels, 23% to calamities, 22% to crime and 19% to celestial apparitions.[11]

This is not to say that early printed news reports were always fanciful to the point of fantasy. There are also sober examples of single-event reports in the archives, e.g. documenting that on 7 November 1492, a 'thunder-stone' (meteorite) fell on Ensisheim, near Mulhouse in Alsace. This really happened, and the rock can still be seen. The occurrence was celebrated with a printed broadsheet, written in verse by the poet Sebastian Brant.[12] Despite the poetry, the sheet has a remarkably modern, newspaper-like appearance, Brant's text being surrounded by woodcuts illustrating the event. Such integration was not to become the norm for centuries. As in other cases, the sheet stands alone, a single publication; it does not herald a series. There are more examples, such as a sober newsbook of 1529, dealing with *New tidings from Speyer About the acts of the Prince*.[13] In 1542, a single-topic publication – *Hevy Newes of an Horryble Earthquake near Florence, Italy* – straightforwardly reported the event. A broadsheet, printed but beautifully hand-coloured, *New Tidings from the Japanese*

Island, noted the arrival in Milan of four Japanese ambassadors in company with a Jesuit monk in 1586.[14] And so on ...

An example of a serious news publication carrying multiple news reports also survives in the archive. In 1548, a *Zeyttungg* (i.e. *Tidings*) was published in the midst of a short early war of religion between the Catholic Holy Roman Emperor, Charles V, and Lutheran princes of the Schmalkaldic League. Charles won. The *Zeyttungg* led with a 1547 account of '*Truthful News of Conquest of Placentz and Parma* ...' describing it as '*Some Well-known history so to speak in Italy*'.[15] It was not solely devoted to this, however, as it carried other reports including a second item on page one, 'concerning Ludovico III Gonzaga, the Ruler of Mantua'. In this way it presented something of the variety of a newspaper but the 'so to speak' perhaps echoes a hesitation over a supposed incompatibility of history and immediacy.

The word *Relation* (German for 'narration', derived from Latin and with an implication of evidence) was, like *Tydings – Zeyttungg –* often to appear in titles hinting at sobriety by foregoing vivid adjectives. (*Zeitung* is modern German for 'newspaper'.) Yet sometimes adjectives were legitimate. News of the earthquake was indeed 'heavy'. The '*True and frightening new tidings from Silesia in this year of* [15]*42*' were also indeed frightening: the outbreak of plague to the east.[16] Unlike the flesh-creeping tales of a distant and otherwise preoccupied 'frightening bloodthirsty' Dracula, such accounts could act to evoke empathy or to give warning. Dracula and his ilk, however, simply appear to have outsold them. The key word in newsbook titles was to be '*strange*', as in '*strange newes*' and the like. The broadsheets and the newsbooks were usually more concerned with sales than with the seriousness and social value of their reporting. Sensationalism, in the mold of *Dracule Wajda*, was their norm and Dracula serves to remind us that many features of journalism that some might consider undesirable, such as sensationalism (or valuing impact over accuracy, or framing events through a prism of 'us vs them', or many others) have been a part of the news for as long as there has been a concept of the news, because they are what people tend to like, which is to say it is because they are what sells.

Moreover, making disasters, crime and the supernatural their staples also helped them to avoid the worst of censorship and repression, in much the way that later, similar types of content have helped some types of ostensibly news-based publications to avoid controversy, in order to maximise marketability. Coverage of natural disasters, as in the *hevy newes* example, or of the horrors of plagues, could be retailed without interference in the centuries under discussion here, but in general, politics could not. Purveyors of such news were not welcomed by the authorities. Newswriters, thought a Venetian ambassador to Rome in the 1700s, 'have always recounted everything with scabrous indecency', but, on the other hand, on occasion this 'indecency' could actually be, in official eyes, not necessarily a bad thing. It was better for newswriters and publishers to be considered mendaciously distracting rather than truthfully threatening. 'The government', a contemporary of the ambassador observed, 'only want the [gazetteers] to write trifles and lies that won't stir anything up'.[17]

For most forms of publication, the move from manuscript to print, whether wood-block or moveable type, was unequivocally advantageous. The production of manuscripts had been highly organised – texts broken into parts for multiple scriveners to copy simultaneously, and specialised illuminators, book binders and marketing 'handlers'. Nevertheless, with print, texts could be made widely available in editions of hundreds as opposed to dozens, and they were always going to duplicate the original more accurately. Above all, even at Gutenberg's printing rate of less than ten impressions-per-hour (iph), with the slow attendant effort of hand-setting the text from the cases of types (or carving it on a wood-block), printing was miraculously quicker than hand-copying – and by 1455, the year he printed *The Bible,* he was working his six presses 12 to 14 hours a day, producing 800+ impressions. And, of course, as well as the speed advantage, printers were cheaper than scribes. Across the ever-expanding plains of this new literacy, however, there were durable bolt-holes to which oral culture fled. After all, most folk were illiterate and the printed sheets, however popular and sensational, were inaccessible to them. The minstrels persisted as an available public alternative to printed news for some time.

On the other hand, manuscript scriptoria in monasteries and elsewhere were soon rendered redundant, although individual scriveners, providing writing services which included private news reports, were not. Knowledge was power, then as now, and printing's capacity to democratise it by 'crying the news' on the streets was not welcomed by the powerful as an unmitigated good. Quite the contrary. Merchants, for example, were careful with their information. There is an early 16th century watercolour of the South German banker, Jakob Fugger, with an accountant making an entry in a ledger, by hand of course. In the background is a filing cabinet, its drawers marked with the names of the towns where Jakob did business via his factors. Their job embraced producing handwritten reports of local conditions for the use of the head-office in Augsburg. Writing being more secure than printing, Fugger's clerks then copied these commercially sensitive intelligences to produce manuscript newsletters – 'advices' or '*advissi*' – for the network of factors and other trusted clients.[18] Privately distributed newsletters of this kind were also to persist for centuries. There is perhaps an argument to be made that in many ways during this period much of what we might, from a modern perspective, think of as 'news' was not in fact of any possible relevance to the largely illiterate mass in medieval or early modern society. As with the case of these private, business-oriented information channels, those who did need (and/or were allowed to have) such information acquired it without any need for public news-media in the modern sense.

Secular authorities were always unhappy about any serious communication channel they did not totally control and, in their own communication systems, they also tended towards secrecy. As in the merchant's counting house, so in the prince's court. By the time of Gutenberg, couriers – salaried letter carriers – were common in royal households. The reports of ambassadors 'sent to lie abroad for the good of their country' at such courts were sent via private couriers, too, and violation of their letters was held to be transgressive (as were attacks on their person). That diplomatic communication ought to be privileged, although not yet enshrined formally in emerging international law, was well understood. In general, across Europe, rulers developed postal networks, using established coach routes, first for themselves and then opened more widely. The English Royal Mail, for example, was established by Henry VIII in 1516, but by then the Holy Roman Emperor's system had been operating for 20 years.

Yet despite all the secrecy, the more public possibilities of the newsletter were not entirely ignored. As the Turks threatened Venice in 1536, a *gazzete* – the smallest of coins – would buy you a handwritten sheet on the situation. Alternatively, if you could not read, payment of the coin might allow you to join a crowd hearing it read out by the *gazzetiero* – or *reportisto* – who had composed it. A *gazzete*'s worth of news, a *gazeta dele novita*, became, simply, a gazette. Also called *avvisi*, they were most popular in Rome and Venice, only rarely appearing north of the Alps. They were often written on two sheets. One, which could be based on leaked official information, was devoted to sobriety, while the other retailed the tittle-tattle of scandal. An obituary of a Roman noble, for example, read: 'he had lived with no confession, communion or extreme unction ... he ruled like a lion, lived like a wolf and died like a dog'.[19] The gazetteer reported jubilation at the funeral. An affiliation with spying (which still lingers) infected the status of the *reportisto* with the public, but with little effect on their popularity. The *avvisi*, however, although vendible enough to yield an income, were not regular. Again, they were more sensationalist than sober and, most curiously, their authors seemed never to give much thought to printing, rather than writing, their sheets. In fact, because they were, or could have been, in competition with print, instead they too inhibited the exploration of the printed option. *Avviso* and *Gazette* as print titles, though, were eventually to join *Tidings* and *Accounts* and *News* – strange or otherwise – as news publication titles.

Secrecy aside, authorities were also well-aware of the contrary value of print to improve communication with those they ruled, effectively from the moment of its proliferation as a technology. The French and English *occasionnels* and royal proclamations, often printed on broadsheet, were being regularly issued, several in any given year. When deemed to be good for public relations, the texts of normally secret treaties and the like might also be printed and made public. Monarchs sometimes even resorted to printing pamphlets which made a public case for their actions. For these reasons, the official/independent boundary could be hard to maintain. *Dracule Wajda*, for example, was politically sanctioned by the Hungarian crown and then reprinted by entrepreneurial publishers. The Polish authorities published a *Neuer Zeitung*, a digest of '*New Tidings from Lithuania and concerning the Muscovites ...*', in 1513.[20] As official publications, however, they were not independent sources of information and, although they were sober, they cannot be regarded as news. On the other hand, in the same year as the Polish *Zeitung*, the English printer Richard Faques (Fawkes /Fake) produced the earliest known 'newsbook' in English – *hereafter ensue the trewe encountre of Batayle lately don betwene Englāde and Scotlande* (Flodden Field, 9 September 1513).[21] He, not the Crown, was the initiator, but this crucial distinction was difficult to maintain, as 'publishers' were often either directly employed or closely involved with the court. (And their outputs were still irregular.)

For Henry VIII, publications came to constitute an important element in his campaigns for his divorces and for his religious positions. Somewhat ironically given his later break with the papacy, the earliest of these to bear his name as author, *The Assertion of the Seven Sacraments*,[22] was a reply in Latin to Martin Luther's first heretical publication attacking the Pope.[23] Luther replied in *Against Henry King of the English*.[24] Such pamphlets were no more considered news than was fiction or other non-fictional publications – scientific, philosophic, geographic, etc. In general, they proffered arguments in 'the marketplace of ideas', retailing naked opinion on a single subject.

Henry's publications were part of a wider pamphlet war, waged for hearts and minds during the Reformation. The printers were to fuel the violence of the schism with a flood of broadsheet *placards* for public posting, bringing the vitriol of often vulgar debate to the walls of urban squares and streets.[25] Luther himself, however, led the way with the pamphlets. In 1522, he had raised the flag of church reformation, in German, not Latin, with the publication of *To the Christian Nobility of the German Nation*.[26] The majority of publications were to be in the Protestant cause. The Church, despite its taste for printed indulgences and devotional texts, was soon alarmed by the printing houses' outputs. The pamphlets showed printing to be a pact with the devil in the eyes of many Catholics. The faked 'horrible media' – producing journalism found offensive whatever its veracity – was then to be fought, futilely, with censorship. Reading *Omni libri et scriptae*, written by Martinus Lutherus, for instance, might have entailed excommunication or even execution, but that did not stop him producing dozens of publications, sometimes in editions of several thousand copies. As was said at the time, '*notabitur Romae, legetur ergo*' – if it's banned in Rome, it's bound to be read. And even his finely engraved printed portrait was sold by the thousands to his supporters, as a sort of holy pin-up.

There were, however, in essence no *newspapers* in this period. In these years, the world might have been moving into modern times. Reformation and Renaissance might have been remaking it, in no small part in the name of rational fact. Printed news, however, was not much involved in this seismic change. Eschewing sobriety and toying with veracity might have made commercial sense, but it left the field free to be occupied by publications branded as reporting, but actually significantly closer to fictional imaginings. And the not insignificant matter of draconian censorship enforced during the struggles of the Reformation pushed the printers further in this direction. The authorities worried about the news, but fake news, the more trivialised the better, served well both the censor and the censored newswriters who were profitably unconstrained by 'truth', despite their claims to the contrary.

Moreover, as we have seen, instead of the newspaper as a platform for debate, there were pamphlets offering opinion and, of course, opinions were not news. They were not to be seen in news publications as a regular item for many decades after newspapers finally established themselves, with difficulty, in the second quarter of the 17th century. Handwritten *avvisi* were news but they were not printed.

'Strange newes': Printed news 1485— **25**

Newsbooks and broadsheets were printed, but as one-offs and not periodicals. The manuscript newsletters of merchants and the communications of the state were secret. In sum, though, most social needs were being met by these various forms of news communication. Newspapers, as such, were not needed. But perhaps the most telling inhibitor was, after all, the popularity of the 'absurd exaggerations' of newsbooks and broadsheets.[27] Not only is fake news as old as the news, surviving examples demonstrate that it was more popular. It was more the norm. As *news* was commoditised in the marketplace of print, fakery in a broad sense was ever-present.

The newsbooks were often garishly illustrated with crude woodcuts, just as *Dracule Wajda* had been. Their titles made claims to offer 'newes', 'tydings', 'current occurences', but it was sensation that pushed sales. Their approach echoed *meistersinger* Beheim's and that of the printers of the Dracula newsbooks who followed him. The reports, even when quite clearly grounded in fact, were sensationalised. The witchcraft panic which swept Europe in the 16th and 17th centuries really did consume as many as 60,000+ lives[28], but the news reports of this slaughter merely credulously milked every last detail of the supposed 'crimes', and of the disgusting cruelties involved in punishing them. It was a reality horror show, and endlessly reported as such. Other types of crime-story, so to speak, were also newsworthy. Solitary murders, of – for instance – a Mr Tate in 1624, became *The crying Murther: Contayning the cruell and most horrible Butcher of Mr. Tate*, illustrated with a woodcut of his killers wandering about with various bits of his corpse – an arm here, his torso there.[29] Another mainstay was miracles: in 1619, in Lyon, a child dead for 24 hours was resuscitated '*par l'intercession de la vierge*' – Virgin Mary revives corpse. Scoop![30]

Centuries before the development of the tabloid, the newsbooks endlessly tabloidised their content. Every report was 'strange' or 'wonderful', even when it concerned natural, explicable and familiar events such as a flood:

> *Wofull Newes from Wales, or the lamentable loss of divers Villages and Parishes (by a strange and wonderful Floud) within the Countye of Monmouth in Wales: which happened in January last past, 1607, whereby a great number of his Majesties subjects inhabiting in these parts are utterly undone.*[31]

And, often, when there was '*newes*' it was also '*strange newes*': '*Newes and Strange Newes of a tempestuous spirit which is called by the Indians a hurycano or whirlwind*'. News of the weather, and more generally the sky, often a staple of the newsbooks, becomes of particular interest when it (apparently) occasions such 'strange' inexplicable reports. For example, there is a *canard* – sold as was usual as a '*veritable conte*' – about a dragon, a '*serpent de merveilleuse grandure*', flying in the skies over Paris in 1579.[32] In 1583, in England: *Wonderful and strange newes* [was reported] *out of Suffolke and Essex where it rayned wheat the space of six or seven miles.*[33] In Germany, the city of Rosenberg was apparently in considerable trouble in 1593. The newsbook on the subject was a good buy, replete with titillations: *Strange Signes seene in the Aire,*

Strange Monsters Behelld on the Lande, And Wonderful Prodegies both By Land And Sea, Over, In and About the Citie of Rosenberge in High Germany ... truly translated out of the High Dutch copie.[34] The *'wonderful prodegies'* included the obligatory monstrous birth, in this case of four babies born at once. The quadruplets and their mother all died and were put in a coffin too heavy to lift, but which, when opened, was found to contain – Shock! Horror! – only four drops of blood!!

The claim that this sort of thing was any sort of news was sustained by branding it as 'true' or '*véritable*', for all that, in practice, this was endlessly undercut by the unsubstantiated – dare we say – 'facts' presented in the texts that followed. Reporting the supernatural was, unsurprisingly, a winning formula with credulous readers. This was, to modern eyes, the most absurd and most faked aspect of the newsbooks' bread and butter.

On balance, though (and, arguably, not totally unlike some modern tabloid or tabloidised content), at least a kernel of reality prompted much of what newsbooks retailed. The witches, after all, did burn. And there was, in truth, amongst the proliferation of clearly fabricated reports, news which contemporary ignorance often found strange and supernatural, but for which we have ready explanations, looking back. For example, one spring week in 1613 brought: *Strange newes from Lancaster, containing an account of a prodigious monster burne in the township of Addlington, with two bodies joined to one back.*[35] Unfeasible monster births of this type were another newsbook staple, but this report of an instantly recognisable case of conjoined twins suggests that not all were faked. Not to ignore the broadsheets' and newsbooks' imaginative excesses, even the most outlandish tale might have proved to be triangulatable.

> *TRUE AND WONDERFULL.*
> *A Discourse relating*
> *A STRANGE AND MONSTROUS*
> *SERPENT, OR DRAGON,*
> *Lately Discovered and yet living*
> *to the great Annoyance and divers*
> *Slaughters both Men and Cattll, by his*
> *strong and violent*
> *Poyson ...*
>
> *this present*
> *Month of August, 1614.*[36]

Such accounts bore the trappings of the truth brand. The killer serpent was to be found *In Sussex, two Miles from Horsam, in a Woode called St. Leonards Forrest, and thirtie Miles from London,* and moreover, as for witnesses, the writer promised that:

> the persons, whose names are hereunder printed, have seen this serpent, beside divers others, as the carrier of Horsham, who lieth at the White Horse, in Southwark, and who can certify the truth of all that has been here related.

John Steele.
Christopher Holder.
And a Widow Woman dwelling near Faygate.[37]

It is far from ridiculous to think that if you wanted, you could go and find the carrier in the White Horse pub who would tell you about the widow living near Faygate. But that would be no more convincing a way to prove the serpent existed than it would be now. In effect, just trust the journalist. After all, could this 'serpent' have been an escaped hamadryad – a king cobra? The Governor and Company of Merchants of London trading into the East Indies', the East India Company, had received its Royal Charter by 1601. Time enough for a returning 'John Company' ship to have brought the strange and monstrous serpent, native to India, home to England.

Generally speaking, we don't know very much about how these publications were received but, despite such deployment, it seems probable that their claims of the truth of the strangenesses they reported was not universally accepted. The age was credulous, but it was also absorbing rationality. As the newsbooks reached their highpoint of popularity, Ben Jonson's 1625 satire, *The Staple of News,* can be taken to reflect the thinking of the literati about them. He has its lead character, a news publisher and printer, excuse the writers:

> Why, methinks, Sir, if the honest common People
> Will be abus'd, why should not they ha' their pleasure
> In the believing Lyes, are made for them.[38]

As they began with the likes of Dracula, so news publications had continued until Jonson's day. And today, denials and protestations notwithstanding, they yet provide the template that allows mainstream journalism to sell embellishment, exaggeration and misrepresentation as triangulated accounts of events – as news: 'strange newes'. Of the newsbooks' 'strange' staples only the supernatural has slipped from mainstream coverage, and even that is alive and well among the mendacities of fake news publications and spurious news websites.[39]

While, as we argued in the foreword, sobriety and/or formality of tone is neither a cure for journalism's problems nor a sign of their absence, it is worth noting that sobriety was always present as a road not so much taken. Historians and chroniclers, after all, had from antiquity utilised a sober tone, and had sought to triangulate their narratives with witness accounts and other evidence. This was history rather than news, dealing with the past rather than the present, and thus totally unconcerned with timeliness, that touchstone of the news. However, it might prompt the question, if this was already how history was often written, why wasn't journalism, the so-called 'first rough draft of history',[40] ever written the same way? There would seem to be one lonely surviving prototype of the historical method being applied to report on an event as it happened, to highlight this as a road less travelled on; but it is also a very early signpost to the contemporary concept of the news report. Modern medievalists consider this text as 'Formally bizarre … the only journalistic history we have from Europe in the 12th century'.[41] The manuscript concerns the assassination of 'Good' Count Charles of Flanders in the city of Bruges on the morning of 2 March 1127[42] and was written by Galbert, a notary, who lived through the aftermath of the murder.

Galbert of Bruges had been moved to write up a report which was neither gossip nor, as he well understood, history. He had no word for what he was doing – setting down an account of contemporary events in a tone essentially describable as sober. But we can recognise it as news in the modern sense. Galbert was being a journalist, before there was such a thing.[43]

In Latin, on dated wax tablets, he fabricated (in its original sense of making) a report of the tumultuous civil disorders of the days after the killing.[44] Galbert knew he wasn't writing as an historian. He knew he was no Thucydides painstakingly gathering evidence from informants long after the events described. He was a witness and the events were now: 'I had to wait for moments of peace during the night or day to set down in order the present account of events as they happened'.[45]

He begins:

> In the year one thousand one hundred and twenty-seven, on the sixth day before the Nones of March, on the second day that is, after the beginning of the same month ... about dawn, the count at Bruges was kneeling in prayer in order to hear the early Mass in the church of Saint Donatian. The office of the first hour was completed ... and when the count, according to custom, was praying ... those wretched traitors, already murderers at heart, slew the count, who was struck down with swords and run through again and again.

Here, centuries before any news media appeared in Europe literally *avant la lettre*, is the journalistic ideal of: Who? What? When? Where? And, how? Had modern clocks existed in his day, the account reads as though he surely would have given us the minute. Galbert's text was, as far as the record goes, without precedent, and without progeny until after the Middle Ages were deemed to be long-over. For all that the English-speaking world, apart from medievalists, largely ignores its existence, Galbert's Latin *De multro ... on the murder etc. of the glorious Charles ...* must stand, amazingly, as a proto-template for journalism of record a full half-millennium before anything like it appears in Europe again. It is the most striking indicator that a different cultural position for the dissemination of news could have developed but did not. It is thought only one manuscript was produced; and forgotten.[46]

So, why does such an innovation wither on the branch? A lack of interest or demand, of course, but why would there be no interest or demand? For the same reason that if somebody had invented the modern clocks alluded to in the previous paragraph, that innovation would not have taken off either. For the same reason that even after the rise of moveable type it still takes more than a century for anything resembling a newspaper to emerge, even though no element necessary for one's production is missing. Simply put, there was no social need for it. A faith-based, largely illiterate medieval society, with no firm grasp on current events or the modern concept of evidence, needs sober journalism like a fish needs a bicycle.

The coming of print, despite technicist belief to the contrary, did not create a literate public. Mass-communication of the news does not arise in a society in which there is no mass with any need to know the news, even if the technology is at hand to provide it. And even though other specific needs had occasioned the development of print, there was no social drive to apply it to producing newspapers. It is only later, as will be related in subsequent chapters, once society has changed and developed, producing a citizenry with actual needs and uses for details of current events beyond simple diversion, that any medium comes to offer such information on such events.

Between *De multro* and the advent of the first recognisable newspapers, in the first decade of the 17th century, lie no less than 465 years or so – and even after the three hundred years between Galbert and Gutenberg and Michel Beheim are laid aside, there are still 15 decades of delay to account for. The significance of this for us today is that no distinction between what the news soberly promises and what it actually delivers was insisted upon, generally accepted, or even, in a sense, noticed. Its long gestation allowed the newspaper, when it finally appeared, to be relaxed – very relaxed – about both sobriety and veracity. Even though they could not have prevented present difficulties, nonetheless the effects of the news having been born not out of these qualities, but rather out of, if not mendacity then certainly sensationalism, still resonate in the modern media landscape.

Notes

1 Despite the popularity of relatively straightforward stories of the single famous 'great man' (always 'man') inventor and a singular moment of invention, there are always – as in Gutenberg's case – ghosts lurking in the media's technological history. With printing, as is usually the case, society, not technology, is the prime determinant of successful fully-diffused innovation. This is why there are traces and hints of experimenters in Avignon and Prague and perhaps elsewhere, shadowy contemporary rivals to Johannes Gensfleisch zur Laden zum Gutenberg. As with the other rival forgotten 'inventors' involved in the introduction of subsequent media technologies – serendipitously producing the same 'invention' at virtually the same moment each time – Gutenberg may well not have been alone in responding to emerging social needs in the town and in the Church by reaching for the idea of moveable type. All are stirred not by 'eureka' insights but by an identical social need. Received understanding, however, is clear regarding the 'invention' of printing, i.e. Gutenberg, Mainz, the late 1430s, eureka and hey presto (Winston, Brian [2005]. *Messages*. London: Routledge, pp 1–9.).
2 Pettegree, Andrew (2017). 'Broadsheets: Single-sheet publishing in the first age of print. Typology and typography' in *Broadsheets: Single-Sheet Publishing in the First Age of Print* (Andrew Pettegree, ed.). Leiden: Brill, pp 1–32.
3 Eisenstein, Elizabeth (1993). *The Printing Revolution in Early Modern Europe*. Cambridge: Cambridge University Press, pp. 13–17.
4 Bahn, Eugene & Margaret Bahn (1970). *History of Oral Interpretation*. Minneapolis, MN: Burgess Publishing Company, p. 72.
5 Hall, Joseph (1914) *The Poems of Laurence Minot*. Oxford: Clarendon Press: Oxford University Press, p. xii.

6 Miller, Elizabeth (2003). 'Beheim and the Dracula connection' [conference paper]. https://kutztownEnglish.files.wordpress.com/2015/09/jds_v5_2003_dickens_and_miller.pdf [accessed 13 August 2018].
7 Stoker, Bram (1897). *Dracula*. Westminster: Archibald Constable and Company.
8 Johnson, Samuel (1758). 'Corruption of news-writers', *The Idler*, 30, 11 November. www.johnsonessays.com/the-idler/corruption-news-writers/ [accessed 6 September 2018].
9 Pooley, Eric (1989). 'Grins, gore, and videotape – The trouble with local TV news', *New York Magazine*. http://evaluatingconversations.weebly.com/if-it-bleeds-it-leads.html [accessed 31 January 2020].
10 Trepow, Kurt (2000). *Vlad III Dracula: The Life and Times of the Historical Dracula*. University of Michigan: Center for Roumanian Studies.
11 Bellanger, Claude *et al.* (1969). *Histoire Générale de la Presse Française: Tome 1*. Paris: Presses Universitaires de France, p. 44.
12 Brant, Sebastian (1492). *Von dem Donnerstein vor Ensisheim....* Straßburg: Johann Prüss. https://bildsuche.digitale- [accessed 20 August 2018]; Roland, Ingrid (1990). 'A contemporary account of the Ensisheim meteorite', *Meteorotics*, 25, pp. 19–22.
13 Wacher (1529). *Newe zeyttung von Speyr Von handlung der Fürsten ein reytten vnd erscheynung 1529*. [Held in the Bavarian State Archive, Nuremberg]. www.Europeana.eu/portal/en/record/9200386/BibliographicResource_3000149337072.html [accessed 20 August 2018].
14 Anon [Michael Nanger?] (1586). *Newe Zeyttung auß der Insel Japonien/ New Tidings from the Japanese Island*. [British Library shelfmark C.40.a.19]. www.britishmuseum.org/research/collection_online/collection_object_details.aspx?objectId=1423510&partId=1 [accessed 20 August 2018].
15 Anon (Timothy Hudson: Rare and Early Newspapers) (n/d). 'Exceedingly rare 1548 newsbook ... Over 460 years old ...' [advertisement]. www.rarenewspapers.com/view/643799 [accessed 16 August 2018].
16 Rurscheyt, Anton (1542). *Warhafftige vnd erschrockenliche Newe Zeyttung, inn Schlesien geschehen inn disem 42* [Österreichische Nationalbibliothek, Vienna]. www.europeana.eu/portal/en/record/9200332/ABO__2BZ184959101.html [accessed 20 August 2018].
17 Falise, Mario (2004). 'Information and politics in the seventeenth century' in *Court and Politics in Papal Rome, 1492–1700* (Gianvittorio Signorotto & Maria Antonietta Visceglia, eds.). Cambridge: Cambridge University Press, pp. 217, 222.
18 Steinburg, Sigfrid (1969). *500 Years of Printing*. Harmondsworth: Penguin, p. 240.
19 Felise, Mario (2004). *Information and Politics in the Seventeenth Century: Court and Politics in Papal Rome, 1492–1700* (Gianvittorio Signorotto & Maria Antonietta Visceglia, eds.) Cambridge: Cambridge University Press, p. 222.
20 Bernhard, Jim (2007). *Porcupine, Picayune, and Post: How Newspapers Get Their Names*. Columbia, MO: University of Missouri Press, p. 10.
21 Dibdin, Thomas (1816). *Typographical Antiquities: Or the History of Printing in England, Scotland and Ireland, Vol. 3*. London: John Murray, p. 361 (Faques sometimes printed his name as 'Fake'.).
22 Henry VIII/Thomas Moore (1521). *Assertio Septem Sacramentorum adversus Martinum Lutherum*. Basel: Frobein.
23 e.g. Luther, Martin (1517: printed January 1518). *Amore et studio elucidande veritatis: hec subscripta disputabuntur Wittenberge. Presidente R.P Martino Lutther* [aka: *The 95 Theses*]. Nuremberg.
24 Luther, Martin (1522). *Contra Henricum Regem Anglie/ Against Henry King of the English*. Wittenberg: Petri.

25 Jouhaud, Christian (1987). 'Readability and persuasion: Political handbills' in *The Culture of Print: Power and the Uses of Print in Early Modern Europe* (Roger Chartier, ed.; Lynda Cochoran, trans.). Princeton: Princeton University Press, pp. 235–260.
26 Luther, Martin (1522). *An den christlichen Adel deutscher Nation*. Wittenberg.
27 Andrew, Alexander (1859). *A History of British Journalism, Vol. I*. London: Richard Bently, p. 34.
28 Levack, Brian (2006). *The Witch-Hunt in Early Modern Europe*. London: Longman.
29 Olasky, Marvin (n/d). 'Central ideas in the development of American journalism', *World Magazine*. www.worldmag.com/world/olasky/centralideas/appa.html [accessed 15 June 2019].
30 Bellanger, Claude et al. (1969). *Histoire Générale de la Presse Française: Tome 1*. Paris: Presses Universitaires de France, p. 43.
31 Anon (1607). *Wofull Newes from Wales, or the lamentable loss of divers Villages and Parishes (by a strange and wonderful Floud) within the Countye of Monmouth in Wales: which happened in January last past, 1607, whereby a great number of his Majesties subjects inhabiting in these parts are utterly undone*, qt. in Mason Jackson (1885). *The Pictorial Press: Its Origin and Progress*. London: Hurst & Blackett, p. 13.
32 Bellanger, Claude et al (1969). *Histoire Générale de la Presse Française: Tome 1*. Paris: Presses Universitaires de France, p. 53.
33 Anon (1583). *Wonderful and strange newes out of Suffolke and Essex where it rayned wheat the space of six or seven miles*, qt in Alexander Andrews (1859), *A History of British Journalism, Vol. I*. London: Richard Bentley, p. 35.
34 Ettinghousen, Henry (2015). *How the Press Began. The Pre-Periodical Printed News in Early Modern Europe*. www.janusdigital.es/anexos.htm2015 [accessed 15 August 2018].
35 Anon (1613) *Strange newes from Lancaster, containing an account of a prodigious monster burne in the township of Addlington, with two bodies joined to one back*, qt in Alexander Andrews (1859), *A History of British Journalism Vol. I*, London: Richard Bently, p. 27.
36 Anon (1614). *TRUE AND WONDERFULL. A Discourse relating A STRANGE AND MONSTROUS SERPENT, OR DRAGON, Lately Discovered and yet living*. https://en.wikisource.org/wiki/True_and_wonderfull [accessed 15 August 2018].
37 Ibid.
38 Jonson, Ben (1625). *The Staple of News*, Act 1, Sc 5. http://hollowaypages.com/Jonson1692news.htm [accessed 13 March 2012].
39 And, also, it can still be found in the mainstream. The broadsheet London *Daily Telegraph*, for example, the voice of British conservatism, continues to report strange meteorological sightings. Only, from the mid-20th century on into the present, these are not caused by dragons but by 'Unidentified Flying Objects'. 2009 was a particularly good year for this: Copping, Jasper (2009). 'UFO sightings over Britain more than triple this year', *Daily Telegraph*, 19 September. www.telegraph.co.uk/news/newstopics/howaboutthat/ufo/6209733/UFO-sightings-over-Britain-more-than-triple-this-year.html [accessed 9 January 2020].
40 The phrase is often attributed to *Washington Post* publisher and president Philip L. Graham, but its actual first use is disputed/unknown: Shafer, J. (2010). 'On the trail of the question who first said or wrote that journalism is the first rough draft of history. *The Slate*. https://slate.com/news-and-politics/2010/08/on-the-trail-of-the-question-who-first-said-or-wrote-that-journalism-is-the-first-rough-draft-of-history.html [accessed 13 August 2018].
41 Rider, Jeff (2001). *God's Scribe: The Historiography of Galbert of Bruges*. Washington, DC: Catholic University of America Press, p. 1.

42 Galbert of Bruges (2009 [1127]). *The Murder of Charles, the Good Count of Flanders.* New York: Harper Row, p. 13; Galbert of Bruges (2005 [*1127*]) *De multro, traditione et occisione gloriosi Karoli comitis Flandriarum/The Murder of Count Charles of Flanders* (trans. James Ross). New York: Columbia University Press.
43 Nichols, Bill (1991). *Representing Reality: Issues and Concepts in Documentary.* Bloomington, IN: Indiana University Press, p. 50.
44 Galbert of Bruges (2009 [1127]). *The Murder of Charles, the Good Count of Flanders.* New York: Harper Row, p. 13; Galbert of Bruges (2005 [*1127*]) *De multro, traditione et occisione gloriosi Karoli comitis Flandriarum/The Murder of Count Charles of Flanders* (trans. James Ross). New York: Columbia University Press.
45 Ibid.
46 We owe our knowledge of it to 17th century reprints.

2

'NEWES': THE COMING OF THE NEWSPAPER 1600—

> 'For the better information of the people'
> *Marchmont Needham (1620–1678)*
> *Journalist, Publisher and Pamphleteer*

By 1600, the news began to concern itself with war and politics (and business), at the expense of wonders in the sky and monsters on the ground. Although born in sensationalism and spectacle, a more regularly appearing sobriety was also proving to be vendible – selling not 'strange newes' but, simply, 'newes':

> Tuesday, Ianuary 30.
> This day the King was beheaded, over against the Banquetting house by White-Hall. The manner of Execution, and what passed before his death take thus. He was brought from St James about ten in the morning, walking on foot through the Park, with a Regiment of Foot for his guard, with Colours fflying, Drums beating, his private Guard of Partisans, with some of his Gentlemen before, and some behind bareheaded, Dr Juxton late Bishop of London next behind him, and Colonel Thomlinson (who had charge of him) to the gallery in Whitehall and so into the Cabinet Chamber where he used to lie at his Devotion … The Scaffold was hung with black, and the floor covered with black, and the Axe and Block laid in the middle of the Scaffold. There were diverse companies of Foot and Horse, on every side the Scaffold, and the multitude that came to be Spectators, very great. The King, making a Pass upon the Scaffold, looked very earnestly upon the block.

Samuel Pecke, printer and publisher, produced this carefully-witnessed, fact-filled report for the 288th edition of his *Perfect Diurnal of Some Passages in Parliament*, dated 29 January to 5 February, 1649. The *Diurnal* sequenced such daily reports and published them in weekly batches. So, as the execution was on a Tuesday, Pecke ran the story with no headline beyond the dateline on page three – the cover page being the masthead presented over a woodcut of the parliament in session, and the second page being devoted to what happened in Westminster on the Monday.

It is the tone which is extraordinary, in context. In the broadsheets and the newsbooks everything was 'horrible', 'wonderous', or, most commonly, 'strange'. Here was an event without precedent in English history, a virtual deicide in the eyes of many at the time, and it contains but the one adverb – 'earnestly'.

> After which the King, stooping down, laid his necke upon the blocke, and after a very little pause, stretching forth his hands, the executioner at one blow severed his head from his bodiy. Then his body was put in a coffin and covered with black velvet; and removed to his lodging chamber in Whitehall.[1]

And, without break, the next paragraph begins: 'The House of Commons this day, according to given orders, sat early, and the Dutch Ambassadors, having sent them a transcript of their Embassie in English, the House spent much time in hearing the same read …'. Pecke was, as were many of his fellow newswriters by this time, at last and albeit unwittingly, channelling not the sensationalist *Meistersinger* Michael Beheim but the sober notary Galbert.

In 1605, in the Protestant Imperial City of Strasburg, Johann Carolus had published what is received as the first newspaper: *Relation aller Fürnemmen und gedenckwürdigen Historian/ Account of All Distinguished and Commemorable News*, although in format it was more newsbook than broadsheet. Carolus had a business selling regular news, copied by hand, to subscribers. Writing for clients semi-privately, he was midway between a Fugger newsletter scribe and a manuscript *avviso* gazetteer. In fact, the reports he copied would appear to have come, at least in part, from *avvisi* to which he himself subscribed. The clients for his service were his fellow burghers, including the municipal authorities. His great idea – at last – was that, using the same title for his newsletters every time but numbering and dating them, he should print copies every week instead of writing them out by hand. As he explained, in a petition to the municipal council for the privilege of a news-publishing monopoly:

> I have recently purchased at a high and costly price the former printing workshop of the late Thomas Jobin and placed and installed the same in my house at no little expense …. For several weeks, and now for the twelfth occasion, I have set, printed and published the said advice in my printing workshop, likewise not without much effort.[2]

Despite his declaring himself 'your graces humble and obedient citizen', the magistracy did not award the privilege. Nonetheless, the multi-report, regular, dated news publication had arrived.

We had been moving towards this since the *Zeyttungg* of 1548, at least. Single report newsbooks were the norm at that time but it was only 40 years on that (between 1588 and 1593) a *Relatio Historica* began to appear regularly, twice a year.[3] The publication's alternative title was the *Messerelation* because its author, Michael von Aitzing of Cologne, shrewdly produced it specifically for sale at the semi-annual Frankfurt *Buchmesse* – Bookfares.[4] Von Aitzung offered a sober overview of the previous six months, though still confusing, in approach and title, the historical with the contemporary (much as Galbert had). 1592 saw the arrival of an even more substantial book recording mainly military events over the previous four years. Written in Latin by Michael ab Isset, it adopted a suitably learned title derived from the name of the messenger of the Roman gods, *Mercurius*. The *Mercurius Gallobelgicus* transformed itself into a periodical via updates by various authors published in twice-yearly new volumes until 1635.[5] Again, this was history as much as it was news, not least because of the implied permanence signaled by it being bound. And, from 1596, Samuel Dilburn published in Switzerland a *trewlichte* [sober and political] *Kurtze Beschreibung* (*Short Copy* – a digest) speeding up the periodicity from six months to one.[6] The 'then' of its predecessors was becoming the 'now'.

The earliest surviving copy of a Carolus *Relation* dates from 1609, and its sensitivity to time marked a breakthrough. Instead of a newsbook's crude woodcut, there was a beautifully embellished engraved title page announcing reports from *Schott und Engelland* in the west to *Hungern, Polan und Moldau* in the east and from *Hiffpanie, Franchreich* and *Italien* in the south. Stressing present rather than past, it carried four date-lined items – *alles auff das trewlichte wie*: from Cologne (8 January), Rome (20 December 1608), Vienna (*16. Ditto*), Prague (*29. Ditto*) – and there was nothing 'strange' about any of them.[7]

This did not mean that occasional single-report serious news publications now ceased. For example, in Amsterdam, on 17 May in the same year as Carolus's petition, a printer named Abraham Verhoeven published a broadsheet image of the siege of Antwerp, a significant event in the never-ending religious conflict then engulfing the Netherlands. And this was not a crude woodcut either, but a wonderfully detailed aerial view of the besiegers and the city, printed from a copper-plate. The banner read (Verhoeven enlarged his market with French editions):

LE VRAI PORTAIT COMME LES REBELLES …
metre le siège devant la ville d'Anvers le 17.[8]

'The True Picture of how the Rebels … lay siege to the city of Antwerp'. By the 1620s, he was integrating such engravings into an intermittent newsbook series, but Carolus's *Relation* had moved the goal-posts on regularity.

All titles continued to be used. *Tidings* or *Zeitung*, *Advises* or *Avvisi*, *Accounts* (narrations) or *Relationen*, *Journal* or *Gionali*, however, gave no necessary indication of immediacy. They could all contain delayed materials – 'late intelligences' – and so a term emerged more directly to reflect contemporaneity. Adding a sense of time to the old word for 'flow' – current – the Dutch publishers took the lead in acknowledging the perishability (as it were) of news, and the crucial importance of regularity, by naming an unbound dated news periodical carrying a diet of reports a *Coranto*.

So, overall, what was the environment which engendered this development? Why the early 1600s?

Basically, it is a central technicist illusion that, as Marshall McLuhan put it: 'We shape our tools and then our tools shape us'.[9] This concept ignores the history of technology which, rather, reveals that supervening social necessities condition the systems engineering leading to technological developments even as the suppression of their radical disruptive potential constrains the speed of their diffusion.[10] The machines become common only because they fit our agenda and service our objectives. Fernand Braudel's understanding of this phenomenon is far more apposite. He saw social changes in terms of 'accelerators' – factors pushing such advances – and 'brakes' hindering them.[11] Urbanisation and the Church's need for uncorrupted texts produced the supervening social necessities encouraging systems engineers such as Gutenberg to depress the Braudelian accelerator in the first place. The press's speed increased from the less than ten iph Gutenberg had achieved to (a best-estimated) peak of 240 sheets.[12] Printing on blanksheet allowed for four smaller pages of text per impression. The sheet was then folded and cut (ergo, quarto), speeding output yet further. But, as we have seen, as far as news was concerned, from the 1450s, other available communication channels – oral, private – satisfied demand. Their effectiveness had inhibited the potential for more consistent public distribution of printed intelligence. The literates' demands for news were being met by these various news sources; and, in a landscape of illiteracy, older modes of orality persisted, e.g. with the minstrelsy and the publicly declaimed *gazzetto*, into the 16th century.

And illiteracy apart, there were other suppressive pressures of an ingrained culture of secrecy sustained by the scribes of merchants, ambassadors and thrones. Even some public opinion was not unsympathetic to the principle of official secrecy. 'The affairs of princes which they do not want broadcast should not be bandied about': Tobias Peucer wrote this in a University of Leipzig PhD thesis on news-gathering from 1690 – the earliest surviving media studies research paper known. Come to that, he added, it was also 'ridiculous' and 'foolish' to bandy about 'how many purple and gold garments (each prince possessed)'. This was knowledge which 'profits no-one' – except of course the printer.[13] And, of course, there was also the increasingly restrictive censorship, both sacred and secular, contributing to seriously stunting printed news's development. The censors were always particularly sensitive to news, implicitly assuming its disruptive power. But events – the Reformation and the conflicts that flowed from it – were to release the brake.

In 1555, the Peace of Augsburg calmed the first phase of the religious wars. A truce between the Catholic Church and the allied Schmalkaldic Lutheran princes was agreed. Although vicious conflicts continued in France and the Low Countries, elsewhere throughout Europe the compromise held. As the century turned, though, the peace was fraying. The Turks were harassing Europe's southern flank. In 1600 they invaded Styria (a part of present-day Austria). Within the Hapsburg lands where his writ ran, the Jesuit-educated Archduke of Austria, Ferdinand II, had already begun to tear away at the protections the Protestants had secured at Augsburg. In Upper and Lower Austria, Bohemia, Croatia, Slovenia, and parts of Hungary, Reformed books and pamphlets were burned. Reformed pastors and teachers were exiled. Indeed, exile or forced Catholic confession became common. In 1607, Ferdinand was appointed by the Emperor Rudolph as deputy to the Imperial throne and, in 1619, he was elected Emperor. By then, though, his zealotry had enflamed the east, and what would be the bloodiest conflict of pre-20th century Europe, the Thirty Years' War, had begun. Eight million are estimated to have died in the German lands, one-third of the total population, in the name of faith. The Peace of Augsburg was broken.

The supervening social necessity that finally produces the newspaper is the democratisation of the need to know occasioned by this ever-deepening disaster: the need to know where the fires of the stakes burned and where the hanging trees stood; where the armies advanced, the battles were fought, the sieges laid, the alliances made, and the truces brokered. Luther had claimed the right of a free conscience – in effect not just in matters theological. A century later, Milton was to call for this as a demand for 'the liberty to know, to utter, and to argue freely according to conscience, above all liberties'.[14] It was in the wash of such rhetoric, and in the loosening of the censoring powers of authorities distracted by war, that the demand for serious, ever more timely news flourished ever more insistently. Meeting increasing demand for news in the first decades of the 17th century required no major technological advance in the wooden press. A Sam Pecke could easily print (and sell) 2,500 copies of his eight page (maximum) *Diurnal* a week; that is 20,000 pages on 2,500 blanksheets – a couple of (long) days' work. He was not alone in achieving such circulation. And the conflicts of the time created the demand to sustain it.

The formal cause of the thirty-year armed conflict occurred in May 1618 when rebel Czech Protestants ignominiously threw Frederick's emissaries, come to enforce his will upon them, out of a 20-metre high window – the 'Defenestration of Prague'. The month following, a regular weekly publication, a *Courante uyt Italien, Duytslandt, &c.*, began to be published in Amsterdam.[15] Time-sensitivity as evidenced by its title supports a claim that this *courante* might better be the earliest example of a newspaper – not, despite their periodicity, Carolus's newsbook-style publications of the previous decade. A translation was made into English, signed by the publishers, George Veseler and the writer/engraver Peter van der Keere. For nearly a year, from 2 December 1620 to 18 September 1621, 15 editions crossed the Channel to London and were distributed without any official sanctions. The continental war and sober, regular news in its modern form arrived together.

Censorship, although about to falter, was still everywhere, making the provision of information problematic. In England, print needed the imprimatur of the printers' guild – the Stationers' Company – reinforced by the power of the Tudor court of the Star Chamber to censor all unlicensed printing activity via bans, fines, and/or imprisonment. When Thomas Archer, a London publisher, sought to break into the market uncovered by the *courante* with his own translated and unlicensed publication, he was imprisoned. This was, however, merely a hiccup. Within a month of his incarceration, he was released, undeterred. On 24 September 1621, Archer and fellow publishers Nathaniel Bourne and Nathaniel Butter (a senior figure in the Stationers' Company, thought to be the model for Jonson's satirized protagonist) issued another *Corante, or, news from Italy, Germany, Hungarie, Spaine and France out of the Hie Dutch Coppy printed at Franckford* ....[16] It was 'to be sold at their shops at the Exchange, and in Popes-head Pallace'. After some format experiments, a weekly edition was made available as an unbound quarto running from eight to 24 pages. The war meant the corantos had much news to retail. The first edition that Veseler and van der Keere sent to London carried reports of the initial major salvo of the conflict – the great battle at the White Mountain outside Prague. The tone was Galbertian:

> Letters out of Nuremberg make mention that they had advice from the borders of Bohemia, that there had been a very great Battle by Prage, between the King and the Duke of Beyeren and many 1000 slaine on both sides, but that the Duke of Beyeren should have any folks with him in Prage is yet uncertaine.[17]

About 25% of the report's words are devoted to the protocols establishing veracity, although 'the letters from Nuremberg' merely repeat hearsay from 'the borders of Bohemia'. As with the serpent near Horsham, the fellow in the pub and the local unnamed widow, so here too: a nod to an established convention. A further 25% reveals ignorance – what is going on 'is yet uncertaine'. The event itself gets the remaining 50%. So here is the news – regular in appearance, sober in tone, significant in content. All this was far from 'strange newes' – but that the 'newes' be 'trewe', ensured it was still, in practice, targeting an untriangulable idea.

In fact, the increasing pressure of a market-driven need for timeliness exacerbated its problems. The report of the Battle of the White Mountain contains, with commendable honesty, a measure of confusion as to the whereabouts of the losers: if any Protestants had retreated to Prague was 'as yet uncertaine'. But deadlines must be met if publications are to be current and marketable and such ignorance did not stop the presses. A weak obligation to truth was further weakened, but it was this need for contemporaneity more than any propensity for sensationalism which encouraged this. Triangulation is sacrificed simply to beat the competition. When demands for sensation in a lively marketplace of ideas are added, the need for recent datelines compounds the dangers of journalistic error. Timeliness was to make the news perishable, as it were – like fresh fruit. And like fresh fruit it could be sent to market unripened. Although not quite the enemy of sobriety that sensationalism is, having to be current is not its friend either. For example:

Despite a measure of harassment from the authorities, Butter and Bourne had established their own coranto of foreign news. On 20 October 1631, they had duly reported the death of the initially triumphant Catholic field-marshal Johannes Tserclaes, Count of Tilly, 'the monk in armour', who had prevailed at the White Mountain. On the untriangulated basis of the information which had come to them, they had pronounced him dead – but with a caveat:

> Indifferent Reader, we promised you (in the front of our last Aviso) the Death and Interment of Monsieur Tilly, which we now performe; notwithstanding that the last Antwerpian Post hath ruemored the contrary, against which you may balance each other, and accordingly beleeve.[18]

And why not have the cake and eat it? Butter said he was only 'the writer, or the transcriber rather, of the newes'.[19] He could not be held accountable for the fact that Tilly was actually alive and well at this point. The soldier was to be wounded in an encounter with the Protestant King of Sweden, Gustavus Adolphus, at the Battle of Rain-am-Lech in Bavaria and to die, probably of tetanus, 17 days later, on the 30 April 1632 – six months after Butter and Bourne had invited readers to draw their own conclusions regarding reports of his demise.

Clever writers turned cynicism and doubt to their own purposes: 'the uncertaintie likewise and varieties of reports is such that we know not what to believe .... And what is given out today for certain is tomorrow contradicted'.[20] Given the slowness of communications at this time, it was possible to publish a species of retroactive scoop in the form of 'late intelligences' specifically designed to undercut or correct the news already carried to market by rivals. For Ben Jonson, the public opened themselves to this abuse of the press through their 'hunger and thirſti after publſh'd pamphlets of news, ſet out very Saturday'.[21] And, of course, this hunger and thirst also blurred the distinction between 'newes' and 'strange newes' – between news and fake news. Perceiving a dichotomy between them continued to be as tricky as it had been from the outset.

In the accumulated reports of the new regular news publications, sobriety now appeared promiscuously side by side with sensationalism. As well as reporting on commercial matters such as 'The Turkish Pyracies', for example, Butter and Bourne had not been above finding space for '… certaine prodigies seene in the Empire'.[22] This was 'Times Newes', as Jonson called it in the printed edition of *The Staple of News*. Speed might have encouraged error but, of course, this does not mean that fictional imaginings were no longer also a factor. They continued to flourish. 'Times Newes' was still nothing but 'a weekly Cheat to draw Money'. The supposed reports were 'made at home, and no syllable of truth in them; than which there cannot be a greater Diſeaſe in Nature, nor a fouler Scorn put upon the Times'. But Jonson had no surer way of spotting fakery than do we.

Before the English Civil War, the authorities harassed news vendors simply for the act of publishing, whether their products were sober or trivial, politics or gossip, truth or lies. The Star Chamber was ever ready to censor. The Polish ambassador, for example, treated all coranto coverage of his country as a species of (Trumpian) '*fake news*', and, in response to his complaints, news publications of any kind were banned (i.e. could not be licensed) from 1632 on. It was six years before Butter and Bourne successfully petitioned for this prohibition to be lifted. But a century on from Luther's attack on papacy, the authority of censors had finally begun to falter. The world was in flux. Even the ancient concept of the Divine Right of Kings was not as self-evident as it once had been. The continent was in flames, and in England too the King's assertion of absolutism became a matter to be determined by force of arms.

In June 1641, deeply at loggerheads with Charles I, the newly assembled and unbiddable 'Long Parliament' (as it was to become known) abolished the Star Chamber. The wings of the Stationers' Company were also clipped and, as well as the continuing foreign war reports of the corantos, regular news of local events appeared in print, in English, for the first time: 'by strange alteration and vicissitude of times we talke of nothing else but what is done in England'.[23]

A year later, in August, Charles raised an army to remove the Parliament by force of arms and in the Civil War that followed the English press found its full-throated voice. Bandying about the doings of domestic princes rapidly became its prime activity, and this was to distinguish it from its continental equivalents for long after. On the continent, the sense that news publications should essentially act as critics of authority, whistle-blowers or muckrakers was less well articulated and explored. But in England, this became the prime legacy of the Civil War to the Anglophone press. The contrast was stark. The father of the French periodic press, Théophraste Renaudot, who founded *La Gazette de France* in 1631, was in fairly regular touch with Louis XIII: 'was it for me to examine the deeds of the government? My pen was only the grafting tool', he wrote.[24] A decade later, across the Channel, Marchmont Needham, a Civil War pioneer of English journalism, was in the exact opposite business. His motivation was to expose 'the deeds of the government' – that is, the misrule of King Charles I: 'I tooke up my pen for disabusing his Majesty, and for disbishoping and dispoping his good subjects', as he was to write.[25] But in doing so Needham was in effect having journalism take on another obligation. Beyond sobriety, truthfulness, and topicality (however much or little those were in fact on offer), in hands like his the press began to lay claim to being the answer to Juvenal's ancient question: 'Who guards the guardians?' Who holds authority to account? Needham was clear. He was in the business of nothing less than 'taking off vizards and vailes and disguises'. The argument could be made that in some admittedly limited respects, ideologically if not practically, this approach, or at least its rhetoric, was an ancestor of the investigative journalistic tradition.

Between 1642 and the King's execution in Westminster in 1649 some 200 or so English news-titles appeared and, although many tended still to be sold as bound news-books and were sheltered by one side or another, they met the other requirements of the newspaper – regular, periodic, numbered, multiple reports, etc. The King and his court had established themselves in Oxford and a weekly digest of news in support of his cause appeared from January 1643: the *Mercurius Aulicus* [*Court Mercury*] *Communicating Intelligence from all Parts, to all parts of the Kingdome, touching all Affaires, Conditions, Humours and Defigns*. It was largely written by Sir John Berkenhead and took the established form of a diurnal, ostentatiously announcing it was printed on Sundays to upset the Puritans in Westminster; but, despite its motto about 'humours and defigns', it was in tone at first very like Pecke's *Perfect Diurnall*. The third issue of the *Aulicus* added an *'AGAINE'* to the title (*Mercurius Aulicus AGAINE Communicating Intelligence ...'*) to indicate it meant to stay in the public eye and Berkenhead did manage to produce 118 editions. It soon adopted a more sober *Affaires of the Court to the reft of the Kingdome* as its motto, but its contents and tone were to move in the other direction – more tabloid than broadsheet:

> You have heard last week of the affrights and terrours which the prevailing faction in the pretended Houses [of Parliament] are fallen into, by reason of the sad condition of their affaires in the most parts abroad and shall now heare of the confusions and distractions they are in at home.[26]

The 'party newspaper' was born.

The Parliament, always 'the pretended Houses' in the pages of the *Aulicus*, yielded much news of faction and stresses in Westminster but overall this reporting – and the persistent editorial stance of Berkenhead along these lines – represented wishful thinking. Westminster might have been troubled but the verdict of history is that they were in better shape than was the King's party. The *Aulicus* exacerbates that slanting of the news, primarily as sensation, which had become a commonplace in the century and a half since it was first printed. Its reporting function, under the stress of war, was contaminated by an unremittingly distorted agenda. The paper also well represents the increasingly common blurring of the line which had previously been maintained between news publications and pamphlets, organs of opinion. Its editorial purpose was less *Communicating Intelligence* than assertions to undermine the enemy. Reporting on events as plainly as possible was not to be its prime business. The paper's voice slipped into opinionated charges of hypocrisy and the like without missing a beat:

> And to let you see what devout Soules these Members are for the Protestant Religion, we must tell you (as for this day we are for certaine advised) ... there are two troops more of *Popish* Wallones lately come over to serve these pious Reformers.[27]

Parliament withstood several months of such provocation before unleashing Marchmont Needham.

The anti-royalists in Westminster ranged in opinion from those who wished merely (as it were) to curb Charles's tyrannical behaviour and the threat of Papism, to outright revolutionary republicans who wanted the throne abolished. All sides found they were engaged in a propaganda as well as a hot war. As Dr Johnson was to note decades later: 'among the calamities of war may be justly numbered the diminution of the love of truth, by the falsehoods which interest dictates and credulity encourages'.[28] Any need for sober reporting was undercut by the conflict, ensuring that, after truth, sobriety would be its next casualty following close behind. Needham 'tooke up' his pen in August of 1643 initially as editor of the *Mercurius Britannicus*, the main mouthpiece of Parliament's supporters, and in that moment the English approach to the news, in all its obstreperousness, crazed competitiveness, and passion for 'taking off of vizards, vails and disguises'[29] manifested itself. It has never gone away.

Needham was a radical journalistic innovator. He set headings for his paper's stories down the side of the page identifying them by cross referencing their first words in the body of the text as an index of these 'incipits', an early move towards headlines and stand-firsts. He was to augment the quasi-scoops of 'late intelligences' with a prototype of the modern investigative report by publishing Charles's secret cabinet papers. These had been captured in King's horse's paniers after his disastrous defeat at the Battle of Naseby in June 1645:

> I will shew you more Tricks here [wrote Needham], than ever Hocus-Pocus did … at Bartholomew Faire … it will yield us at least a Moneths sport; and I mean to anatomize every Paper, week after week, till I have gone quite through; keeping still to my old Motto, 'For the better Information of the People'.[30]

In the event, Needham ran eight weeks of leaks. But, even more fatefully for Anglophone journalism's future, he was to build on Berkenhead's blurring of the line between pamphlet and news.

Obligation to be 'trewe' had suggested a neutrality which journalists were happy to claim, but this blurring rendered that stance fraught. The 'truth' rhetoric had them as 'transcribers' of verifiable realities, not retailers of opinion. Even when they themselves bore witness, they claimed that they were disengaged – 'flies on the wall rather than flies in the soup' (as it were).[31] The pose of unattached observer generally served to legitimate reporting, although a certain consanguinity with spying was noted when 'intelligencers' (reporters) emerged in the later 17th century as operatives distinct from publishers/printers. It was to become a given and, by the end of the century, neutrality was embedded as an element in the claim of truth. Joseph Addison insouciantly spoke to this in the voice of 'Mr. Spectator' in the first edition of his (and Richard Steele's) *Spectator* magazine in 1711: 'I live in the world as a Spectator of mankind rather than as one of the species'; but this denial of subjectivity is another supposed given of journalism which cannot bear too much scrutiny.[32]

Berkenhead and Needham, though, were more elephants in the room than unnoticed flies on the wall. Instead of, say, Pecke's neutral third-person editorial voice, which might be thought unavoidable if any pretence of being unbiased is to be maintained, both of them used the first person and a colloquial, accessible mode of address. It suffused their papers. Needham scattered his writings with twice as many 'I's and 'we's as Berkenhead. '*Aulicus* [he wrote], we have learned to reply as well as you can answer'.[33] An instance: after the King's defeat at the Battle of Marston Moor in 1644, Berkenhead discounted a Roundhead report that 10000 arms had been captured: 'Captaine *Hamiltons* letter sayes 3000, you may say 3 millions, and have it voted true'.[34]. Needham was not impressed: '[Berkenhead] sais we tell lies …. I thought you had no time to see any lies of ours you are so busie making your own'.

Overt subjectivity in the form of personal invective did not become routinised in the peacetime mainstream English press, but another aspect of subjectivity, in the form of the pamphlet-style editorial opinion (which Needham also inserted into his pages), did:

> Where is King Charles? What's become of him? The strange variety of opinions leaves nothing certain: for some say, when he saw the Storm coming after him as far as Bridgewater, he ran away to his dearly beloved in Ireland; yes, they say he ran away out of his own Kingdome very Majestically …. Because there is such a deale of uncertainty; and therefore (for the satisfaction of my Countrymen) it were best to send a Hue and Cry after him. If any man can bring tale or tiding of a wilfull King, which hath gone astray these foure years from his Parliament, with a guilty Conscience, bloody Hands, a Heart full of broken Vowes and Protestations …. Then give notice to Britannicus, and you shall be well paid for your paines: So God save the Parliament.[35]

Berkenhead was outfaced. All he could say to this scandalous 'Hue and Cry' editorial was that Needham had misspelled (a concept barely in place at the time) *Britannicus* with two 'n's. Such pettifogging was not going to gag Marchmont.

Events were against Berkenhead. Faced with the reality of Charles's weakening position, he articulates – quite clearly – a Trumpian approach to negative news: he cries 'fake' – 'false intelligences', 'lyes' – at every turn. The *Aulicus* more or less ceased to deal with the doings of the court or the Royalist state of arms. Behind the continued deployment of the protocols of the news, its focus was to undercut and delegitimate the account of the Cavaliers' mounting failures, as these were being reported by the *Britannicus* and other hostile Parliamentary titles such as the unbound one-penny quarto *Mercurius Civicus LONDONs INTELLEGENCER OR, Truth Impartially Related Thence to the Whole Kingdome to Prevent mif-information.*[36] The *Aulicus* ceased publication in 1645 as the pretence could not be maintained after the shattering defeat at Naseby.

Needham's side was winning but his innovative 'tearing down' approach to journalism nevertheless got him into trouble. His jocular call for a hue and cry to capture the King was deemed too 'saucy' by the less radical peers still sitting in the House of Lords in the Long Parliament; and his career throughout the period of uncertainty following Naseby was to see him change sides more than once, the vehemence of his rhetoric undiminished, whoever his paymaster. Each time, he was saved by his pen, being deemed too effective not to be used.[37] In 1646, he was imprisoned and the *Britannicus* banned for another too-'saucy' editorial.

A year later, ignoring that the wind had changed irrevocably in the Parliament's direction, he contrived to throw himself on the King's mercy (the King being held at Hampton Court, still intriguing for a rescue by a continental Catholic or Scottish Presbyterian army). Needham quickly produced an unlicensed, shamelessly Royalist (and completely sensationalist) diurnal, the *Mercurius Pragmaticus* with tales, for example, of Baptists cutting the throats of their newborn babies to ensure they entered heaven.

After the King's execution, Needham was caught by the Puritans in May 1649 and, thinking about it in prison over the next six months, he decided to return to Parliament's side, supporting Cromwell and the Commonwealth. With Cromwell's censor, John Milton, as his licensor, in 1650 he was given a monopoly of news, producing the *Mercurius Politicus*. Needham returned to the more sober (if it can be so described) *Britannicus*. The *Politicus* was again a diurnal: *Comprising the summe of all intelligence, with the affairs, and designs now on foot, in the three nations of England, Ireland, and Scotland*; but did often begin with his innovative editorials, e.g. 'Wee have noted the third error or default in Policy, to be a keeping the People ignorant of thofe ways and means that are effentially necef/ary for the preservation of their Liberty'.[38] And, then, in 1660, he went too far again for conservative opinion, warning that the exiled Charles Stuart, the beheaded King's son, was seeking to avenge his father's execution. Marchmont's career as a regular diurnalist came, finally, to a halt (although he did get one last pardon!).

Needham, although a far-from-neutral propagandist, was nonetheless the father of English journalism from every point of view: a writer of vivid brilliance with unerring news-sense, fearlessly speaking truth to power in innovative and effective ways, and a person of utterly elastic principles (beyond causing trouble). Centuries later a wit would write words which can stand as his epitaph:

> You cannot hope to bribe or twist,
> Thank god! The British journalist.
> But, seeing what the man will do,
> Unbribed, there's no occasion to.[39]

The sequence of Needham's *Mercuries* – from *Britannicus* though *Pragmaticus* to *Politicus*, show the extent to which fake news had, in effect, become inseparable from the news.

Such blurring is the source of journalism's most egregious problems. The existential choice that journalism has always faced was not so much grounded in the clear binary between truth and falsity (simple to navigate – don't lie). Rather it involved negotiating a continuum that runs from recorded triangulated observations to increasingly untethered imaginings (much more complicated) causing unavoidable confusion and blurring. Checking was (and is) crucial but it was not (and never became) obligatory. Needham commented in one edition of the *Britannicus*: '*Aulicus* is woefully betrayed by his intelligencers this week'. The protocols required that sources be cited, not that their accuracy be checked; and then, too, editorials, whose very essence crosses the line between verifiable fact and assertion required no triangulation either.

Hence, as well, the use of correspondents, originally readers were invited to send in news items. This procedure also precluded due diligence. 'Sir', wrote one to a Restoration editor, 'in your last you desired me acquaint you what non-conformists, papists and others were indicted at quarter sessions ....'[40] The editor did not (could not?) cross-check. Triangulation was not a factor.

By this time the news, triangulated or not, was only one element in these publications. Fake news fabrications aside, contents included advertisements, advice columns (whose patness seemed often to smack of inauthenticity), salacious sex scandals (especially during the Commonwealth in satiric *nocturalls* such as the *Mercurius Fumigosus*), cartoons, puzzles, and, with slow but increasing regularity, editorials. By 1670, the only thing lacking in English was a generally agreed term to describe such publications but in that year, this was provided by at least one reader who contacted the editor of *The London Gazette* to complain that he 'wanted the news paper [*sic:* two words] last Monday' and did not get it. By 1688, the words were finally conjoined in print:[41] newspaper:

> [f. News *sb.*] A printed, now usul. daily or weekly, publication containing the news, advertisement, literary matter and other items of public interest. (OED)

The term stuck. Despite all contaminations, it was largely sober in tone, significant in content and its higher ambitions were eventually to acquire a positively theological tinge: 'speaking truth to power',[42] 'comforting the afflicted and afflicting the comfortable, etc.'[43] Its freedom to pursue such high-minded purposes, according to the pseudonymous 18th century pamphleteer 'Junius', was 'the palladium of all the civil, political and religious rights'.[44] For Thomas Carlyle (quoting Edmond Burke) the press was a 'Fourth Estate more important than they all'.[45] For John Kennedy, the press was 'the recorder of man's [*sic*] deeds, the keeper of his [*sic*] conscience [to which] we look for strength and assistance'.[46] The centrality of the press to the ordering (or disordering) of western societies has been a matter of (mainly positive) received opinion, and with reason.

Although paradoxically the right of expression is of less utilitarian value than the other rights to life and liberty, Junius's belief in the press's centrality to their preservation has been amply affirmed by time. Journalism played this role, for instance, in the American and French Revolutions in the 18th century; in the 19th in political struggles such as the Chartist agitation for a representative democracy in Britain and in anti-slavery campaigns in the United States, as well as in the resistance to the Nazi occupation of Europe in the 20th century. The US papers and broadcasters, many above- and more (proportion-wise) under-ground, spoke out loudly for civil rights in the 1960s.[47] Examples proliferate as such speaking truth to power was, and is, the press's best *raison d'être*. It is no wonder that *bien-pensant* opinion is positive:

> If a nation expects to be ignorant & free, in a state of civilisation, it expects what never was & never will be [wrote Thomas Jefferson]. The functionaries of every government have propensities to command at will the liberty & property of their constituents. There is no safe deposit for these but with the people themselves; nor can they be safe with them without information. Where the press is free and every man [*sic*] able to read, all is safe.[48]

Nothing, perhaps, better attests to the press's social efficacy than the authoritarianism (or worse) of its most outspoken enemies. This is, after all, the press Napoleon apparently believed was 'more to be feared than a thousand bayonets' – 'the enemy of the people' according to Trump (and Hitler, and others). But the hostility of authoritarians (and worse) cannot be seen as being merely of a piece with their general paranoia. Contrast the received *bien-pensant* opinion as to the importance of free expression to democracy with the public opinion of the news media. As repeatedly expressed in surveys over many decades, it is a given of such inquires that journalists rank with used car dealers and other such reprobates. Moreover, in our present environment of all-pervasive news media, investigators are now finding the people are not only distrusting but bored. This is, we are arguing, a consequence – indeed, the most dangerous consequence – of the unfulfillable promises made by the press through the centuries between us and Needham.

Notes

1 Pecke, Samuel (2005 [1649]). *A Perfect Diurnall of Some Passages in Parliament, No.288 29 January – 5 February 1649* in *British Literature, 1640–1789: An Anthology* (Robert DeMaria, ed.). Oxford: Blackwell.
2 Webber, Johannes (2005). 'The early German newspaper: A medium of contemporaneity' in *The Dissemination of News and the Emergence of Contemporaneity in Early Modern Europe* (Brendan Dooley, ed.). London: Routledge, p. 70.
3 Aitzen, Michael von (1588). *Relatio historica Deß, so sich nach dem Abschied der Cöllnischen …* https://books.google.co.uk/books?id=O3g8AAAAcAAJ&pg=PA47&lpg=PA47&dq=Michael+von+Aitzen+Relatio&source=bl&ots=Rj0xOCvLRT&sig=5KyTIxQloNONzGkJgZx0sZR6mGY&hl=en&sa=X&ved=2ahUKEwjE6OajuojdAhXqLMAKHc7xBqkQ6AEwAnoECAcQAQ#v=onepage&q=Michael%20von%20Aitzen%20Relatio&f=false [accessed 25 August 2018].
4 Eaman, Ross (2009). *Historical Dictionary of Journalism*. Langham MD: Scarecrow Press, p. 9.
5 Michael ab Isselt (1592). *Mercurius Gallobelgicus sive rerum in Gallia et Belgio potissimum Hispania quoque Italia, Anglia, Germania, Polonia, vicinisque locis ab anno 1588 usque ad Septembrim anni praesentis 1592*. https://books.google.co.uk/books?id=wAtTAAAAcAAJ&printsec=frontcover#v=onepage&q&f=false [accessed 24 August 2018].
6 Dilbaum, Samuel (1596). *Jahrs. Kurtze Beschreibung etlicher fürnemmer Sachen*, August. https://books.google.co.uk/books?id=BCK3lfO5Yw8C&printsec=frontcover&dq=Samuel+Dilbaum&hl=en&sa=X&ved=0ahUKEwield2H9f3cAhWsJcAKHcCSAKcQ6AEIOzAD#v=onepage&q=Historical%20Relation%20or%20Narrative%20&f=f [accessed 21 August 2018].

7 Carolus, Johann (1609). *Relation: Aller Fuernemmen und gedenckwuerdigen Historien: so sich hin und wider in Hoch- und Nieder-Teutschland, auch in … verlauffen und zutragen möchte*. <http://digi.ub.uni-heidelberg.de/diglit/relation1609/0005/image> [accessed 21 August 2018].

8 Verhoven, Abraham (1605). *Le Vrai Povtrait*. https://en.wikipedia.org/wiki/Abraham_Verhoeven#/media/File:Blokkersdijk_1605.jpg [accessed 22 August 2018].

9 Culkin, John (1967). 'Education in America: A schoolman's guide to Marshall McLuhan', *The Saturday Review*, 18 March, p. 70.

10 Winston, Brian (1998). *Media Technology and Society: From the Telegraph to the Internet*. London: Routledge, pp. 1–9.

11 Braudel, Fernand (1979). *Civilization and Capitalism, 15th–18th Centuries* (Siân Reynolds, trans.). Los Angeles: UCLA.

12 Pollack, Michael (1972). 'The performance of the wooden printing press', *The Library Quarterly*, 42:2, April, pp. 218–264.

13 Attwood, Ron & Arnold De Beer (2001). 'The roots of academic news research: Tobias Peucer's "*De relationibus novellis*" (1690)', *Journalism Studies* 2:4, pp. 485–496, 490.

14 Milton, John (1644). *Areopagitica and Of Education*. London, p. 35.

15 Morison, S. (1980). 'The origins of the newspaper'. *Selected Essays on the History of Letter-Forms in Manuscript and Print*. Cambridge: Cambridge University Press, p. 345.

16 Archer, Thomas, Nathaniel Bourne & Nathaniel Butter (1621). *Corante…*, 24 September et seq. https://quod.lib.umich.edu/e/eebo2?rgn=subject;type=simple;q1=Europe+--+History+--+1517–1648+--+Early+works+to+1800 [accessed 24 August 2018].

17 Veseler, George & Peter van De Keere (1620). *Corrant out of Italie etc*. Amsterdam, 23 December.

18 Cranfield, Geoffrey (2013). *The Press and Society: From Caxton to Northcliffe*. Abingdon, Oxon: Routledge, p. 8.

19 Andrews, Alexander (1859). *A History of British Journalism, Vol. I*. London: Richard Bentley, p. 31.

20 Boys, Jayne (2011). *London's News Press and the Thirty Years War*. Woodbridge, Suffolk: The Boydell Press, p. 76.

21 Jonson, Ben (1625). *The Staple of News*, Act 1, Sc 5. http://hollowaypages.com/Jonson1692news.htm [accessed 13 March 2012].

22 Steinburg, Sigfrid (1969). *500 Years of Printing*. Harmondsworth: Penguin, p. 166.

23 Raymond, Joad (2005). *The Invention of the Newspaper: English Newsbooks, 1641–1649*. Oxford: Oxford University Press, p. 146.

24 Smith, Anthony (1979). *The Newspaper: An International History*. London: Thames & Hudson, p. 30.

25 Needham, Marchmont (1645). *Mercurius Britannicus August 12–19*, qt in Joseph Muddiman (1906), *A History of English Journalism to the Foundation of the Gazette*. London: Longman.

26 Berkenhead, John (1643). *Aulicus*, 6–12 August. www.reportingtheenglishcivilwar.com/week-1-1-8-january-43/mercurius-Aulicus-week-32-6-12-august-43/ [accessed 20 August 2018].

27 Berkenhead, John (1643). *Aulicus, 27 August – 2 September*. www.reportingtheenglishcivilwar.com/week-1-1-8-january-43/mercurius-aulicus-week-35-27-august-2-september-43/ [accessed 20 August 2018].

28 Johnson, Samuel (1758). 'Corruption of news-writers', *The Idler, 30*, 11 November. www.johnsonessays.com/the-idler/corruption-news-writers/ [accessed 6 September 2018]. The thought was repeated 160 years later by US Senator Hiram Warren Johnson and appeared in print a decade after that: 'When war is declared, truth is the first casualty' (Ponsonby, Arthur [1928]. *Falsehood in Wartime*. London: Allen Unwin).

29 Andrews, Alexander (1859). *A History of British Journalism, Vol. I*. London: Richard Bentley, p. 51.
30 Needham, Marchmont (1645). *Mercurius Britannicus*, xc, 21 July.
31 The phrase is the late Henry Breitrose's.
32 Addison, Joseph (1711). 'Thursday, March 1st 1711'. *The Spectator*, 1:1, 1 March, p. 1; (see p. 42).
33 Berkenhead, John (1644). *Mercurius Aulicus*. 26 August – 1 September.
34 Berkenhead, John (1645). *Mercurius Aulicus*. 28 July – 4 August.
35 Needham, Marchmont (1645). *Mercurius Britannicus*, xcii, 4 August.
36 qt. in Frank, Joseph (1961). *The Beginnings of the English Newspaper 1620–1660*. Cambridge, MA: Harvard University Press, p. 41.
37 Macadam, Joyce (2011). '*Mercurius Britannicus* on Charles I: An exercise in civil war journalism and high politics, August 1643 to May 1646'. *Historical Research*, 84:225. Oxford: Blackwell.
38 Needham, Marchmont (1652). *Mercurius Politicus*, 102, 13–20 May.
39 Woolf, Humbert (n/d). *The British Journalist*. www.poetrynook.com/poem/british-journalist [accessed 9 January 2020].
40 Sutherland, James (2004). *The Restoration Newspaper and its Development*. Cambridge: Cambridge University Press, p. 6.
41 Bernhard, Jim (2007). *Porcupine, Picayune, and Post: How Newspapers Get Their Names*. Columbia, MO: University of Missouri Press, p. 174.
42 Anon (American Friends Service Committee) (1955). *Speak Truth to Power. A Quaker Search for an Alternative to Violence: A Study of International Conflict*, 2 March.
43 Dunne, Finley Peter ['Mr Dooley'] (1902). *Observations By Mr. Dooley*. New York: R.H. Russell, p. 132.
44 Anon (*stat Junius umbra*), 1772. 'Dedication to the English Nation', *The Letters of Junius*. London: Henry Woodfall Sampson, p. iv.
45 Carlyle, Thomas (1840). *On Heroes, Hero Worship and the Heroic in History* (reprinted: *Collected Works*). London: Robson & Sons, p. 194.
46 Kennedy, John. 'The president and the press: Address before the American Newspaper Publishers Association'. New York, April 27, 1961. www.jfklibrary.org/Research/Research-Aids/JFK-Speeches/American-Newspaper-Publishers-Association_19610427.aspx [accessed 3 February 2020].
47 See for example: Burrowes, Carl (2011). 'Property, power and press freedom: Emergence of the fourth estate, 1640–1789', *Journalism & Communication Monographs*, 13:1, pp. 1–66; Grimes, Charlotte (2007). 'Civil rights and the press', *Journalism Studies*, 6:1, pp. 117–134. www.tandfonline.com/doi/abs/10.1080/1461670052000328258?src=recsys&journalCode=rjos20[accessed 3 February 2019]; Shannon, Martin & David Copeland (eds.) (2003). *The Function of Newspapers in Society: A Global Perspective*. Santa Barbara, CA: Praeger; Smith, Anthony (1979). *The Newspaper: An International History*. London: Thames and Hudson; Simkin, John (2014). 'Anti-slavery newspapers' https://spartacus-educational.com/USAsnewspapers.htm [accessed 3 February 2019]; Bellanger, C. (1969), *Histoire Générale de la Presse Française*, Paris: Presses Universitaires de France; Darnton Robert & Daniel Roche (eds.) (1989). *Revolution in Print: The Press in France, 1775–1800*. Los Angeles, CA: UCLA Press; Stone, Harry (1996). *Writing in the Shadow: Resistance Publications in Occupied Europe*. London: Cassell; Williams, Francis (1957). *Dangerous Estate: The Anatomy of Newspapers*. London: Longmans, Green & Co.; Simkin, John

(2014):'Chartist newspapers'. https://spartacus-educational.com/CHnewspaper.htm [accessed 3 February 2019]; Mott, Frank (1962). *American Journalism: A History, 1690–1960*. New York: Macmillan; McMillian, John (2010). *Smoking Typewriters: The Sixties Underground Press and the Rise of Alternative Media in America*. New York: Oxford University Press.

48 Jefferson, Thomas. 'All is safe', Letter to Charles Yancey, January 6, 1816. http://tjrs.monticello.org/letter/327 [accessed 9 January 2020].

3

'BOOMING A NEWSPAPER': NEWSPAPERS AND NEWS-MEDIA 1800—

> 'Many a good newspaper story has been ruined by over-verification'
> [ATTRIBUTED]
> *James Gordon Bennett Jr. (1841–1918)*
> *Newspaper Proprietor*

Journalism's insisting on its own truthfulness, while failing to create and regularly utilise procedures and protocols to ensure its delivery (even in the necessarily incomplete forms available to it), always portended distrust and disaster. Because of this, the history of the misuse of the press is just as easy to trace as any heroic account of it.

The rhetoric of the press's claim to being essential to a free society dates back, as we have seen, to Luther's explicit demand for a right of free conscience and John Milton's impassioned plea: 'Give me the liberty to know'.[1] But such liberty cannot be easily constrained if it is to have meaning. Certainly the exercise of free speech cannot be limited only to that which is deemed socially positive. Constraints requiring this need censors to enforce that and censors and freedom do not mix. If it is to have meaning, the essential freedoms contained within the overarching freedom of expression, such as speaking truth to power etc., must include the right to be offensive, trivial, sensationalist, bigoted, biased, and even to present fictional imaginings as truth. (The last item may seem somewhat out of place at first glance, but it does belong here.) And being free to do all and any of that can embolden abuse.

A century on from Milton, and the need for a limit on free speech was being acknowledged but, also, it was understood that the limit has itself to be limited. As a journalist, Thomas Trenchard, and a Whig MP, John Gordon, put it in a London journal of 1721 (under the pen-name 'Cato'): 'Freedom of Speech … is the Right of every Man [sic],' but this right extends only 'as far as by it he [*sic*] does not hurt and controul the Right of another'. The position taken is that this 'do no harm' principle 'is the only Check which it ought to suffer, the only Bounds which it ought to know'.[2] The essential problem, however, is that harm might be thought to require that the news's effect is negative in measurably damaging ways, but establishing this is as hard as determining what is truth.

Where, then, does that leave fakery? The reality is that lies, fictions, are not necessarily harmful even when presented as truth. In fact, they might be entertaining and why should 'the honest common people ... not ha' their pleasure [i]n believing lies that are made for them?'[3]

It is not necessarily much of a stretch to say that fictional imaginings coming to be presented as news, and being relatively easily embedded into the press's more usual behaviour is, like pornography or bigotry, an inevitable consequence of freedom of speech. And it is here, in the perhaps somewhat confusing borderlands of that freedom, that fake news, in the broad sense in which we are using the term, has taken root and flourished. This, though, does not mean that naked lies have been, or are now, an everyday salient feature of journalism. In fact, specific glaring mendacities cut from mainstream media's whole cloth are rare enough to stand out as notorious:

THE NEW YORK SUN
FRIDAY MORNING, AUGUST 21, 1835
Celestial Discoveries. – The Edinburgh Courant says – 'We have learnt from an eminent publisher in this city that Sir John Herschel, at the Cape of Good Hope, has made some astronomical discoveries of the most wonderful description, by means of an immense telescope of an entire new principle'.[4]

In the week following, every edition of *The Sun* carried full reports of amazing observations of wildlife on the moon following up the '*Edinburgh Courant*' which had itself culled them from a 'supplement to the *Edinburgh Journal of Science*'. This was exactly the sort of 'eminent' learned publication where, ever since 1665 (in the pages, say, of *le Journal des sçavans* or the *Philosophical Proceedings of The Royal Society*) similar advances in scientific knowledge had been announced.

As protocol demanded, then, the Edinburgh newspaper and journal were the basis for the New York paper's claim of authenticity but, alas for truth, neither existed – any more than did the telescope or the moon creatures. The whole hoax was designed, in the fervid 1830s market of one-cent New York popular papers, as a spoiler to draw attention (and sales) away from *The Sun*'s new rival, the *New York Morning Herald*, which had been founded three months earlier by James Gordon Bennet Sn. The hoax was splashed across the former's pages in order to boost circulation in the face of the *Herald*'s very successful launch.

The 'story' was instantly exposed as a fiction but the paper's circulation increased by a third while it ran. Such a fabrication stands at one end of the reporting/ imagining continuum. Despite being published in a newspaper, the coverage was so close to fiction as barely to occupy journalism's interstitial position at all. But it was presented as a news story, however much it might have been, in the modern sense, fabricated; and it was not, after all, 'pure' fiction. It was a fiction contaminated (as such stories usually are) by verifiable truths. Herschel, for example, was the most famous astronomer of the day. There was, and is, a Cape of Good Hope (and the moon – and telescopes to point at it). The hoax is an outright lie but it is more tethered to reality than, say, reports of wars 'in a galaxy far, far away'. It is a rare example because its basic mendacity was manufactured in house and that, as far as the record goes, very seldom occurs. On the other hand, such tethering is a journalistic commonplace, especially given the press's unfortunate readiness to mirror Renaudot's relationship with Louis XIII and let themselves be a conduit for uninterrogated official information. (This includes, of course, the Anglophone press, at least on occasion.) But, again, the instances of this purveying of 'official' barefaced lies are rare enough also to be notorious:

In October 1924, Britain's first Labour government under Ramsey Macdonald, barely ten months in office, was forced to go to the country. Four days before the General Election, the London *Daily Mail* splashed '**CIVIL WAR PLOT BY SOCIALIST MASTERS**' across the seven columns of its front page and ran a double-column unsigned lead story headlined:

MOSCOW ORDERS TO OUR REDS
GREAT PLOT DISCLOSED YESTERDAY.

———

'PARALYSE THE ARMY AND THE NAVY.'

———

MR MACDONALD
WOULD LEND RUSSIA OUR MONEY!

———

DOCUMENT ISSUED
BY
FOREIGN OFFICE

———

AFTER 'DAILY MAIL'
HAD SPREAD THE NEWS

The communication giving the orders arrived in London, apparently via a secret agent in Riga, as purportedly coming from the Chair of the Communist International (Comintern), Grigori Zinoviev, who was charged with fomenting overseas revolutions on behalf of the USSR. The legitimacy of the document was confirmed by the paper's subordinate deck: 'ISSUED FROM THE FOREIGN OFFICE'. Irrespective of its provenance, though, it was a forgery.

Leaving spies in Riga aside, the document outlining the plot to foment revolution was almost certainly the work of somebody in the British Secret Service, passed, (as was admitted much later) to the paper by partisan elements in the civil service.[5] It was intended to influence the election, which Labour duly lost – though not provably because of the newspaper's hysteria, it must be added. But, unlike *The New York Sun*, *The Mail* did not do the imagining; it did not own – originate – the forgery. That was done outside its walls, which puts the paper's coverage a step away from the New York hoax. The moon creatures and telescope did not exist but the British Foreign Office did, as of course did Zinoviev, Comintern, and its overseas interventionist policy. The Zinoviev story is, once again, an impure lie shot through with trace elements of significant truth, but the paper's only homemade misfeasance was its failure to triangulate – not the initial fabrication of the untruth. Its lie was only the false implication that it had forced the authorities into releasing the document 'after' the paper had 'spread the news' when it was merely doing their bidding.

This is still not to say, however, that the *Mail* made a habit of inventing naked lies wholesale. Certainly, under its Nazi-sympathising publisher, Lord Rothermere,[6] and subsequently, it fed its predominantly elderly British petit-bourgeois readership a daily diet of distortions on everything from radicals, to immigrants, to health-scares, to sex-scandals, but that is not quite the same thing as lying. This notorious incident, though unusual, does nonetheless serve to spotlight journalism's more usual interstitial distortions. Essential to the *Mail's* falsification was not only the lie itself and the paper's failure to triangulate, but also the partialities of its contextualisation – what we would today call 'spin'. It is the unrevealed biases determining what will appear – the 'inferential frame' being brought to the assigning, editing, and publishing processes – which lie at the heart of the matter.[7] The *Mail's* coverage of the Zinoviev Letter can stand as a classic instance of how this, a far more everyday phenomenon than mendacity and outright hoaxing, works.

Let us take just one facet of the paper's spin. The big story of the decade's first years had been the fully reported, and well-photographed, famine which had claimed millions of Russian and Ukrainian lives post-revolution and civil war. It had provoked an extensive western relief effort that continued into 1923. Ignoring this context thus skews the *Mail's* third subordinate deck: 'MR MACDONALD WOULD LEND RUSSIA OUR MONEY!' (Note the punctuation!) The socialist British Prime Minister Macdonald had recognised the USSR, infuriating the right and its mouthpieces such as the *Mail*. Red scaremongering, of course, prevented any mention that, in this, he was following the footsteps of the previous Liberal Party government, by expanding the first UK/Soviet trade agreement, which had been signed in 1921. And he had arranged a loan as part of a negotiation around repayments of monies the last Tsar had borrowed earlier during the First World War.[8] There was, then, a loan all right, but that was a fact deprived of necessary context, in this routinised variant on fakery: silence, via deliberate omission or unthinking ignorance, can work just as well to provide spin as any published misrepresentation.[9] Misleading the public does not require committed mendacity. Needham's inky fingerprints are all over that exclamation point.

Moreover, in the intervening centuries the press had acquired one further trick which had not occurred to him. His importation of subjectivity had legitimated breaches of the neutrality that eventually could seem essential to ('good') journalism. Despite this and other transgressions littering the history of the news, neutrality, objectivity, etc., had become a given of the rhetoric around journalism, but the journalistic 'fly-on-the-wall' rhetoric of detachment – insofar as it had ever really reflected practice – was slowly being, de facto, abandoned. The press had been learning how to make the news. And this willingness to intervene in the world in order to generate content – a technique that is now seen as entirely legitimate, and sometimes even laudable – became an everyday given. How it might threaten the truth-telling ambitions of the press was unacknowledged

James Gordon Bennett Sr had brushed off *The New York Sun*'s antics, eventually becoming the dominant player in the city's news market. Within a decade of its appearance his *New York Morning Herald* had a daily circulation of 12,000, yielding revenues of over $10 million a year in today's money. By this time, Gutenbergian flat-beds had given way to rotary presses capable of 15,000 iph. The driver for the technological advance, as ever, was a matter of social circumstances. The industrial revolution and the emergence of a necessarily increasingly literate mass-workforce in the west, with a taste for sensation, had encouraged the arrival of steam engines in the printing house. And, like Needham before him, Gordon Bennet Sn, was able to meet new demand with content innovations. He secured the attention of the city's moneyed class by introducing the first systematic coverage of Wall Street as a newspaper reporter's beat, but just as significantly, he had an unerring eye for sensation as the mainstay of his mass-readership. He found ways to satisfy popular tastes without resorting to fiction.

Covering a sensational murder of a young prostitute, Ellen Jewitt, in a Manhattan bordello in April 1836, Gordon Bennet took it upon himself to interview a police witness, Rosina Townsend, the brothel-keeper, and crossed the police line at the murder scene to do it. 'Why do you let that man in?' he reported a bystander asking a police officer. 'He is an editor. He is on public duty', Gordon Bennet has the officer replying. What follows is a referent – something happening in the world to be reported – which was entirely dependent on his activity – the interview:

> Rosina …
>
> …. sat on the sofa, talking – talking – talking of Ellen – Ellen – Ellen … 'I am going,' said Mrs Townsend, 'to have a funeral sermon preached next Sunday on poor Ellen. Poor thing …' 'By all means have a funeral sermon and let it be at Arthur Tappan's tabernacle.' No, that would not do. Arthur Tappan is an abolitionist – and Rosina detests abolition. Oh! Virtue! Oh! Morals! Oh! The age of civilization![10]

Gordon Bennett Sn was here no spectator. He had instigated the event and was part of it. He knew he had crossed more than one line.

Had he been reporting testimony the woman had given in court, Gordon Bennett's account would not have broken new ground. In fact, a feature of newspapers of the time was legal testimony (usually heard in Magistrates' courts) in cases of minor infractions such as drunk and disorderly charges. These, reported verbatim in the papers, were often presented as a source of humour. Bennett's intention was more (albeit tendentiously) 'high-minded' than that: 'Let us not suppose but courts and juries and justices have a right alone to examine a matter affecting our morals'.[11] (Certainly not when, as the press had always known, stories about sex and murder sell, especially when the two are combined.) Despite the whiff of hypocrisy, the contrast with observational reporting is profound. Court reports – events that would have occurred with or without the journalist's presence – are of a different order from interviews which have to be, in the original sense, fabricated by the journalist as an explicit or implicit protagonist. As a new technique for providing content – especially exclusive content – this could not be ignored. Within four years, Gordon Bennett Sn became the first journalist to interview a US President, Martin van Buren.

The use of the interview, for all its ubiquity, nevertheless caused a measure of concern for most of the rest of the century. In the 1860s, sober journalists could think interviewing was 'a kind of toadyism or hucksterism' or 'the joint production of some humbug of a hack politician and another humbug of a newspaper reporter'.[12] In 1884, W. T. Stead, the editor of the [London] *Pall Mall Gazette* wrote that interviewing was still seen as a 'monstrous departure from the dignity and propriety of journalism'.[13] He was pleased to note, however, that this hostility was a 'superstition' and that it was on the wane.

It is not surprising to find Stead holding such a view. He claimed that he had 'acclimatised' the British press to this American practice; and its value to journalism from the 1830s to his time, even if regarded in some quarters as dubious, could not be gainsaid:

> BUNDER UJIJI, ON LAKE TANGANYIKA, CENTRAL AFRICA, NOVEMBER 23, 1871....
> ... There is a group of the most respectable Arabs, and as I [Henry Stanley] come nearer I see the white face of an old man among them. He has a cap with a gold band around it, his dress is a short jacket of red blanket cloth, and his pants – well, I didn't observe. I am shaking hands with him. We raise our hats, and I say:
> 'Doctor Livingstone, I presume?'
> And he says, 'Yes.'
> ... finis coronat opus.[14]

Stanley's expedition to Central Africa, however, was not only (or even primarily) to conduct an exclusive interview (which, in this initial published account, consisted of just five words) with David Livingstone. He was, rather, engaged in making the news. Meeting Livingstone was a scoop but Needham had run those. Stanley's report, however, unlike Needham's leaks of secret state documents, consisted of created content which would not have existed had he not provoked the event he reported – which was, in terms of column inches, his own adventures getting to Ujiji. It was like Gordon Bennett Sn in his encounter with Mrs Townsend but it was even more interventionist (as it were). The (literal) lengths he went to in order to get the content – many column inches were devoted to the trek – is a perfect example of this ever-expanding interventionism of newspapers of the later 19th century. It is an example of a technique even more fabricated (first meaning) than the interview: the newspaper 'stunt'.

Stanley was in Africa funded by Joseph Levy, the publisher of *The* [London] *Daily Telegraph* and by Gordon Bennett's son, James Jr., who was now running the *New York Morning Herald*. They were well-rewarded for their investment as Stanley provided them with many broadsheet pages retailing an exclusive account of his adventures. But Gordon Bennett Jr. famously (and, of course, 'reportedly') claimed that: 'many a good newspaper story has been ruined by over-verification', and the Livingstone scoop, the greatest he published, is also an example of this. Dr Livingstone was not actually 'lost' as such, but rather merely out of contact.[15] Avoidance of 'over-verification' is a journalistic given, the unspoken motto of the tabloids but also a principle not unknown to more sober platforms. Such 'stunts' of all kinds were an essential mark of the new sensationalist transatlantic journalism these men purveyed. It was the essence of what would become known in the USA as the 'Yellow Press'.[16] Over the centuries to this point, leaving aside fictional imaginings, the walls surrounding disengagement as a crucial aspect of the reporting process had been first eroded by the deployment of overt subjectivity (the use of the first person). Then observationalism was breached by the arrival of editorials, enlarged by interviewing and finally, in effect, more or less totally demolished by such 'stunts'. The unceasing thirst for content fed journalism's propensity to go beyond personal expression, editorializing, and interviewing. James Gordon Bennett Jr proudly and publicly boasted: 'I make the news', not something his predecessors had ever promised to be doing.

Stunts could be socially valuable 'exposés', or they could be about far more trivial 'human interest' (as we would today term reports of 'soft' news). Take the most famous 19th-century American female reporter, Elizabeth Cochran, writing under the byline 'Nellie Bly'. Her career illustrates both these aspects of the stunt – the valuable and the trivial. Her first exposé was to duplicate the investigation of a male reporter who had infiltrated a mad-house posing as an insane person. Shockingly, in 1887, she did the same with a women's asylum for Joseph Pulitzer's *New York World*. The 'tombstone' headlines on the page-one column read:

BEHIND ASYLUM BARS
--
The Mystery of the Unknown
Insane Girl
--
Remarkable Story of the Successful
Impersonation of Insanity.[17]

Her reporting did not involve interviewing, but rather what a modern sociologist would call 'participant observation' (or perhaps, 'ethnography'). Her story caused a sensation. Like Bennett Sn, but unlike Addison, she was no spectator. But more than Bennett, she endured, and vividly reported, the mistreatments of the genuinely mentally ill.[18] The *World* was to claim the city doubled its appropriation to the asylums as a result of the paper's intervention. Such outcomes could, of course, be ambiguous; they need not be positive, or even real. But, for all the 'common-sense' pervasiveness of the assumption that such demonstrations of media power (for good or bad) are common, they are not. As we shall see, the question of media effect is far more complicated than that.

Bly went on to expose conditions in factories, laundries, tenements, matrimonial agencies, and homes for unmarried mothers. She illegally bought a baby, in order to expose a particularly disgusting trade in newborns.[19] She also engineered stunts, however, in a softer, more 'human interest' mode. She auditioned for a chorus line: 'She Wears a Scant Costume', headlined the paper with a line drawing of her in same.[20] She presented herself as being ill and reported that 'according to the decision of seven reputable New York physicians I am suffering from seven different complaints'.[21] And in late 1889 she raced round the world in an effort to better the 80 days it took Jules Verne's fictitious hero to do it. It took her 72 days, six hours, 11 minutes and 14 seconds. Pulitzer thought the news of her triumph was worth a special edition ('**Nellie Bly Extra**') and a whole front-page splash.[22] Others thought otherwise. The US press's trade magazine, *The Journalist*, for example, thought the whole thing ridiculous: 'a young woman sent around the world for no practical purpose will work to greater advantage in booming a newspaper than a dozen men sent after the facts'.[23] Pulitzer was unrepentant.

He, and the 'New Journalism' he espoused, were not limited to exposés and human interest stunts. Also allowed were 'campaigns' on any matter deemed important, and these could be, as with reporters' interventions, serious attempts overtly to fix the socio-political agenda or, alternatively, express purely attention-grabbing ambitions. Perhaps the most conspicuous outcome of the latter is the base of the Statue of Liberty in New York's Lower Harbour. The figure itself, a gift from the French intended to honour the centenary of the American Revolution, needed a plinth which no US authority wanted to fund. As the 110th anniversary embarrassingly approached, Pulitzer took the matter in hand: 'The World is the people's paper and it now appeals to the people to come forward and raise this money'. 120,000 did and, in 1886, the torch was finally held aloft, illuminating the way to the New World for the 'huddled masses yearning to breathe free'. Pulitzer did not have to 'claim' impact. The presence of the pedestal is evidence of it on its face; but it is, of itself, no proof of journalism's usual capacity to impact on society, the triangulation of which is very much harder to demonstrate. On the other hand, on balance, the tolerance for intervention obviously significantly increased the possibility of printing fictional imaginings, and certainly exponentially expanded the scope for spinning reports.

Pulitzer's rival, William Randolph Hearst, felt he could engineer more than a plinth. His ambitions for America were imperial and in 1897 and '98, with a Cuban revolt against Spanish colonial rule increasing tension between Spain and the US, he used his rival paper to Pulitzer's *World*, the *New York Journal* (and his other titles such as the *San Francisco Examiner*), to splash one incendiary story after another, pushing for an open conflict with Spain. 'SPANIARDS SEARCH WOMEN ON AMERICAN STEAMERS' was the caption on an 1897 front page sketch of a naked young woman being examined by a bunch of moustachioed Spaniards on board her American ship in Havana Harbour. Hearst had sent Frederic Remington, a famous western frontier artist known for his heroic images of men on horses – cowboys, Wells Fargo riders, cavalrymen, 'Indians' – to cover the war he was determined to provoke. Remington had cabled him that: 'There will be no war. I wish to return'. Hearst famously cabled back: 'You furnish the pictures, and I will furnish the war'. Remington duly furnished the nude, etc., and the war duly broke out in April 1898.

Hearst was to deny that he ever sent the cable and certainly his was not the only voice clamouring for a conflict, but let us follow his example and refuse to kill the story through over-verification. The point, in any case, is that interventionism had become an entirely permissible procedure for mainstream journalism, thereby aiding and abetting a tolerance for filling pages, sensationally, with material contrived by the journalists themselves. Even when mendacity was not involved, the results could backfire. W. T. Stead, for example, was, apart from being Britain's leading advocate for the New Journalism, a non-conformist minister's son and a teetotal lay-preacher. An outspoken member of the 'Purity Lobby', he leant his paper to campaigning for its causes, notably including efforts at exposing the evils of prostitution in late Victorian London. With the wife of a high-ranking churchman, he 'bought' a young girl and ran 'The Maiden Tribute of Modern Babylon' as the *Pall Mall Gazette's* splash, releasing the story on 6 July 1885. The girl's family was to claim she thought she was being hired as a servant and Stead, who had done himself no favours with the sensational salaciousness he had deployed in his reports, was sentenced by a judge to three months hard labour for procuring.[24]

All these scandals were reported to the public in written form, often accompanied by artistic illustrations. As such, they inevitably reflected the subjectivities of the reporters, illustrators, editors, and proprietors who produced them. This has never changed – despite the rhetoric of observationalism that journalists continued to deploy as the press absorbed the technological advances of, first, photography and cinematography, and then wireless telegraphy in its various forms.

The photographic camera was introduced as a species of scientific instrument, more thermometer than pencil or paintbrush. The story photography told about the world was, supposedly, **the** story. This technology apparently provided evidence of the referent, directly 'read from the book of nature'. François Arago, the French radical politician and mathematician who, in 1839, persuaded the Chambre des Députés to buy-out Louise Daguerre's patented photographic system and give it to the world, was explicit: the camera joined 'the thermometer, barometer, hydrometer, the telescope and the microscope' as the latest wonder device able to take an objective measure of reality.[25] It was elevated as a tool of science and, as such, was quickly held to be incapable of telling 'lies'. The analogy was, of course, spurious, and photography was as readily available for manipulation as were words or drawings. Nevertheless, the received notion quickly became the adage that 'the camera doesn't lie' – that photographs were, as the philosopher Charles Peirce was to put it a few decades later, 'physically forced to correspond point by point to nature'.[26] Given the press's claim on the real, the meshing of print and photography was a marriage made in journalistic heaven. News publications soon took notice of photography.

Despite its claims as evidence, however, photography did nothing to quell scandals about veracity and authenticity; in fact it added to them. The photographic image became a mainstay of the emerging popular (tabloid) press, but many an iconic photo has been relentlessly subjected to accusations of manipulation. For one thing, there was, of course, no guarantee that the referent had not been tampered with, i.e. that a photograph had not been staged. Were the Russian cannon balls on the road, photographed by Roger Fenton during the Crimean War in 1855, laying there following the aftermath of an artillery barrage? Or were they placed there by Fenton and his assistants? (There are shots of the road both with and without them.) And is AP photographer Joe Rosenthal's 'The Raising of the Stars and Stripes on Mount Surabachi', taken during the Second World War battle for the Island of Iwo Jima, a lie because he photographed a second raising, restaged at the behest of the military commanders, 90 minutes after the original, smaller, and therefore less photogenic flag was run up a flagpole without much effort? Ultimately, does it matter? All the marines in the image were killed in the battle to secure the island.[27]

The problem is not just with war photography. The quintessential image of mid-20th century Paris as the capital of romance is, arguably, Robert Doisneau's photograph of a couple he caught kissing by the Hotel de Ville under the disapproving eye of a bystander. But this too involved restaging. Doisneau, commissioned to provide *Life* with images of lovers in Paris, saw a young couple – aspiring actors as it turned out – kissing in public and engaged them to do it again in a number of locations. The bystander, an Irish tourist, was not disapproving. He was vexed at losing his traveling companion. Françoise Bornet, the woman in the photograph, has said: 'The photo was posed, but the kiss was real'.[28] As with 'The Raising of the Stars and Stripes on Mount Surabachi', where such interventions leave the photograph in terms of judging it as honest, truthful, etc., would seem to be at least somewhat open to question.

Within the photograph's frame nothing of the pre-photographic moment can be known; at best it can only be ambiguously deduced. And this has always been the case: from the outset, even if the referent was uncompromised by intervention, its relationship to the final image could easily be rendered tendentious by this uncertainly. For all its received status as evidence 'on its face', the photograph's meaning cannot definitively stand alone – and this is without reference to the endless possibilities of manipulations post- as well as pre- the photographic moment. The wonder here is that, just as much as with deliberate deception in written news-stories, instances of the use of retouching or other manipulative darkroom techniques to create fully fraudulent fictions in news photography – making the camera unequivocally 'lie' – were (as far as the received history goes) rare. Examples are far more readily to be found, say, in the images produced by Stalin's propaganda machine than in the archives of the west's mainstream press. But a degree of darkroom manipulation has always been regarded as acceptable, and spinning a photograph's meaning came far more commonly to rely on captioning than chemistry. Whether thanks to cognitive dissonance, an unconscious faith in the honesty of others, or some other factor(s), it came to be generally assumed that, although manipulation was possible and the camera could 'lie', a photograph nevertheless usually reflected the untampered scene before the lens. This perhaps accounts for the glacial slowness with which iconic photo scandals have tended to develop, often over the course of decades.

There is an argument to be made that cognitive dissonance in the age of digital image manipulation, however, cannot protect the tendency to assume photographic image integrity very much longer (if, indeed, it can still be said generally to do so). With electronic image capture, the photograph loses all claim to be of any greater reliability as evidence than any other mode of representation. Witness the present ubiquity of suspicions that images, found in the news or elsewhere (such as on social media), are 'probably photoshopped'. That being said, it is also true that despite all this, many people continue to take many photographs at face value, so perhaps such assumptions are not as near to dying out as might be expected.

Digital image manipulation has, after all, actually been around for a while. The first commercially available computer system to enable instant pixel-by-pixel manipulation was the Scitex, introduced in the 1980s. Scandals rapidly followed. *National Geographic*, for instance, used its Scitex to reposition the pyramids at Giza for the front cover of its February 1982 edition. The magazine was quickly forced to promise that: 'Scitex will never be used again to shift any of the seven wonders of the world'.[29] In 1993 a monk, who was abandoning his Order in order to marry, had been photographed by Rupert Murdoch's [London] *Sun*, disobligingly wearing jeans and a shirt. So, explained a spokesman to the industry's UK *Press Gazette*: 'We have superimposed [a] monk's habit to make it clear to readers that the story is about a monk'.[30] Though such causes célèbres were/are rare, the integrity of the photographic image, which was never actually guaranteed by the equipment, now could not be safely assumed at all.

It is, anyway, not these manipulations which highlight photojournalism's fractured claim on the real. However directly 'taken from the book of nature', news photographs always require contextualisation if ambiguity is to be reduced, let alone avoided altogether, and therein lies the major difficulty. The photograph-as-news needs context, that is to say: text in a caption of one sort or another. But as Roland Barthes notes, such captioning 'loads the image, burdening it with a culture, a moral, an imagination'.[31] The text dissolves the underpinning scientism of the photograph as evidence, even without consideration of the unknowability of the pre-photographic moment, and certainly before the coming of Scitex, Photoshop and the like. As elsewhere, a key difficulty for 'truth' is context: is the photograph of a punch still the truth if it doesn't mention that it was staged, or that it was thrown in self-defence, or some implausible explanation such as that it was thrown with the full consent of both parties, to settle a bet? As with other types of telling/showing somebody a 'fact', context can be everything.

Far from closing down the slippage between referent and representation, the photographic image can exacerbate it. News photography, according to its rhetoric, should be firmly on the reporting side of the ravine, instead of which it is actually as deeply trapped in the interstitial fissure before the cliff of fictional imagining as is the text. It is every bit as threatened by the seductions of fakery. It can't, and shouldn't, be trusted. We ask even of the most vivid of images in the photojournalism archive, how much was the 'decisive moment' that secured the image the result of happenstance, as the reporting of events requires? Or, alternatively, how much intervention was needed? Did Robert Capa really click the shutter of his Leica just at the instant when 24-year old loyalist militiaman, Federico Borrell Garcia, was fatally wounded during the Spanish Civil War? Or is the story of the image not quite so straightforward? As with other kinds of reporting, it is difficult to be entirely free from doubt.[32]

And, of course, what of the moving image?

That film could be as newsworthy as photography had been obvious from the moment of cinematography's diffusion. The British pioneer Bert Acres had filmed the 1896 Derby (horserace) for distribution to the emerging Kinetoscope parlours, and film of events was to prove attractive to the cinema's first audiences. For instance, Frederick Villiers, a British journalist, claimed to have taken some footage while covering a Greco-Turkish war in 1897. More certainly, since, unlike Villiers, their work has survived, Edison cameramen were on hand to record the removal of the Spanish flag from the battlements of the Morro fortress in Havana, during the Spanish-American war in 1899. In this period, war footage was born.

The contaminations of fakery, however, were just as much to hand as ever. Never mind Villiers, in 1897 the new medium's most enthusiastically playful exploiter, Georges Méliès, staged an incident from the same Greco-Turkish war. Using ten extras to represent both armies, he re-enacted an attack, on a wall erected in his Parisian studio, and billed it as *The Surrender of Tournavos*. And in the midst of his trick film output he found time to continue with other 'artificially arranged scenes'. Undeterred by the fact that cameras were forbidden in Westminster Abbey, Méliès spared no expense ($10,000, claimed the ads[33]) in making a *Reconstitution of the Coronation of Edward VII* – 30-plus actors including a King Edward lookalike. He was also undeterred by the existence of actual footage of the coronation procession outside the Abbey, using instead a shot of toy carriages and horses before a model of its exterior. Even when actual coverage was available to the public, releasing suitably captioned – i.e. titled and intertitled – films, using actors to recreate scenes yet purporting to be documenting current news stories, was not unusual. The Chinese Boxer Rebellion was staged on a roof in Philadelphia (1902), and boys from a military school in New York re-enacted an engagement during the Russo-Japanese war (1904).[34]

The use of models, too, was normalised in cinematic news-reporting. For its contribution to the Spanish-American war coverage, Vitagraph, a major production company, released *The Battle of Santiago Bay*, shot on a tabletop using cut-out photographs of the warships. On one occasion, film of a model even out-performed at the box-office the actual footage of an event. The 1906 San Francisco earthquake and fire was quickly 'reconstituted' by the Biograph company using a detailed model of the city, and the vividness of the model burning − despite the unfeasible size of the flames − proved more compelling for audiences than did the aftermath shots which had actually been filmed on location.[35] Misrepresentations and de facto fakery, however, required neither models nor actors. Untampered-with footage could be ripped from its referent merely by altering a film's title. Nothing so vividly demonstrates the accuracy of Barthes' view of the caption.

For all that fakery or misrepresentation of one sort or another was 'a matter of common practice'[36] in the production of newsfilm (or supposed newsfilm) around the turn of the 20th century, there is little evidence of the degree to which these subterfuges were believed − though there is some. For example, in 1909, Vitagraph depicted in a reconstitution the wireless officer of a ship that was involved in an at-sea collision shirking his duty at the time of impact. He had in fact been at his Morse key, and sued for defamation. The case turned on the audience's imputing documentary value to the image, as actually depicting his behavior, and the court held that this was in fact the case. By the end of the first decade of the century, however, reconstitutions declined. The norm for newsfilms, what the French termed actualités, quickly came to be footage shot on location as events occurred. The fake news film fad nevertheless gave big-screen news-reporting a reputation for untrustworthiness and mendacity from which it never quite escaped. As a popular song of the day had it of these Kinomatograph productions:

> As a fabrication-mill, it is the greatest thing
> Two hundred lies a minute.[37]

Actualités, initially single-shot films, stood alone in distributors' catalogues. They were the equivalent of the early newsbooks and broadsheets, and as had happened with the newspaper, so with the newsreel three centuries later. Using a term − newsbriefs (faits divers) − taken from the French press in 1908, Pathé began putting newsfilms together in a single reel: Pathé-faits divers. The following year the collection was marketed as a *Journal* (newspaper): *Pathé Journal*. The term used in English was 'newsreel' and it can be defined as being exactly similar to the newspaper in content, differing only in medium: 'a disparate selection of news stories held on a single reel of film, and released in cinemas weekly or twice-weekly'.[38] Coverage of calamities − not with models in a studio but on location − became as much a staple to them as stories of the supernatural had been to the newsbooks centuries earlier. 'In the course of newsreel history, catastrophe, whether natural or man-made, has generally furnished the most colourful and dramatic subject matter'.[39]

And, after reconstitutions had been laid aside early on, like their mainstream print counterparts, the newsreels were not given to over-manipulation of the footage, except in authoritarian regimes where they were seen as an essential propaganda tool. In the western newsreels, eschewing such state control, the films were not overtly messed with, either when being shot or when being processed and edited. In the dubbing theatre, though, it was a different story. There, newsreel scripts functioned as the most burdensome of Barthesian 'captions', vigorously imposing cultural spin, moral takes and imaginative explanations – often more vividly than did the visuals alone.

The cinematic record of the Second World War begins with a perfect, and notorious, example of the importance of this 'captioning' – contextualisation by commentary. In a false-flag operation, Nazis – dressed in Polish military uniforms – seized and destroyed Sender Gleiwitz, a German broadcasting transmitter on Polish soil, on the night of 31 August 1939. Stridently blaming the Poles, as part of structured flow of stories detailing atrocities against Germans living in Poland that the Nazi press had been carrying for months, the destructive aftermath of the fake attack was filmed as evidence of a *causus belli*. The account of 'Polish terror', etc. appeared in the *Ufa-Tonwoche* newsreel a week later. Journalists at UFA, under the watchful eye of Joseph Goebbels, needed do nothing more than mouth the lie in their script. No darkroom trickery altered a frame.

Nor did such distortion – or at least a measure of it – require mendacious footage. It was obvious that maintaining public morale necessitated that the evacuation of the defeated British Expeditionary Force (BEF) from the beaches of Dunkirk be reported as other than it was – a defeat. **The British Movietone News** story, 'Epic of Dunkirk', reflects how the norms of 'captioning', as a means of giving the image unambiguous meaning, had become completely routinised. In four shots, a general, a staff officer, and a civilian exit a building. The soldiers then walk a few feet to a waiting car. The commentary goes well beyond mere identification:

> Lord Gort's appearance in London is the best sign that the evacuation of the BEF from Flanders is virtually completed for we can be sure that this lion-hearted commander would have remained with his troops had there existed any anxiety for the outcome of the great withdrawal.[40]

Without the context the commentary provides, the four shots, even at the time, told the audience little. Presumably the 1940 cinema audience would have been able to recognise Lord Gort as the C-in-C of the BEF (and the unnamed civilian, Anthony Eden, as the Secretary of State for War), but the location cannot be clearly identified as London; what they had been doing was unreported; where Gort was going was not stated; the nature of the occasion was a secret. And as for signs of 'lion-heartedness', there were none. It is in these partialities that the creation of a simulacrum of information lies. This is the importance of the newsreel legacy for modern audio-visual news media.

The newsreels are a sign that increasing the data available for the journalist to share with her audience does not necessarily increase the ability of journalism to report the world, or to avoid distortions when so doing. Paradoxically, moving images, despite the density of the information they carry, worked to weaken the reputation of news media as serious social force. The cinema's impact on society was deemed to be so powerful that, without much question, films – including news films – were subject to a form of censorship, in licensing, which the press had sloughed off centuries before. In effect, free expression in the media, limited of course by the rule of law, was revealed as a press privilege. New media could expect to be regulated. This did not help the reputation of the newsreels. A head of the British Board of Film Censors (a trade body) proudly declared in 1937 that not one film of any social significance was showing in London.[41] As newsreels were dying in the 1950s, their function usurped by television news, the Hollywood wit Oscar Levant offered a definition of them which can stand as their epitaph: 'a series of catastrophes, ended by a fashion show'.[42] They were themselves ended by the catastrophe (for them) of electrical signalling systems – by broadcasting.

The speed of the news flow from the referent to the consumer has always been conditioned by the technology in play. The post was crucial as a means of gathering information and – especially in non-Anglophone countries where newspapers were less 'cried on the street' than they were sold through subscription – for distributing it, too. Pre-the electrical age, the semaphore systems with their line-of-sight towers were far quicker than the mail, capable, for example, of getting a message (at a vast cost in personnel) from Paris to Strasbourg in under an hour.[43] As point-to-point systems, they were, though, extremely limited and, moreover, as a state military asset, they were barred both to the press and to the public.

The possibilities of using electricity to communicate without direct contact had been first mooted with the development of the electric battery at the dawn of the 19th century, but the possibility of using it as the basis of a signalling system was rejected by, for example, the British Admiralty as unneeded: they had the semaphore, anything else was 'wholly unnecessary'.[44] The introduction of steam trains (using single tracks for traffic in both directions) in the 1840s, however, produced the social necessity requiring speed of communication. Rail safety demanded a faster, indeed, an effectively instantaneous signalling system, and this was to be provided by the electric telegraph, the 'invention' of which (as is usually the case) required systems engineering rather than any new science. It was still, like the semaphore systems, limited to point-to-point communication but, opened to the public, it was realised that the point-to-point disadvantage could be overcome by using a human messenger, the 'telegraph boy', for delivery over the last mile or two. It was still far quicker than the mail. For the press, long committed to contemporaneity, it was a godsend.

Topicality had always been critical but the telegraph now ensured that the news was indeed fresh fruit, truly perishable, worthless if delayed. 'Late Intelligences', a species of scoop to in effect undercut one's rivals, was no more.

Now 'deadlines' were king and the time scale in which errors, misrepresentations, etc., could occur was impacted, that is: shortened and thereby exacerbated. Where once they had been titled 'Posts', now newspapers appeared with 'Telegraph' in their mastheads. In the west, these advances also encouraged their owners to pool their resources, setting up news agency wire services which, because they served outlets with a variety of viewpoints, in some respects cemented the sober claims of the press to be observational, unbiased, objective. By that time, sober or sensationalist, newspapers had become a capital-intensive industry existing in a business landscape of similar large, limited liability companies. A small Detroit proprietor, E. W. Scrips, got it into his head to start, or buy up, papers in other cities, beginning with one in Cleveland in 1878. Soon he had a chain, the first in the world, of media outlets, eventually owning 34 papers in 15 states and thereby started the news-media down the path that would lead to the rise of the press barons of the 20th century and the media conglomerates of the 21st.

The general introduction of a plethora of devices – all patented, in the US, in the quarter-century after the end of the Civil War – was occasioned and facilitated by such economic developments across the board: ten storey 'sky-scraper' buildings with Otis safety elevators, and offices illuminated by Edison electric lights, with Cutter rolltop desks, Remington typewriters, Baldwin calculators, McKinnon and Cross 'fountain' pens, Heyl staplers, and Fay paperclips. In common with other capitalist enterprises, the press embraced these, but the systems engineering which had produced them also produced an application which heralded what would develop into a journalistic medium to rival print: Bell's (and Elisha Grey's) 'speaking telegraph', with multiple reception points connecting through 'exchanges' – the telephone.

The threat was not readily apparent as only in Budapest was any attempt made, against the technology's grain as a person-to-person communication system, to use the telephone as a species of mass medium. Starting in 1893, by the turn of the 20th century, over 6,000 subscribers could dial up on the hour and listen to a news bulletin. Emulators elsewhere in Europe and in the US failed to take off and the Hungarian experiment itself terminated in 1923. But we should note that its short history contains no record of faked or distorted coverage.[45]

By the time Telefonico Hirondel closed in Budapest, the telephone's capacity to convey sound instantaneously over distance had been liberated from the wires. For the first time since Gutenberg, a technological alternative to the print's news monopoly appeared at a scale and with a speed nothing, certainly not the newsreels, could match: radio. And once again, the same problems, intrinsic to the nature of reporting the news, were to play out in a new medium.

Notes

1 Milton, John (1644). *Areopagitica*: A SPEECH OF Mr. JOHN MILTON For The Liberty Of UNLICENC'D PRINTING, To The PARLIAMENT Of ENGLAND. London, p. 35.
2 'Cato' (1721). 'Letter No 15', *London Journal*, 4 February.
3 Op cit.

4 Anon (Richard Locke) (1835). 'Celestial Discoveries', *The New York Sun,* 21 August, p. 1.
5 Bennett, Gill (2018). *The Zinoviev Letter: The Conspiracy that Never Dies.* Oxford: Oxford University Press, p. 12.
6 e.g. The *Mail*'s proprietor, Viscount Rothermere's signed editorial 'Hurrah for Blackshirts', 15 January 1934.
7 Glasgow Media Group (1980). *More Bad News.* Abingdon, Oxon: Routledge & Kegan Paul, p. 107.
8 Bennett, Gill (2018). *The Zinoviev Letter: The Conspiracy that Never Dies.* Oxford: Oxford University Press, pp. 10, 25; Steiner, Zara (2007). *The Lights that Failed: European International History, 1919–1933.* Oxford: Oxford Universty Press, p. 173.
9 And persistence can compound this. To celebrate the 95th anniversary of the hoax, the *Mail* simply rehashed the story using (as is usual with contested stories) a flimsy chain of supposedly 'recently' uncovered 'new evidence': Walters, Guy (2019). 'Was the red plot letter that helped kick Labour out genuine after all?' *MailOnline,* 12 October. www.dailymail.co.uk/news/article-7566421/Was-red-plot-letter-helped-kick-Labour-GENUINE-all.html [accessed 7 November 2019]. No, it remains just as faked as it had been 95 years earlier.
10 Gordon Bennett Sr, James (1836). *The New York Herald.* 16 April, p. 1.
11 Ibid.
12 Lasky, Melvin (2000). *The Language of Journalism: Vol. 1 Newspaper Culture.* New Brunswick, NJ: Transaction, p. 164.
13 McNair, Brian (1999). *Journalism and Democracy: An Evaluation of the Political Public Sphere.* Abingdon, Oxford: Routledge, p. 88.
14 Stanley, Henry (1872). 'The end crowns the work'. *The Daily Telegraph,* 3 July, p. 1 et seq.
15 He was ill but, a year before, his last letter home was date-lined Ujiji, a settlement in today's Uganda on the shores of Lake Tanganyika. The place was known to Europeans who had first reached it a decade earlier. It did take Stanley some months of trekking to get there from Dar-es-Salaam but he made his way to the lake and came back with his copy pretty directly.
16 A cartoon, 'The Yellow Kid', ran in Joseph Pulitzer's *New York World* but the strip was poached by William Randolph Hearst for his *New York Journal*. Hearst hired another artist to keep it going in the *World*, so the two 'Yellow Kids' finished up in court – and the papers in which they ran (and their rivals) were tagged as the 'Yellow Papers'; hence 'Yellow Journalism' and eventually the 'Yellow Press'.
17 Bly, Nellie (1887). 'Behind asylum bars'. *The New York World,* 9 October, p. 1.
18 Ibid.
19 Anon (n/d). 'Nellie Bly of The New York World'. http://dlib.nyu.edu/undercover/nellie-bly-new-york-world-0 [accessed 10 January 2020].
20 Bly, Nellie (1888). 'Nellie Bly on the stage'. *The New York World,* 4 March, p. 15.
21 Bly, Nellie (1889). 'Nellie Bly's doctors'. *The New York World,* 27 October, p. 1.
22 25 January 1890.
23 qt in Brian, Denis (2001). *Pulitzer: A Life.* New York: John Wiley, p. 148.
24 Fisher, Trevor (1995). *Scandal: The Sexual Politics of Late Victorian Britain.* Stroud, Gloucestershire: Alan Sutton, p. 89.
25 Eder, Maria (1972). *History of Photography*, (E. Epstean, trans.). New York: Dover, pp. 238–9.
26 Peirce, Charles Sanders (1931–58). *Collected Papers I-VIII* (C. Hartshorne, P. Weiss & A. Burks, eds.). Cambridge, MA: Harvard University Press, CP2–281.

27 From its exhibition in 1855 until 2011, Roger Fenton's photograph 'Valley of the Shadow of Death' was unquestioned. But then the documentary filmmaker Errol Morris drew attention to the implications of an identical Fenton image of the ravine without the cannon balls (Morris, Errol [2011]. *Believing Is Seeing: Observations on the Mysteries of Photography*. Harmondsworth, Mddx: Penguin). AP photographer Joe Rosenthal's 'The Raising of the Stars and Stripes on Mount Surabachi' appeared in hundreds of US Sunday papers on 25 February 1945 (Albee, Jr Parker & Keller Cushing Freeman [1995]. *Shadow of Suribachi: Raising The Flags on Iwo Jima*. Santa Babara, CA: Praeger).

28 '*Le baiser de l'hôtel de ville*'/'The Kiss by the Hôtel de Ville'; Driscoll, Molly (2012). 'Robert Doisneau: The story behind his famous photograph "The Kiss"'. *Christian Science Monitor*, 14 April. www.csmonitor.com/Technology/Horizons/2012/0414/Robert-Doisneau-The-story-behind-his-famous-Kiss%5baccessed%255 [accessed 30 March 2019].

29 Goldberg, Susan (2016). 'How we spot altered pictures,' *National Geographic*, July. www.nationalgeographic.com/magazine/2016/07/editors-note-images-and-ethics/ [accessed 30 March 2019].

30 Frost, Chris (2003). *Designing for Newspapers and Magazines*. Abingdon, Oxford.: Routledge, p. 150.

31 Barthes, Roland (1977). *Image, Music, Text* (Stephen Heath, trans.). New York: Hill and Wang, p. 26.

32 Robert Capa took 'Loyalist Militiaman at the Moment of Death, Cerro Muriano' on 3 September 1936. Since the 1970s, the photograph has been subjected to endless forensic examination (Whelan, Richard [2002]. 'Robert Capa's Falling Soldier: A detective story', *Aperture*, 166, Spring).

33 $300,000 current value.

34 Fielding, Raymond (1972). *The American Newsreel, 1911–1967*. Norman, OK: University of Oklahoma Press, p. 25ff; *The Derby*, Birt Acres, UK , 1895; *Raising Old Glory over Morro Castle*, Edison Co., USA, 1899; *La prise de Tournavos/ The Surrender of Tournavos*, Georges Méliès, France, 1897; *Le Sacre d'Édouard VII/ The Coronation of Edward VII*, Georges Méliès, France, 1902; *Boxer Rebellion, Russo-Japanese War* (Barnouw, 1974, pp. 24ff); Musser Charles (1997), *Edison Motion Pictures 1890–1900*. Washington: Smithsonian Institution Press p. 482; *The Battle of Santiago Bay* [now lost]; *San Francisco Disaster*, Bioscope, USA, 1906.

35 Chambers, Ciara, Mats Jönsson & Roel Vande Winke (2018). *Researching Newsreels: Local, National and Transnational Case Studies*. Abingdon: Palgrave, p. 1.

36 Fielding, Raymond (1972). *The American Newsreel, 1911–1967*. Norman, OK: University of Oklahoma Press, p. 27.

37 Popple, Simon & Joe Kember (2003). *Early Cinema from Factory Gate to Film Factory*. London: Wallflower, p. 50.

38 McKernan, Luke (2014). *The War and the Newsreel*, p. 1. https://lukemckernan.com/wp-content/uploads/war_and_the_newsreel.pdf [accessed 10 July 2019].

39 Fielding, Raymond (1972). *The American Newsreel, 1911–1967*. Norman, OK: University of Oklahoma Press, p. 34.

40 *Movietone*, 3 June 1940.

41 Dickinson, Margaret & Sarah Street (1985). *Cinema and the State: The Film Industry and the British Government 1927–1984*. London: BFI, p. 8.

42 Fielding, Raymond (1972). *The American Newsreel, 1911–1967*. Norman, OK.: University of Oklahoma Press, p.153.

43 Flichy, P. (1991). *Une historie de la communciation moderne: Espace public et vie privée*. Paris: La Découverte, pp 19–23.
44 Ronalds, Beverley (2016). 'The bicentennial of Francis Ronalds's electric telegraph'. *Physics Today*, 69:2, 1 February. https://physicstoday.scitation.org/doi/10.1063/PT.3.3079?journalCode=pto [21 June 2019].
45 Hollins, T. (1984). *Beyond Broadcasting: Into the Cable Age*. London: BFI, p. 35.

4

'OH, THE HUMANITY!': LEGACY NEWS MEDIA 1900—

> 'The public interest, convenience, or necessity'
> *United States Code: Radio Act of 1927, 47 U.S.C. §§ 81–119*

At 8pm on 30 October 1938, the CBS Radio Network reported that the Martians had invaded New Jersey:

> *Announcer:* We are bringing you an eyewitness account of what's happening on the Wilmuth Farm, Grovers Mill, New Jersey.
> *Reporter:* Ladies and gentlemen (am I on?). Ladies and gentlemen, here I am … I'll give you every detail as long as I can talk. As long as I can see. More state police have arrived. They're drawing up a cordon in front of the pit, about thirty of them. *[HISSING SOUND FOLLOWED BY A HUMMING THAT INCREASES IN INTENSITY]* … A humped shape is rising out of the pit. I can make out a small beam of light against a mirror. What's that? There's a jet of flame springing from the mirror, and it leaps right at the advancing men. It strikes them head on! Good Lord, they're turning into flame *[SCREAMS AND UNEARTHLY SHRIEKS]* … it's spreading everywhere. It's coming this way. About twenty yards to my right … *[CRASH OF MICROPHONE … THEN DEAD SILENCE]*[1]

And thus news of the Martian invasion of the Earth reached the American public who, according to press reports the next day, panicked in their millions. Of course, there was no such invasion, only a fictional radio-play presented in the format of a news-broadcast.

Telling such lies simply isn't at the heart of broadcast journalism's problems. Radio's archive of hoax-type scandals is even slimmer than print's. But the student of its history needs realise that the reason for the absence of outright mendacity presents as a cure even worse than the disease. Radio was regulated. It illustrates yet more clearly than did film-licensing that such media freedom as existed, existed more for the press than for newer media. Radio's infrastructure was everywhere firmly in the hands of the state and a case can be mounted that the state – even in the case of the liberal bourgeois democracies – was not loath to extend its reach to content. The received understanding was that this was more than justified by the supposed power of the new medium – as perfectly illustrated by the millions who panicked at CBS Radio's little joke.

Except that they didn't – so it wasn't.

According to Frank Stanton, the father of radio audience research in the US, and CBS's expert at the time, nobody much was actually listening to *The War of the Worlds* broadcast – a play transmitted in a drama slot, clearly announced as such, with its emulation of the news transparently 'faked' and crudely unconvincing.[2] Stanton exaggerated – but not by much. Ratings were in their infancy but an audience of only 1%–2% of households was noted – 600,000 homes. The papers' splashes the following day contained a lot of hearsay about panic and hysteria but no triangulated evidence to back up the headlines. The same lack characterises the flawed sociological account of the episode which secured its reputation as a major incident.[3] Nevertheless, even into the 1990s media sociologists were still claiming: 'What occurred that October night was one of the most remarkable media events of all time'.[4]

All the parties had a vested interest in establishing that a panic had actually occurred. CBS was more than willing to have the efficacy of their medium so dramatically demonstrated to potential advertisers. And, conversely, the press, seeing the broadcasters as serious rivals for the advertisers' dollar, was eager to have the FCC clip their wings on the grounds of their recklessness. Producer Orson Welles, then 23, was of course equally happy to burnish his reputation as a go-to enfant terrible. And the sociologists[5] were excited to legitimise media studies.

They began work in earnest months after the transmission. In total around 165 people (all inhabitants of New Jersey, the site of the drama) were interviewed for the study, up to a year after the broadcast, the vast majority later rather than sooner. They were chosen largely 'because they were known [to the investigators] to have been upset by the broadcast'.[6] The scale to record audience responses on the questionnaire, which was the main research instrument, was conflated so that 'frightened, 'disturbed', or 'excited' all became 'panicked'. In fact, the actual *The War of the Worlds* transmission says very little to the power of the medium. What it does indicate is how easily a sociological investigation can be seriously flawed and yet be highly regarded. The programme also, in its uniqueness, highlights that radio was no more given to outright fraud than were the papers. In the annals of fake news, the show stands with *The Great Moon Hoax* of 1835 – just as much a fiction, and just as unconvincing. Most tellingly, unlike *The Hoax* it was not 'indexed' as anything other than a drama in a drama slot, rather than as a news bulletin. Authenticity was not required and – not least because the show had been produced at speed and at little cost beyond a script and the actors – not much was forthcoming. It was, as Welles announced at the end, his little Halloween prank.

The newspapers' response to it illustrates their continued unwillingness to ruin stories by over-verification. At this time, with the world drifting towards war and the radio increasingly exploiting spot news coverage, the papers were eager to convince the government that this upstart rival was out of control and tighter regulation was urgently needed.[7] The fake news here is not an interplanetary invasion, but the reports of a panic that didn't actually happen. Welles wasn't claiming a real invasion, but the papers were reporting a fake panic.

The broadcast is, however, an important marker on the road to current hysteria about fakery. It might not stand up as a proof of media power but it does have considerable significance nevertheless. Leaving aside a scattered handful of hoaxes and pure fictions, anything approaching comprehensive fakery has been, as we have seen, a rarity in the mainstream press. It was not unknown – although still rare – in news photography (being primarily caused by false captioning). At least initially, dubious 'reconstitutions' were a commonplace in news film. But the received history of the radio bulletins reveals the absence of any notorious mendacities at all. This obviously begs the question, why no such scandals?

There is a clear and, for anyone who (like the authors) asserts the critical importance of free speech, uncomfortable explanation for this difference. The not-so-secret ingredient is state control. Radio news bulletins were licensed to a greater degree than any other medium. The very earliest radio regulation in America, dating from before the Great War, prohibited operators from 'knowingly transmitting any false or fraudulent distress signal or call or false or fraudulent signal call, or other radiogram of any kind'.[8] And so it was that the US regulators, having found no evidence of panic at the time (because there was none), nevertheless did eventually state that *The War of the Worlds* transmission was 'not in the public interest'. (It took them 28 years to get round to doing so.)

However, the constraints of the regulatory environment for real news bulletins was an ever-present consideration from the off and few other scandals occurred. In the 1970s the transmission of real fake news (so to speak) occasioned action. One station was given a year's probationary license renewal following a fake weather forecast and another, which had faked the kidnapping of its morning DJ as a publicity stunt, did have its licence totally revoked. The rarity of such cases makes clear that faked radio news was not a ubiquitous problem for the American federal authorities. The primary reason was simple; instead of the Commission censoring output, the owners of the licences it awarded (and the networks of content providers they established) had to maintain powerful internal compliance offices to afford protection against the possibility that output would not meet the public interest, necessity, and convenience tests. At a stroke, the circle was squared: self-censorship ensured radio was, in effect, censored, but by the broadcasters themselves and not by the government. The First Amendment was, apparently, safe.

The free air propagation of radio-signals – wireless – used a finite natural resource: the frequency range physically available to enable transmissions. And, from the point of view of the American traditions of free speech, that posed a very real problem. The technology simply could not be effectively deployed as a mass medium without external control allocating these frequencies. Broadcasting without regulation, therefore, would have been impossible and, as the resource was natural and, like the very air, inalienable, the state was, logically, its obvious regulator. Moreover, it was the signalling needs of the great 'Dreadnaught' battleships at the end of the 19th century which constituted a supervening necessity driving engineers to produce 'wireless' communication from devices littering the physics labs of the day. Morse-coded telegraph signals were first transmitted ship-to-ship during the summer manoeuvres of the British and Russian Imperial fleets in 1895. Wireless was everywhere a military technology first, and civilians needed a state licence to own and operate any trans[mitter/re]ceiver apparatus.

The first demonstration of wireless telephony (not to be confused with wireless telegraphy) once again required only smart systems engineering. An experiment, in 1906, was targeted at commercial shipping at large in the mid-Atlantic. Operators were startled to hear singing through the headphones of their transceivers but the advance was barely noticed, and was emulated only once on dry land. Otherwise, just as the *Telefonico Hirondel* in Budapest had in effect sought to ignore the point-to-point logic of the telephone, so were the implications of the nature of wireless telephony sidelined. Its potential, as was proving to be usual with new communication techniques, was effectively suppressed.

The biggest perceived problem was, obviously, its lack of privacy when compared to wired communications by telegraph or telephone. Wireless was OK for ships signalling SOS at sea, but useless for land-based business, industrial, or personal use. It was, therefore, not particularly commercially viable as a business itself. Sending untargeted wireless messages was positively revolutionary. Indeed, one of the few instances of it, to defeat a news blackout, was the proclamation, in morse, of an Irish Republic from the roof of the Dublin Post Office during the Easter Uprising against the British in 1916. Otherwise wireless telephony, like wireless telegraphy, remained a military asset, albeit one in wide use from 1914 on. In the Great War, it was deployed not only by the navies but also on the battlefields, and even in the air by the emerging air-forces.

Then, finally, in the peace, realisation dawned. Wireless telephony was not a faulty messaging system but a mass medium. Indeed – *anyone could listen* and in short order they did – through the headphones of a 'cat's whiskers' receive-only decoder, of a kind many thousands of ex-military wireless operators knew well how to tune. The trajectory of urbanised social entertainment needs, which had industrialised popular theatre and produced the cinema, now served to establish wireless telephony as a new mass medium. In the Netherlands, the US, Great Britain – from Canada to the Argentine to Czechoslovakia, transmitting stations were licensed and soon moved on from merely replaying records to programming live shows of various kinds. The last impediment to rapid mass diffusion was brought to market – a receive-only set with a loudspeaker, not headphones. It required no training to operate. The device was (in English) christened a 'radio' – and the medium (in many languages) shared that name: radio.

The military legacy, however, reinforced by the constraints of physics, produced an emergent environment which did not necessarily bode well for radio's future as a medium of free expression. In the peace, operating any civilian wireless transceiver, whether commercially or as a species of hobby, unsurprisingly still required a licence from the government. In the light of the bandwidth limitation, the burgeoning numbers of both public and commercial entities being rewarded licences really did require that their operation be, at least technically, carefully organised and restricted. In 1926 in the US the government began allocating specific wavelengths, in order to prevent aural chaos.

This, though, assuredly did not mean nationalising the commercial licensees' businesses. The possibility of public ownership and direct government control of communications (except for the postal service) had never been embraced in America, and although with radio the idea was briefly revisited, it was again dismissed.[9] Public funding of the medium was available only from the few institutions, public universities for example, that happened to be awarded licences. The majority of licensees were commercial interests coming from all sectors of the communication industries.

At one stage the electrical manufacturing companies effectively gave away the programming in order to sell the receivers but this, obviously, could not survive market saturation. Keen consumer advertisers, including the press, also acquired licences in order to sell their wares but, particularly from a long-term perspective, 'giving away' content meant taking on an expense where one could instead turn a profit. The business model built on the sale of programme sponsorship, soon augmented by also selling spot advertisements, allowed anyone with a radio to listen for nothing. The government did not license listen-only receivers, as they did not talk over each other. Physics did not demand state intervention there. And so American radio was to appear to be almost entirely self-regulated. The protections of the First Amendment appeared to apply to the programme-makers, but broadcasting was nonetheless not quite like the press in this regard. The award of a licence by the Federal Communication Commission (FCC; the government's regulatory agency after 1934) was conditional. Although inhibited by the First Amendment, the FCC's rules on content echoed the interventionism of the initial legislation. Licences had to be operated in the problematically undefined and vague 'public interest, convenience, or necessity'.

As early as 1922, the process of providing something to listen to was being described as 'broadcasting' – a late 18th century agricultural term for planting by scattering seed. The term was apt. As with film, radio was assumed to have tremendous power to plant ideas in the mind of the masses. The use of persuasive media messages as propaganda in order to condition opinion and maintain morale had been a feature of the Great War, on all sides. In the peace that followed, ever-increasingly consumerist societies, especially America, were suffused with advertising to shift products and services. Sophisticated branding of consumer goods had, over the previous half-century, become a commonplace. Tens of millions a year were spent on ads in magazines, newspapers, and on billboards.[10] To explain the phenomenon, American sociology in the 1920s reached for metaphors: media messages were 'magic bullets', having a 'hypodermic needle effect'. The audience could do nothing but accept what they were being 'injected' with. An assumption that authority needed to protect the public was a largely unchallenged corollary of such an understanding. That at the same time authority could cauterise messages deemed to be undercutting it was no disadvantage – to the authorities – either. Despite the tradition of free speech, state control of broadcast 'speech' (i.e. the content of radio programming) was thus warranted.

Radio station owners could suffer the total loss of their business if they were personally convicted of a serious crime. There were also legally-enforced technical obligations unknown to the press – the maintenance of detailed operating logs, for instance. By law, until the right-wing were given their head in the 1980s to make a bonfire of regulations, broadcasters had to give air-time to those critical of their editorial stances (the 'equal time' or 'right of reply' provision).[11] In general, occasional interventions against 'hoaxing' notwithstanding, the more significant constraints on content were the fact that transmitting 'obscene, indecent, or profane' programming could always occasion the draconian revocation of a licence. Also important was the vague prohibition against content 'not in the public interest'. The rants of a demagogic evangelical radio preacher, for example, were deemed to be not in the public interest, and on that basis in 1930 he was denied licence renewal of the station he ran. His rant insisting that this was in breach of his First Amendment rights went unheeded.[12]

In 1943, the Supreme Court confirmed the constitutionality of that decision. Felix Frankfurter, the Chief Justice, held that the Act establishing the FCC gave it 'not niggardly but expansive powers.'[13] It was given a comprehensive mandate to 'encourage the larger and more effective use of radio in the public interest'. But the Commission almost never acted, and the illusion of radio's free speech was maintained, sustained by the apparent independence of advertising as a revenue source. The reality, however, was that through the compliance officer system, the industry policed itself so effectively that the FCC did not have to.[14]

Broadcasting's power seemed self-evident. Across much of Europe, radio's potential was utterly corrupted by authoritarian regimes. Mussolini began to use it to broadcast his speeches in 1925 but it was the Nazis who most fully exploited the possibilities of radio. As Hitler came to power in 1933, Joseph Goebbels asserted that: 'it would not have been possible for us to take power or to use it in the ways we have without the radio'.[15] Whatever the truth of this assertion (and few sources in history can be as unreliable as Goebbels), broadcasting expression was different. It might well have been the case that only newspaper owners truly enjoyed freedom of the press. Theatrical performances were licensed – although that became as much a matter of health and safety as of content. It might also be true that freedom to show what you wanted on a cinema screen – even if you owned the cinema – was licensed, content subject to, at a minimum, classification. It was acceptable even in the world's democracies, however, that freedom to broadcast needed to be even more constricted than any of that – so, de facto, you needed official permission to build a transmitter and to switch it on in the first place. And you were then kept on a short leash if you wanted to stay in business. Let us remember what Jefferson had long before suggested, that the propensities of governmental functionaries are, even in a representative democracy, always to command the liberty and property of the citizenry. Broadcasters have never escaped their clutches.

Despite all the constraints, however, news on radio, its agenda exactly echoing that of the press, was immediately an important broadcasting strand. Never mind free speech, journalism's essential commitment to topicality made radio news's popularity inevitable and, despite the initial hostility of the press, the two platforms slowly learned to live with each other. Initially the papers had successfully persuaded regulators to limit radio news, and denied the broadcasters access to their wire services, but as the 1930s progressed it was realised that, while print provided detail which radio could not match, radio gave journalism a new voice of unprecedented vividness and immediacy. The notion that *The War of the Worlds* might cause a panic was grounded, it should be remembered, in its close mimicking of a famous actual news report of the previous year.

7 May 1937, Lakehurst, New Jersey: at 7:25 PM the airship LZ 129 *Hindenburg* collided with its mooring mast as it attempted to dock. Herbert Morrison for Station WLS, Chicago:

> It's burst into flames! Get this, Charlie; get this, Charlie! It's fire … and it's crashing! It's crashing terrible! Oh, my! Get out of the way, please! It's burning and bursting into flames and the … and it's falling on the mooring mast and all the folks between it. Oh, the humanity! [16]

Welles had Frank Readick, the actor who played the reporter in his drama, listen to this carefully in rehearsal. (The performance is the broadcast's only remotely believable moment.)

It is no wonder that such vividness justified regulation. However, to one degree or another, first on radio and then, after the Second World War, on television, this did taint broadcasting's potential as an independent news medium, even when compared with the freedoms the capitalist press enjoyed. This held true however broadcasting was funded – by the sale of ads in the American system; or as in the Netherlands, where funds were raised through broadcasting organisations set up by seven 'pillars of Dutch Society' (e.g. churches, unions, etc.); or as in the UK, where direct taxation was (is) used to pay for programming. The Dutch system was not emulated, but the British solution was. It emerged as the major alternative to the American.

State intervention readily destroyed broadcasting as a reliable source of information in the dictatorships. In the democracies, however, it produced an uncomfortable truth for those who value the free press. It could well be that regulation might have effectively caused the paucity of faking scandals in the broadcasting archive (as well, of course, as containing demagoguery). If so, an obvious question follows: could perhaps the same beneficial outcome have resulted if the press were similarly controlled? But to take such a view is to forget that state intervention cost the concept of a free press, which had been centuries in the making, dear – and nowhere can this be seen as clearly as in the case of the BBC's news and current affairs provision, for all its sobriety of tone and trusted status.

British 19th- and 20th-century telecommunication history was (at least until the 1950s) a more or less obverse of the American. Public telegraphy had been deemed part of the state postal monopoly as, subsequently, was telephony. And, naturally, the General Post Office, which was already issuing experimental transceiver wireless licences, was empowered to control radio. In 1922, it had the major set manufacturers, who operated its 'experimental' licences and had been giving the programming away in order to sell their 'wirelesses', establish a commonly-owned mass transmission monopoly, the British Broadcasting Company Ltd (BBCo). The Post Master General (PMG) had ultimate control over it because his (of course, a male) government fixed its income. In Britain, you not only needed a licence to broadcast but also to receive broadcasting signals. The revenues raised from the sale of these receive-only licences were passed to the company to fund its programming. It was, in effect, an hypothecated tax at a rate which the government set. Any degree of private ownership was eliminated in 1927 when the BBCo was deposed by means of a medieval-style charter issued from the Throne, and a publicly-owned British Broadcasting Corporation replaced it. Radio was nationalised and its output was branded as 'public service broadcasting' – uncontaminated by commercial sponsorship of any kind.

This, though, ignored the press's hard-won principle that its revenues should not be directly handed over by the state.[17] Broadcasting, funded in effect by a system totally controlled by the state, was not fertile soil for the (essential) journalistic function of being a constraint on the state's power. The PMG, a member of the government, anyway lacked the wit displayed by the FCC in laying the censoring role off onto the broadcasters. Unrestrained by any First Amendment considerations, he took it upon himself to ensure the radio's general probity. Public objection was not raised even when his tolerance proved to be extremely limited. Not just obscenity, etc., but anything 'controversial' could be, and was, subject to his interference. Certainly, the newspapers were not unhappy to have him effectively in their corner, limiting the scope of radio news. The PMG stated in the House of Commons in 1923 that he thought 'it was undesirable that the [radio] service should be used for the dissemination of speeches on controversial matters', e.g. prohibiting mentioning the Treaty of Versailles without prior Foreign Office clearance, or (astonishingly) preventing the Chancellor of the Exchequer, his cabinet colleague, outlining the budget on air.[18] The mealy-mouthed voice of authority claimed this was not de facto censorship, only positive 'influence'.[19] Revocation of the licence was to be the constant threat and 'good behaviour' became the BBC's second nature, exemplified by its actions in its foundational moments, as the Company was giving way to the Corporation in 1926.

In the summer before the BBC's Charter came into effect, a General Strike – widely perceived as a pre-revolutionary moment – occurred. It involved even the printers and, for its nine-day duration, the wireless was the only nationally distributed source of news. Although some argued for the government to take direct control of broadcasting, clearer heads saw that the Company would be more effective if it were seen as being 'independent'. Unobserved, John Reith, then chief executive and soon to be first Director-General of the BBC, with some of his senior staffers moved into the office of the government's chief PR operative, to write the radio news bulletins.[20] Reith, who had failed to dent the PMG's view of controversy prior to the strike, was certainly not going to offer a challenge now:

> There could be no question [he was famously to write to his senior colleagues] about our supporting the Government in general, particularly since the General Strike had been declared illegal in the High Court.[21]

Received opinion, as for instance that of the BBC's official historian Asa Briggs, is that Reith's political acumen vouchsafed for the broadcasters 'a precarious measure of independence throughout the strike'.[22] But as the BBC's centennial approaches, never mind its Second World War record and the admitted richness of much of its factual broadcasting archive, this view cannot be sustained. Tom Bell suggests that it is to 'misconstrue' the General Strike episode to see it 'as something of a bumpy start on the road to more substantive independence'. Rather the 'independence' not only was – but still is – 'precarious'. The BBC as a news source 'and the highly circumscribed notion of impartiality it developed in parallel with state institutions' is still defined by those nine days.[23]

For the BBC, 'impartiality' became a question of 'balance', but the problem of balance is that it depends on what is put into the scale's pans. Balance becomes 'bias by elimination'. During the strike Reith claimed he wanted to allow an opposition voice:

> The only definite complaint may be that we had no speaker from the Labour side. We asked to be allowed to do so, but the decision eventually was that since the Strike had been declared illegal this could not be allowed.[24]

In English law, since the 18th Century, it had been held that 'the liberty of the press consists in laying no previous restraints on publications, and not in freedom from censure for criminal matter when published'.[25] On its face, Reith's rationale is totally tendentious. If you take the view that the strike was a 'crime', then, at a stroke, he is suggesting that the reporting of crime – a news staple for half a millennium, as we have seen – was itself some sort of crime to be avoided. Of course, it could be viewed in that way, via laws against aiding and abetting, incitement, and sedition, although by precedent this would have been extremely unlikely. The government had not invoked, for instance, the emergency powers offered by the Defence of the Realm Act, which would have given some substance to Reith's stand. As it was, the applicability of the established 'publish and be damned' norm was still in place to be tested – but Reith did not publish (broadcast), clearly saving the BBC as an organisation, but at the cost, at least, of its independence as a news source. Indeed, its failure to demand, maintain, and exercise independence shadows its claim of journalistic integrity.

The 'illegality' fig-leaf was to cover the reporting's essential lack of balance. (Balance, as we have argued, is itself problematic, but pretended independence while parroting the official line is even more so.) It was to exculpate its behaviour as a disguised but fundamentally partisan official source. Voices suggesting the BBC was actually the BFC – the British Falsehood Company – were drowned out. Instead, the BBC was to acquire a reputation for 'impartiality' as, over the decades, in essence it kept 'controversy' at bay. Its news archive was to be free of scandalous incidents of mendacity – and, although free to report press investigations, it was itself largely free of the investigative activities that had marked the press since the English Civil War. Indeed, such activities were so far outside the BBC's ethos that prior to the Second World War, the only sustained programming strand interested in these types of journalistic functions came from the Talks Department (which produced documentary programming) in the mid-1930s. The result, as George Orwell observed having worked there for two years during the Second World War, was that 'talks are mostly ballyhoo and that no subject of importance ever gets the honesty of discussion that it would get even in the most reactionary newspaper'.[26] The nannying 'Auntie' role following the Second World War is also sidelined in the 'story of the BBC' as it is popularly understood.

But more was going on than just timidity and caution. The BBC also secretly invited the secret service to vet employees in roles, however lowly, deemed to be 'sensitive'. MI5 officers had a room in Broadcasting House for this purpose for half a century, from 1935 until the practice was unmasked in 1985 (by investigative print journalists), and as many as a quarter of all hires were processed by them – several thousand cases a year. MI5 was regularly moved to complain about the workload being thrust on them by the Corporation.[27]

As it began with the 1926 strikers so it has continued. There are other noted examples of bias by exclusion. The author of the 1943 template document which was to be the basis of the post-war Welfare State, for example, the liberal John Beveridge, was kept from freely discussing it on air.[28] The Labour leader of the opposition, Hugh Gaitskill, was not allowed to criticise the Suez invasion in 1956 until it was well underway.[29]

The next major communication technology development, television, confirmed the implications of this history. The clear and present danger in the broadcasting environment even at the level of independence exercised by the press is evidenced by the vanishingly small number of cases of outright fakery on mainstream television. Of course, an unexposed number of subterfuges might well be presented on the screen on a regular basis but the business of filming blurs any ethical line between, say, moving an interviewee's chair to improve a shot and faking an incident outright. Did young Welsh nationalists spontaneously smash Prince of Wales

Investiture souvenir mugs in July 1969, as a BBC news magazine reported, or were they encouraged by the crew so to do? (Actual ineffectual terrorist explosions set off by nationalists objecting to the ceremony, after all, were in evidence.[30])

However, until the time of writing, the government has been constrained – as it was, just, in 1926 – from exercising naked censorship and control, believing that – not least because of the Second World War and the BBC's role in maintaining morale – this would be totally counter-productive with the public (and, indeed, the press). This has allowed for the BBC's reputation for independence and neutrality to be nurtured by a number of factors – its own undeniable day-to-day commitment to sobriety being first among them. Moreover, the fact is that, even if it is, in reality, a part of the state's ideological apparatus, it is so in the context of a polity which says it believes that: 'The liberty of the press is indeed essential to the nature of a free state'.[31]

On occasion this countervailing opinion has been used by the BBC to protect itself. For example, as civil unrest began in Ulster in 1972 – 'The Troubles' – the government, as usual, tried to control the output, but Lord Hill, the then chair of the BBC governors, successfully threatened to go public with it if they did. The government's control is thus impure, as it has to be shot through with freedom. It is generally assumed of the BBC that 'as an institution it has real autonomy', but the reality is that it is kept 'on a short lead'. It is a 'contradictory organisation'.[32] Who moves first – the government or the BBC – is seldom very clear. Overt external bans are avoided but at the cost of the BBC, under pressure, taking it upon itself to abandon coverage. Thus, the BBC's long-running current affairs flagship, *Panorama*, investigated MI5 in 1981, only to have the then Director-General, Sir Ian Trethowan, himself alert the agency, who were invited in to eviscerate the programme.[33]

In general, obfuscation became the mark of the BBC's treatment of major controversial issues. It is still difficult fully to comprehend who did what to whom on a regular basis – although the counter-history of the Corporation, exemplified by these instances and very different to the received understanding of its vaunted reputation as a trusted news source, is being more and more revealed through the release of documents and the work of reporters and media scholars. But what has become clearer as we go to press is that the inhibition which has restrained all political talk of licence removal is weakening. Naked political attacks on the Corporation's very foundation are finally being heard (as they could have been at any time in the BBC's century of existence).

The British did eventually emulate the American example and allow first, in 1955, advertising–supported television under the direction of a dedicated licensing and content-regulating authority. Commercial radio signals from the Continent and the Irish Republic were audible in the UK but listenership remained limited. Legal advertising-supported radio began only in 1973, initially with its own licensing authority.

But the consequences of licensing, without the protection of the First Amendment, were that the commercial broadcaster, although freer than the BBC to produce challenging journalism (amidst its perceived down-market general offering), also maintained compliance officers and was exposed in ways the press was not. Commercial television's moves toward investigative reporting could bring about threats to remove a licence (which needed periodic renewal). For example, during 'The Troubles', Thames Television, the London commercial TV licence holder, exposed the assassination of an Irish Republican Army cell in Gibraltar by secret British Army operatives. The company was threatened that its licence would not be renewed.[34] The cost of a licence to the business of tearing down veils and vizards and disguises is very high. It is then no surprise that the majority of major news exposés over the decades – say the Pentagon Papers or Wikileaks' data-dump– have primarily been the business of the print media and not of far more closely monitored broadcast journalism.

But the cost, without question, buys purity. Regulation is a prophylactic against fakery.

So, no fakery scandals in the UK broadcasters' archives. There is only one acknowledged and widely remembered example of a fake news story from the BBC. In 1957, *Panorama* reported on the impact of an unusually warm spring on the spaghetti harvest in southern Switzerland, using footage of trees heavily laden with strands of spaghetti, accompanied by a commentary suggesting the crop was clearly vulnerable to late frosts. The story, however, was of a piece with the Martian Invasion – except that it was transmitted not on Halloween but on April Fool's Day.[35]

Even without the imposition of special rules conditioning its content, the western press, especially in liberal environments, has, as we have documented above, rarely presented blatant fictions as true accounts. So rarely that they are often remembered by their own discrete titles: 'The Great Moon Hoax'; 'The Zinoviev Telegram'. And these occasional scandals, of course, continue into our own time

Type 'Jimmy's World' into your search engine and you will read Janet Cooke's report in *The Washington Post*, 28 September 1980:

JIMMY'S WORLD
8-Year Old Heroin Addict Lives for a Fix
By Janet Cooke
Washington Post Staff Writer

Jimmy is 8 years old and a third-generation heroin addict, a precocious little boy with sandy hair, velvety brown eyes and needle marks freckling the baby-smooth skin of his thin brown arms.[36]

The story quotes a Drug Enforcement Agency official, the director of the Howard University Drug Abuse Institute, the District of Columbia's medical examiner, a social worker at Southeast Neighborhood House, and a doctor from the National Institute on Drug Abuse. The vividness of Cooke's writing and the contextual detail these experts provided her were enough to win her a Pulitzer Prize the following spring. But various support groups had been seeking to help 'Jimmy' and Cooke was steadfastly refusing to reveal his whereabouts. She said the drug dealers made her fearful for her life. But the prize focussed the attention of the *Post*'s editors and her story unravelled. Under their questioning, Cooke confessed to the fabrication: there was no 'Jimmy'. The *Post* promptly returned the Pulitzer. It was the first such incident in the 64-year history of the prize.

And that is the point.

The paucity of hoaxes amidst a million mainstream stories is what is noteworthy. And in the crowd of journalists in the western democracies, thousands strong, serial liars are just as seldom encountered as are these individual instances.[37] This, though, is not much of a comfort. Every full-scale hoax undercuts the basic authenticity claim of the press but, more significantly, hoax-hunting distracts from the commoner problems of avoiding 'over-verification', retailing biases, selectivity, distorting contextualising and all the rest. The press slowly learned that *newes* can be sold as well as *strange newes*, but strangeness still seduces. Journalism seldom actually drowns in the swamp that lies between the uplands of fiction and of reporting, but, equally, it rarely emerges totally clean.

Notes

1 'The War of the Worlds' (*Mercury Theatre*), Orson Welles, USA, 30 October 1938. www.youtube.com/watch?v=OzC3Fg_rRJM [accessed 5 May 2019].
2 Emory, David (2016). 'Did the 1938 radio broadcast of "War of the Worlds" cause a nationwide panic?' *Snopes*, 28 October www.snopes.com/fact-check/war-of-the-worlds/ [accessed 29 April 2019]; Dunham, Croydon, B. (1997). *Fighting for the First Amendment: Stanton of CBS vs. Congress and the Nixon White House*. Westport: Praeger, pp. 33–34.
3 Cantril, Hadley (with Hazel Gaudet & Herta Hertzog, *uncredited*) (1982 [1940]). *The Invasion from Mars: A Study in the Psychology of Panic*. Princeton, NJ: Princeton University Press.
4 Lowery, Shearon, A.. & Melvin L. DeFleur. (1995). *Milestones In Mass Communication Research: Media Effects*. White Plains, NY: Longman. (pp. 45).
5 They were led by Hadley Cantril, a social psychologist and their report was presented as 'A Study in Psychology' but its protocols were to presage those of sociological inquiry, i.e. interviews not lab-based investigations. (Canrtril, Hadley, (with Gaudet, Hazel & Hertzog, Herta, *uncredited*) (1982 [1940]). *The Invasion from Mars: A Study in the Psychology of Panic*. Princeton, NJ: Princeton University Press.
6 Cantril, Hadley (with Hazel Gaudet & Herta Hertzog, *uncredited*) (1982 [1940]). *The Invasion from Mars: A Study in the Psychology of Panic*. Princeton, NJ: Princeton University Press, p. xiii.
7 Hayes, Joy, Kathleen Battles & Wendy Hilton-Morrow (eds.) (2013). *War of the Worlds to Social Media: Mediated Communication in Times of Crisis*. New York: Peter Lang.
8 Levine, Justin (2000). 'A history and analysis of the Federal Communications Commission's response to radio broadcast hoaxes', *Federal Communications Law Journal*, 52:2, pp. 276, 283. www.repository.law.indiana.edu/fclj/vol52/iss2/3 [accessed 29 April 2019].
9 McChesney, Robert (1995). *Telecommunications, Mass Media, and Democracy: The Battle for the Control of U.S. Broadcasting, 1928–1935*. New York: Oxford University Press.

82 Roots

10 Drowne, Morgan, Kathleen Huber & Patrick Huber (2004). *The 1920s*. Westport, CT: Greenwood, pp. 65–70.
11 *Red Lion Broadcasting Co., Inc. v. FCC*, 395 U.S. 367 (1969).
12 Powe, Lucas (1987). *American Broadcasting and the First Amendment*. Berkeley: University of California Press, pp. 12–23.
13 *National Broadcasting Co. v. United States* (1943) 319 U.S. 190
14 Ibid.
15 Goebbels, Joseph (1938 [1933]). 'Der Rundfunk als achte Großmacht' in *Signale der neuen Zeit. 25 ausgewählte Reden von Dr. Joseph Goebbels*. Munich: Zentralverlag der NSDAP.
16 'The Hindenburg disaster – complete eyewitness radio broadcast'. www.youtube.com/watch?v=cXO7mdBcA48 [accessed 10 January 2020].
17 Direct bribes – the brown envelopes of legend – to British newspapers by the government had ceased to be an everyday occurrence by the 1820s.
18 Briggs, Asa (1995). *The History of Broadcasting in the United Kingdom, Volume II: The Golden Age of Wireless 1927–1939*. Oxford: Oxford University Press, pp. 54–55, 243–245.
19 Briggs, Asa (1995). *The History of Broadcasting in the United Kingdom, Volume I: The Birth of Broadcasting*. Oxford: Oxford University Press, pp. 152–157.
20 Bell, Tom, (2016). *The BBC: Myth of a Public Service*. London: Verso, p. 16
21 Briggs, Asa (1995). *The History of Broadcasting in the United Kingdom, Volume I: The Birth of Broadcasting*. Oxford: Oxford University Press, p. 333.
22 Briggs, Asa (1995). *The History of Broadcasting in the United Kingdom, Volume I: The Birth of Broadcasting*. Oxford: Oxford University Press, pp. 152–157.
23 Bell, Tom (2016). *The BBC: Myth of a Public Service*. London: Verso p. 17.
24 Briggs, Asa (1995). *The History of Broadcasting in the United Kingdom, Volume I: The Birth of Broadcasting*. Oxford: Oxford University Press, pp. 330, 347.
25 Blackstone, William (1979 [1769]). *Commentaries on the Laws of England: A Facsimile of the First Edition of 1765—1769, Vol. 4*. Chicago, IL: University of Chicago Press, p. 151.
26 Anderson, Paul (ed.) (2006). *Orwell in Tribune: 'As I Please' and Other Writings 1943–7*, London: Politico's, p. 86 (qt in Richard Keeble (2017), 'Beyond Room 101', *Journal*, Vol. 11, the Orwell Society Autumn, p. 8).
27 Reynolds, Paul (2018). 'The vetting files: How the BBC kept out "subversives"', *BBC News*, 22 April. www.bbc.co.uk/news/stories-43754737 [accessed 10 January 2020].
28 Briggs, Asa (1995). *The History of Broadcasting in the United Kingdom, Volume III: The War of Words*. Oxford: Oxford University Press, pp. 555–556.
29 Bell, Tom (2016). *The BBC: Myth of a Public Service*. London: Verso, pp. 87–88.
30 Shipton, Martin (2008). 'Militants' key role in coming of devolution left ignored deliberately'. *Wales on Line*, 8 November. www.walesonline.co.uk/news/wales-news/militants-key-role-coming-devolution-2141188 [Accessed 6 July 2019].
31 Blackstone, William (1979 [1769]). *Commentaries on the Laws of England: A Facsimile of the First Edition of 1765–1769, vol 4*. Chicago, IL: University of Chicago Press, p. 151.
32 Born, Georgina (2013). *Uncertain Vision: Birt, Dyke and the Reinvention of the BBC*. Harmondsworth: Vintage, p. 31; Bell, Tim (2016). *The BBC: Myth of a Public Service*. London: Verso, pp. 87–88.
33 Hollingsworth, Mark & Richard Norton-Taylor (1988). *Blacklist: The Inside Story of Political Vetting at the BBC*. London: The Hogarth Press.
34 'Death on the Rock', *This Week*, Roger Bolton, UK, 28 April 1988.
35 'Spaghetti-Harvest in Ticino', *Panorama*, BBC, UK, 1 April, 1957. www.youtube.com/watch?v=tVo_wkxH9dU [accessed 10 May 2019].

36 Cooke, Janet (1980). 'Jimmy's World', *The Washington Post*, 19 April. www.washingtonpost.com/archive/politics/1980/09/28/jimmys-world/605f237a-7330-4a69-8433-b6da4c519120/ [accessed 22 October 2019].

37 e.g. Stephen Glass at the *New Republic* was revealed in 1998 as a fantasist who fabricated all his reports and five years later, Jayson Blair was caught plagiarising and augmenting his at *The New York Times*. (Glass's own story was deemed exceptional enough to be made into a Hollywood feature: *Shattered Glass*, Billy Ray, USA, 2003.) The number of such incidents does not seem to be increasing.

5

ONLINE: DIGITAL NEWS 1980—

'I come from Cyberspace, the new home of Mind'
John Perry Barlow (1947–2018)
Poet and cyberlibertarian

In 1973, Vint Cerf, a brilliant young American computer engineer, was delayed getting to an academic conference at Sussex University in England by the birth of a child. He sent his apologies via the very communication network he was going to discuss, and which he was in the midst of developing with fellow scientists for the Pentagon's Advanced Research Project Agency (ARPA). The system was to be designated ARPAnet, and it is the seed from which the internet grew.

The received understanding that we are currently beset by unprecedented levels of fake news is so thoroughly entangled with notions of the affordances of the technology Cerf and his colleagues were pioneering, that in order to speak of how fake news is being misunderstood, we need to understand the context and legacy of that moment nearly half a century ago. Without this, comprehending the allegedly 'post-fact' world in which we find ourselves cannot, for reasons which we intend to examine, escape the temptation to give such technology – particularly Web 2.0 technology – credit for more power than it intrinsically possesses, and blame for more harm than it has itself caused. We might say that the fault, dear Brutus, is not in our algorithms, but in ourselves, that we are underlings, and feel powerless to control the digital environment.

Computing was a child of nuclear weaponry, developed during the Second World War to meet the design needs of first the A- and then the H-bomb builders.[1] Preserving communications in case of a nuclear attack was a major part of the ARPA project and Cerf and his colleagues were tasked with developing the protocols to form a network enabling ten almost completely incompatible, custom-built early mainframes to work together. As these were rooms full of valves, either within military complexes or at universities engaged in military research, scattered across the United States, this was not a straightforward matter. There had anyway been a measure of hostility to the development of operating control systems – 'languages' that could be shared – but the needs of the Cold War were pressing ARPA to overcome engineering prejudice.[2] The required network was created using recently-introduced, commercially-built, secondary smaller ready-to-run computers which could 'talk' to each other, and which could also be programmed to translate data for the specific mainframes to which they were attached. The key hardware to do this was supplied from Honeywell. It was a so-called 'mini-computer', the size of a small dining-room sideboard: the DPP-516. They cost $360,000 each ($2.4 million in today's money), but this was partly because ARPA specified that they be 'ruggedised' – nuke-proofed – for wartime use.

The ARPAnet mainframes were huge, power-hungry, valved (tubed) machines engaged in work of the highest secrecy, and were only a signpost to today's 'micro' personal computer. The crucial enabler for the latter's rise was solid-state electronics – the development of which did not concern the first computer builders. Bombs aside, in 1948 Bell scientists had demonstrated a trans-resistance amplification effect – a solid state 'transistor' to replace the valves/tubes used in telephone exchanges. As well as this application for telephony, by the early 1950s transistors were also to be found in hearing aids and portable radios: the word 'transistor' enters UK slang as a synonym for such radios. Commercial solid-state development's drivers had more to do with needs originating outside the military-industrial complex, and only quite slowly did the nascent non-state computing industry find computing using solid-state electronics viable. (IBM, the world's leading manufacturer of electro-mechanical business machines, convinced itself 'there wasn't enough sand in the word' to make the solid-state devices they would need if they dropped the valves/tubes.[3])

No fully (i.e. solely) transistorised computer was built in the 1950s. In the decade following, the early 'mini' solid-state devices like the DPP-516 used integrated circuits, which was what solo transistors had by then become. It was not until the late 1970s that really 'micro' (that is, desk-top typewriter-sized) programmable devices emerged from the edges of the US electronics industry – such as that garage in Cupertino. No wonder, as why would anyone need a technology thought to be useful only for tasks such as designing bombs, rockets, and by now – as there had proved in fact to be adequate available supplies of sand – managing stock markets, large-scale accounting, and the like? That everybody might want to compute was rather like the strange notion half a century earlier that radio-telephony's real value was that anybody could listen in. What new capabilities could the desk-top computer offer that would be useful to an ordinary citizen? Typing? Calculations? Telex?

By 1977, computing's radical potential to transform these applications by melding them together had been around for the usual decades so that the 'micro' result – the personal or home computer – could now be diffused without radical societal disruption. Capable of being connected by telephony, these civilian, consumer-durable devices allowed for Cerf's inter-computer communication initiative to be made available to all. A myriad of applications followed.

Initially within the military-industrial complex, those, like Cerf, who were concerned with networking formed themselves into a 'network working group', NWG – which soon became international: INWG. Their agenda was to ensure the smooth operation of the inter-connections, but the scope of their attentions rapidly expanded. The protocols they created to facilitate the work led, in short order, to the development of the 'e-mail' system. The emergence of the NGW was to be of immense significance not only for inter-computer communications but also because it fostered an illusory freedom. The very idea of the net's ungovernability is grounded in this disconnect. Despite the self-evident need to control the development of the protocols to make the system work in the first place, the obvious corollary – that the same process could address the question of the control of content – was ignored. The machines might have been buried deep within the military-industrial complex, but leaving the engineers free to explore their own agenda of what non-state-secret information could be carried, and how, proved critical. The state's secrets were protected and a free-for-all emerged for the rest.

The disconnect was profoundly to condition why the digital has attracted such hyperbole. It was, like print, considered a technology to shape – determine – the world. The central McLuhanite belief that technology does this was apparently strikingly affirmed.[4] The internet and the digital in general became, for the technological-determinist (or technicist), the final proof of a 'Technology Rules, OK' hypothesis:

> Governments of the Industrial World, you weary giants of flesh and steel, I come from Cyberspace, the new home of Mind ... You have no sovereignty where we gather ... Cyberspace consists of transactions, relationships, and thought itself, arrayed like a standing wave in the web of our communications. Ours is a world that is both everywhere and nowhere, but it is not where bodies live ... Your legal concepts of property, expression, identity, movement, and context do not apply to us. They are all based on matter, and there is no matter here.[5]

The hyperventilation of the Grateful Dead lyricist and technicist 'cyberlibertarian' John Perry Barlow's 1995 *Declaration of the Independence of Cyberspace*, although extreme, is not untypical of what has been received understanding and opinion as to the digital's overwhelming societal effects. This largely persists, even now when scattered voices of dissent are, in the face of the palpable failure of this vision, growing ever more noticeable. It would seem only cognitive dissonance allows technological enthusiasm to coexist unproblematically with sensibilities disturbed by the ecological fate of the planet.

The virtuality of the digital world is utterly illusional. The un-weary giants of the digital age are as much of flesh and steel (or its equivalents) as their predecessors. Facebook employs 35,000 people (aka flesh) and its headquarters occupy 3.6 acres.

Microsoft, with around the same number of employees, squeezes into 508 acres of HQ. Google has 5 million square feet and nearly 100,000 workers. And Amazon is America's second biggest employer, with nearly twice that figure, and has, at its headquarters alone, 8 million square feet at its disposal – around 140 American football fields. As for the absence of matter, the now somewhat quaint-sounding poetry of the intangibility of 'cyberspace' notwithstanding, the internet is made of wires and cables and machines called computers. We are indeed concerned with 'transactions, relationships, and thought itself', but they are manifested within and through machinery made by processes producing, incidentally, significant pollutants – cauldrons of hazardous antimony, arsenic, cadmium, chromium, cobalt, lead, mercury, and selenium. It takes five times or more the energy – fossil-fuelled, largely – to build a computer than it takes to make a car or a refrigerator; and they present a major recycling challenge. The world's discarded monitors, processing chips, memory boards, speakers, and mikes currently weigh an estimated 50 million metric tons. Each year Americans are throwing away 30 million computers; Europeans 100 million phones. Much of this garbage has found its way into the hands of the 150,000 inhabitants of Guiyu on the South China coast, a major recycling gulag, the biggest one of several dotted round the Global South ... 'no matter', indeed.

For all that it is generally believed, Barlowesque fantasising ignores these basic realities. The simple fact is that the infrastructure was always (and still is, of course) far, far from immaterial. Networks need physical nodes, in this case Internet Exchange Points (IXs or IXPs), and by 2019 there were 239 of them around the world. Around 500 of the 1,500 geostationary satellites orbiting the globe connect them.[6] And together these nodes are no friends of the earth either: by 2015, global data centres were 'estimated to equate to 2% of global emissions, equal to the emissions from global aviation'.[7] The net, which serves at best a half of humanity at the moment (estimates vary), is already as bad a polluter as planes. And it is, after all, just (as it were) a network. It can, if it were desired, be regulated through its nodes and, again, were authorities to be so minded, tanks could be parked on the capacious lawns of Facebook and its fellows. Its electricity could simply be switched off. (We're obviously not saying that the internet should be switched off. We're simply noting the odd fact that so many people, though apparently aware that it runs on electricity, seem to be under the vague impression that, for some unspecified reason, it can't be.)

But instead the foundational disconnect between the initial content providers (the state) and de facto regulators (the engineers of the INWG and its successors) was mapped onto the parallel shrinking of the machines to desktop-size. The delusion of network independence – of the device as a tool for inevitabley uncontrolled and uncontrollable freedom of expression – was born; and nowhere is technicism more dangerous than in its assumptions about communication. Multiple modes of, essentially, communicating one-to-the-other (or one-to-many) telephonically are (for the (?) half of us who can afford to use them) now deemed to be transformative. However, in the commonly circulated discourses of the 'information revolution' and its all-but-limitless impacts, we are, as a culture, being sold the Brooklyn Bridge.

Communication is now unprecedentedly 'interactive' (as if it wasn't before) creating 'networks of outrage and hope' leading on-and-on to cyborgian envisionings of 'post-humanity'. And all because of the initial disconnect between the users and the networkers and their technicist enthusiasms.

Of course it is true, as Wikipedia suggests, that:

> The Internet has no single centralized governance in either technological implementation or policies for access and usage; each constituent network sets its own policies.

And it also cannot be denied that its impact has been transformative. It has:

> enabled and accelerated new forms of personal interactions through instant messaging, internet forums, and social networking. Online shopping has grown exponentially both for major retailers and small businesses and entrepreneurs, as it enables firms to extend their 'brick and mortar' presence to serve a larger market or even sell goods and services entirely online. Business-to-business and financial services on the internet affect supply chains across entire industries.[8]

But a little historical understanding and logical clear-headedness suggest that these 'new forms' are not meaningfully, in essence, 'new' – the new aspects are at best modes, not forms. For all that such technicist hyperbole is undeniable as a description of surface realities, in structuralist terms, it paints a slanted picture. This is not to suggest that digital's impact can or should be ignored or forgotten. It is clearly of fundamental importance. But it is not radical ('pertaining to a root or roots', OED). It coexists with established entities and the disruptions laid at its door are as much consequences of social as technical forces. Above all, the net is clearly not an unmitigated force for good.

Despite Barlow and received opinion, the internet – simply – could have been better controlled – as is spectrum use; and its contents *could* have been censored (in the broadest sense of the term) in line with the practices governing all other media systems. The disconnect, though, has allowed the fact that free speech has never been without bounds to be more or less ignored. Forgotten is that those using media demonstrably to cross a line, e.g. causing harm, have always been subject to control. Not, though, it would seem, these days; not with this technology; not after the digital disconnect. Not all speech has been, or ought to be, protected. In the west, we have long allowed traffic in all other media to be monitored and unidentifiable sources blocked without believing this destroys free expression, as we understand it. Now, though, the owners and exploiters of the net have been allowed to claim they are not like other media owners, because the internet is not like other media. But, we would argue, this is far more a result of technicist double-think than anything else. The net's absolute 'freedom' is not necessarily so; it is in no way inherent in the hardware. It is far more the product of late capital which has allowed the new 'giants of flesh' and metals (and plastics, etc.) to pretend they are not publishers, do not broadcast, are not culpable transmitters (see p. 152). (We shall look at the legal framework that has allowed this, see p. 150).

Talk has been of a 'better world order being ushered in by the Internet' with a monocausal insistence now on the latest stage of digital diffusion as a prime agent of social change.[9] However, as the 21st century's third decade begins, there have been some signs that an understanding is growing that the technicists' ecstatic vision of freedom is, at the same time, an authoritarian's wet-dream of control. The bottom line is that this ultimate 'technology of freedom'[10] is no such thing. Digital affordances have a potency for surveillance and control allowing for an electronic panopticon of an intrusiveness and secrecy unimagined by Jeremy Bentham. This should certainly give us pause. (In our experience as teachers, the authors have found that western media students fairly frequently express the belief that the internet can't be regulated. This idea is, however, understandably far less common among international students from, for example, China, where the possibilities of government monitoring and regulation of the internet are much more fully, and openly, exploited than they are in the west.) Governments, however 'weary' (and however secretively they may do so in ostensibly 'free' countries), are adopting this technology to use it against their citizens.

For example, in 2018, under the ambitious guise of bringing the internet to 50% of India's population, the government of Prime Minister Narendra Modi, inclining to an authoritarian agenda, brought in regulations which state that:

> if the government objects to an online post, Internet companies must provide information about the creator and sharers of the offensive content to government agencies within 72 hours. Nothing prevents the government from identifying individuals who may be posting information critical of the ruling party under the guise of an investigation.[11]

This is a reality, but it struggles against the common (but deluded) view that the transformative impact of capitalism's latest communications technologies is obviously beneficial.[12]

That, supposedly, today 'the revolution will be tweeted' was first assumed to be a real phenomenon by an American blogger in connection with street disturbances in Iran in 2009. He was undeterred by the number of Twitter users actually signed up in that country at the time – less than 1,000.[13] That 'revolution' did not happen either, but nonetheless the conception of the digital as both an unstoppable force for democracy and, at the same time, a tool capable of destroying it (not least through the production of fake news) was firmly 'tweeted' into public consciousness. Subsequent unrest across the Middle East was branded as a series of 'Twitter Revolutions'. Technicist miasma is seldom dispelled by facts. It seems to have become popular, as a narrative, to ascribe the energy driving any revolutions or revolutionary activity to the power of Twitter.

The popular protests/revolts that engulfed the Arab world following an uprising in Tunisia in 2011 were authoritatively suggested by distant western observers to have 'started with organization, debate and calls to rise up on the Internet'.[14] As, at the same time, these commentators correctly also acknowledged the poverty and technological underdevelopment of the area, only cognitive dissonance allows us to understand their reasoning. Of course, within the *Umma* literacy is a religious necessity and one of the largest of the uprisings of the 'Arab Spring' of 2012, in Egypt, certainly used text to call for protesters to gather in Cairo's Tahrir Square. Specifically, they used handbills. 'The changes in Tunisia and Egypt were not driven by technology. These were revolutions driven by people'.[15] It is only by another trick of the light that this went unnoticed and western-owned digital media instead took the credit.[16] After all, even if a mobile phone told you of the demonstration, you still have to go there. And tapping its screen is of limited efficacy against riot-police, tear gas and/or tanks.

A classic pre-internet instance: In Leipzig, communist East Germany, in 1989, 'it was *commonly known* that each Monday at about 6 p.m., a large number of people would come streaming out of both the Nikolai Church and other nearby churches' into the adjacent Karl Marx Platz [emphasis added]. The congregants, becoming political protestors against the regime, refused to disperse and each week 'common knowledge' grew their numbers until, demonstrations and mass disobedience caused the East German Communist state to collapse. Eventually, in a series of falling dominoes, the entire Soviet system followed suit.[17] Of course, many factors were involved in this – but obviously in '89, not the internet. What was significant is that the word spread; the media – the monopolistic state-controlled media – were of no significance. Media absence, curiously, is overlooked by technicists citing this example.[18] However, phenomena such as 'informational cascading', the dynamics of crowds, fads, and fashion – or in this case revolution – can be more important than any new media input.[19]

By 2019, it was possible to note something of a wave of unrest across the globe among the generation coming of age in the post-2008-crash 'austerity era', but, largely leaving that aside (along with the tempting but not directly relevant theory that perhaps essentially neoliberal media preferred blaming Twitter to blaming politics), the attraction of attributing street disturbances to social media was overwhelming. The rioters, after all, all had smartphones. But, in many countries where the authorities are not loath to track every call and text, it was the case that 'social media is now an instrument of state repression as much as it is a tool of revolt'.[20]

And yet the social power of new media remains very much a given, even among sociologists. Entranced by technicism in general, their interests had long been conditioned by the evolving technologies of communication, but the technical and scientific operation of such systems remained largely unexamined. By the 1980s, it was not at all rare for media sociologists to herald, at least in America, the abundant electronic communication channels then coming into their own as 'technologies of freedom'. This phrase was coined in connection with cable television in the

1970s,[21] but each new platform is greeted with similar enthusiasm. The internet enabled *Networks of Outrage and Hope*[22] even while cognitive dissonance allowed them, increasingly, to be attacked as the enemies of truth.

Yet, so strong is the hold technicism has on us that the 'trick of the light' which suggests they are now always central and absolutely necessary is quite common. To take a western example, social media certainly played a role in the UK riots of 2012, but so too did the person-to-person cascade, as well as 'legacy' media such as local radio. 'I just listened to the radio to find a riot. Simple as that'.[23] Monocausal explanations – Twitter ergo revolution – are clearly inadequate. 'Legacy' media overall should not be forgotten. The term was coined by gung-ho technicists downplaying the old platforms' statistics in the new century. But still in 2019, radio is reaching 90% of the English population, with 5.5 million tuning in to local stations (and not just for news of riots).[24] And it is not alone.

$41 billion was taken at the global cinema box office in 2018, for example. In 2017, the broadcast TV industry was still worth $30 billion world-wide and publishing another $12.4 billion. Even Broadway takes $25 million a week.[25] Of course, massive revenues have also accrued to new media — web-advertising, e-Books, gaming, and social media platforms, etc. – but these new platforms have more reflected than transformed the media's underlying contours. At a deep level, content conforms to older modes. And this is even true of the traditional news media where, arguably, the new has had considerable impact.

In the five years to 2017, newspaper publishing revenue continued to decline steadily, falling by some $7 billion, but it still amounts to some $11.7 billion per annum and, although massively reduced from its historic highs, globally, printed newspaper circulation has remained more or less stable around 500 million over this decade. The alternative to this, digital newspaper publishing (largely with paid subscriptions), has been growing but slowly. On 1 July, 1980, for the first time, an online edition of a newspaper, *The Columbus* (OH) *Dispatch*, was published. But by 2018, 38 years on, only 26 million electronic copies per day were being shifted, some 5% of print's number.[26] (Such a statistic is worth considering, even though, obviously, not all online news comes in online papers.) Change, as ever, is of course underway, but radically disruptive dynamics – despite the hyperbole of those selling the new news media – are not so obvious. Currently *The Dispatch* has a daily circulation of 81,291 and 140,307 on Sundays. James Thurber, who began his journalistic career there, is not yet turning in his grave over its fate.

What the internet has not done – has not remotely affected – are the contours of the 'legacy' of the news. The persistence of older media news platforms, as reflected in the statistical record, suggests that the uses and gratifications they afford might still have potency. Beglamoured talk of the impacts of interactivity, of the end of secrecy, and a 'post-truth' panic about fake news is largely unfounded. That is not to say such outcomes do not exist but rather, more or less, that they always have. The internet actually confirms that, for good or ill, digital news 'runs news still'. The record, as we have etched in the above chapters, shows that news production and consumption have always involved measures of interactivity for consumers, leaks, and a cavalier approach to veracity by producers. Modern affordances facilitate established practices but do not remake them.

To see the potential of interactive narratives, for example, as being somehow revolutionary is to deny the deeply human attractions of time-honored non-interactive narrativity. 'Tell me a story' is not the same as 'I want to intervene in this story'; to hear a story is not the same as, in effect, playing a game, and the former has undeniably universal appeal whatever the attractions of the latter. Both involve the mental 'work' of deconstruction. Receiving any text 'does not necessarily mean passivity. Being receptive can be most active'.[27]

> [A]ll meanings have always grown out of a collaboration between the idiosyncratic subjectivities of authors and audience and the reading conventions of the respective cultures they inhabit.[28]

And news stories are no different. They too are 'in some sense interactive'.

New technology does enhance the possibilities of consumers contributing news content. The early dissemination of information about events by internet users to other internet users became a millennial phenomenon. News of natural disasters, terrorist outrages, war-zones, protests, and riots began to reach the public first in this form and much was made of this: 'When the people formerly known as the audience employ the press tools they have in their possession to inform one another', they become 'citizen journalists'.[29] That this might represent a serious socio-political development, however, stands thus far as a mere technicist conceit. The 'citizen journalist' might have the 'press tools' but they have little of the journalists' understanding of the craft and, untriangulated, the flood of their 'reports' only rarely demonstrates impact on events recorded, directly causing other serious social responses. Worse, they can impede and confuse public understanding and official investigation. Moreover, as a source for professional journalists to process and reprint, citizen journalism is, again, nothing new. Input to the news from readers has always been possible. Such correspondents (at first independent of the editorial team) and/or letter-writers supplied content to the very earliest newspapers (see p. 45).

Today, though, texts – written or audio-visual – can be presented to the consumer who can reorder, augment, amend or remake content to a degree older media technologies did not allow. Certainly, users reordering contents affects meaning. It undercuts the agenda-setting power of, say, broadcasters but so, admittedly to a lesser extent, does randomly reading stories on a newspaper page. Its significance, like that of 'citizen journalism', can be easily overstated. Interactivity 'cannot be taken at "face value"'[30]; with news platforms, its power and impact is, again, largely illusionary:

> interactivity is a technical rendering of neoliberal or advanced liberal power and as such a disciplining technology ... [Its apparent surrender of control is]

the basis of self–policing practice, where a regime of free choice is normalised and individuals become disciplined to accept and exercise their own agency … it is a disciplining into a liberal ideal of subjectivity based around notions of freedom, choice and activity.[31]

Interacting with news stories to augment or otherwise alter them can all too easily become what Slavoj Žižek would see as:

> the perfect example of interpassivity: of doing things not to achieve something, but to PREVENT something from really happening, really changing. All the frenetic humanitarian, politically correct, etc., activity fits the formula of 'Let's go on changing something all the time so that, globally, things will remain the same!'[32]

It becomes *dysfunctional* interactivity – 'interpassivity' is his term.

Largely illusionary, also, is the supposedly transformative impact on journalism of the reduced possibilities of secrecy in the internet world. This ignores that newspapers have been, for example, engaged in setting up exposés – 'stings' to ensure scoops – (at least) since Nellie Bly (Elizabeth Cochrane) spent ten days undercover as an inmate of the New York Women's Asylum in 1887 (see p. 56). And they have also long been in the business of publishing documents containing the secrets of others.

In 2008, a shadowy organisation, without involving the press, dumped 251,000 files of a Swiss bank's clients' private records onto the net. Two years later, the organisation, Wikileaks, now in cahoots with five major newspapers from Spain, France, Germany, the UK, and the USA, began to release 250,000 unpublished diplomatic cables:

> Journalists getting handed a set of 250,000 primary source documents is unheard of. It's profoundly new and it's a profoundly new way that our entire society and our entire culture are trying to grapple with information …. Journalists have to try to understand: What does it mean to get 250,000 primary source cables? … Journalists have certain ways of thinking about what information's important. Their ability to come to terms with what a database is, is a new kind of profound challenge for journalism.[33]

But, as it turns out, not that profound.

Journalists have been dealing with secret primary documentation ever since Needham was handed Charles I's papers after the Battle of Naseby (see p. 42). More recently, in 1971, *The New York Times* offers a prime example. Daniel Ellesberg, the official who made the material available to the paper, failed in his intention to halt the war in Vietnam by his action, but the impact of the revelations of official American perfidy certainly sustained the anti-war movement. Wikileaks' unfocussed dumpings cannot claim as much. At the time of its first mass releases via the papers,

Bill Kelner, the then executive editor of *The New York Times* felt: 'this is just like everything else we've always done. This is not all that new, this is not all that big a deal'.[34] And Max Frankel, *The New York Times* Washington bureau-chief who published *The Pentagon Papers* said: '[T]here are few facts or observations in these [Wiki]leaks that an American official would not confide to a respected journalist'.[35]

Revelations do not seem automatically to have greater impact than does other reporting. Revelations from leaked bank data-sets, for example, do not have much apparent impact on rampant (and probably corrupt) wealth accumulation. The fact is that, throughout the last century and into the present one, keeping a secret was best done with a typewriter and a safe. As Julian Assange, the founder of Wikileaks, has correctly observed: 'The only way to keep a secret is never to have one' (attributed). But should you have secrets – even diplomatic or financial ones – public revelations of them, history suggests, will normally have less significant impact than anticipated.

Notes

1 Ulam, Stanislaw (1972). 'Von Neumann: The interaction of mathematics and computing', in *First USA-Japan Computing Conference* (Nicholas Metropolis, and J. Worlton, eds.). Montvale, NJ: AFPIS, p. 96.
2 The earliest of these assembly programmes, COBOL, was cultivated on the orders of Grace Cooper, a senior naval officer in charge of computer developments for her service.
3 Hanson, Dirk (1983). *The New Alchemists: Silicon Valley and the Microelectronics Revolution*. New York: Avon Books, p. 104 et seq. This is the delusion that: 'We shape our tools and then our tools shape us' (see f/n 9, p. 47).
4 e.g. Shirky, Clay (2008). *Here Comes Everybody: The Power of Organizing Without Organizations*. New York: Penguin.Barlow.
5 Barlow, John Perry (1996). 'Declaration of the Independence of Cyberspace.' Davos, Switzerland, 8 February. https://projects.eff.org/~barlow/Declaration-Final.html [accessed 31 October 2011].
6 Anon (n/d). 'Internet exchange points', *Data Center Map*. www.datacentermap.com/ixps.html [accessed 12 July 2019].
7 Hodgson, Christopher (2015). 'Can the digital revolution be environmentally sustainable?', *The Guardian*. www.theguardian.com/global/blog/2015/nov/13/digital-revolution-environmental-sustainable [accessed 12 July, 2019].
8 https://en.wikipedia.org/wiki/Internet [accessed 13 July 2019].
9 e.g. Shirky, Clay (2008). *Here Comes Everybody: The Power of Organizing Without Organizations*. New York: Penguin.
10 A phrase first coined with equal purblindness by Ithiel de Sola Pool in connection with cable television – 'the television of abundance': De Sola Pool, Ithiel (1984). *Technologies of Freedom*. Cambridge, MA: Harvard.
11 Tharoor, Shashi (2019).'This proposed Internet law sets a terrifying precedent', *The WorldPost* (The Berggruen Institute and The Washington Post).18 January. www.washingtonpost.com/news/theworldpost/wp/2019/01/18/modi/ [accessed 5 October 2019].
12 Morozov, Evgeny (2011). *The Net Delusion: How Not to Liberate the World*. London: Allen Lane.

13 Morozov, Evgeny (2011). *The Net Delusion: How Not to Liberate the World*. London: Allen Lane, p. 1.
14 Castells, Manuel (2012). *Networks of Outrage and Hope: Social Movements in the Internet Age*. Cambridge: Polity, p. 103.
15 Fisher, Alan (2011). 'The "Arab Spring"', social media and Al-Jazeera', in *Investigating journalism: Dead or Alive?* (John Mair and Richard Keeble, eds.). Bury St. Edmunds: Abramis, p. 150.
16 Appleyard, Bryan (2011). 'The net delusion', *New Statesman*, 20 January, p. 20.
17 Lohmann, Susanne (1994). 'The dynamics of informational cascades: the Monday Demonstrations in Leipzig, East Germany, 1989–1991', *World Politics,* 47:1, pp. 42–101.
18 e.g. Shirky, Clay (2008). *Here Comes Everybody: The Power of Organizing Without Organizations*. New York: Penguin, pp .162–164.
19 Çelen, Boğaçhan & Shachar Kariv (2004). 'Distinguishing informational cascades from herd behavior in the laboratory', *American Economic Review,* 94:3, May.
20 Shenker, Jack (2019). 'The wave of global protests is led by children of the crash', *The Guardian (Journal)*, 29 October, p. 2.
21 De Sola Pool, Ithiel (1983). *Technologies of Freedom*. Cambridge, MA: Harvard University Press.
22 Castells, Manuel (2012). *Networks of Outrage and Hope: Social Movements in the Internet Age*. Cambridge: Polity.
23 Adegoke, Yemisi & James Ball (2011). 'I just listened to the radio to find a riot. Simple as that', *The Guardian*, 8 December, p. 15.
24 Anon (RAJAR) (2019). *RAJAR (Radio Joint Audience Research)*, 1 August. www.rajar.co.uk/listening/quarterly_listening.php [accessed 6 October 2019].
25 Anon (*Statista*) (2018). 'Global box office revenue from 2005 to 2018 (in billion U.S. dollars)'. www.statista.com/statistics/271856/global-box-office-revenue/ [accessed 16 July 2019]; Ofcom (2017). *TV and audio-visual: The International Communications Market*. www.ofcom.org.uk/__data/assets/pdf_file/0027/108909/icmr-2017-tv-audio-visual.pdf [accessed 16 July 2019]; Wischenbart, Rüdiger (2019). *IPA Global Publishing Statistics*. www.internationalpublishers.org/images/data-statistics/2012/ipa-global-publishing-statistics-2.pdf [accessed 16 July 2019]; Anon (*Playbill*) (2020). 'Broadway grosses'. www.playbill.com/grosses[accessed 1 May 2020].
26 WAN/AFRA (2018). *World Press Trends 2018: Facts and Figures*. www.wptdatabase.org/world-press-trends-2018-facts-and-figures [accessed 16 July 2019]; Ibis World (2019). *Global Newspaper Publishing Industry – Market Research Report*. www.ibisworld.com/global/market-research-reports/global-newspaper-publishing-industry/ [accessed 22 April 2020].
27 Trinh T. Minh-ha (2005). *The Digital Film Event*. New York: Routledge, p 11.
28 Kinder, Marsha (2002.) 'Hot spots, avatars, and narrative fields forever: Bunuel's legacy for new digital media and interactive database media,' *Film Quarterly*, 55:4, Summer.
29 Jay Rosen (2008). 'A most useful definition of citizen journalism', *PressThink,* 14 July [accessed 19 July 2019].
30 Nash, Kate (2014). 'Clicking in the world: Documentary representations and interactivity', in *New Media Ecologies: Emerging Platforms, Practices and Discourses* (Kate Nash, Craig Hight & Catherine Summerhayes, eds.). Basingstoke, UK: Palgrave Macmillan, p. 50.
31 Jarrett, Kylie (2008). 'Interactivity is evil: An investigation of Web 2.0', *First Monday*, 13:3 March 3. http://firstmonday.org/article/view/2140/1947 [accessed 20 January 2016]. Jarrett follows Foucault's concept of 'disciplining technologies' (Foucault, Michel [1975].

Surveiller et punir: Naissance de la prison/Discipline and Punish: The Birth of the Prison. Paris: Gallimard).
32 Žižek, Slavoj (2002). 'A plea for Leninist intolerance', *Critical Inquiry*, 28:2, Winter, pp. 542–566.
33 Anderson, Chris (2010). 'How WikiLeaks affects journalism', *Council on Foreign Relations*, CFR, 23 December. www.cfr.org/interview/how-wikileaks-affects-journalism [accessed 19 July 2019].
34 Keller, Bill (2009). 'Talk to the Newsroom: Executive Editor'. *The New York Times*, 28 January. www.nytimes.com/2009/01/30/business/media/02askthetimes.html [accessed 30 April 2020].
35 Frankel, Max (2010). 'Shared with millions, it is not secret'. *The Guardian*, 1 December, p. 36.

6

'INFO WARS': NEWS PLATFORMS 2000—

> 'But journalism is like the most honoured professions in other ways'
> *Jay Rosen (1955–)*
> *Journalism academic*

Leaving aside all this talk of interactivity and secrecy, for us a factor obscuring the specific challenges facing the press's role is the hyperventilated discourse around 'post-truth' and the fake news panic. Such attention is paid to this that any needed rethinking at a fundamental level about what journalism can and should be in today's world is sidelined.

The consistent presence of elements of interactivity and a tradition of revelations scarce do the press dishonour. Not so a shared history of mendacity. This is not, it should be remembered, a matter of the overt parodying of news formats for satiric effect. Comedic 17th century *Nocturnals* aped the sober *Diurnals* establishing a tradition that persists to this day: see *The Onion* – 'America's finest news source'.[1] These are obviously 'indexed' (that is, characterised in the mind of the reader) as parody and news consumers must themselves beware of their nature. The tradition is alive and well on the net, of course. During the election campaign of 2016, the fact-checkers at BuzzFeed News noted some 750 fake stories, 50% of which were non-political and largely of the *Nocturnal* variety, i.e. gory and/or scatological tales: man accidently shoots off his own penis; woman wins the lottery and defecates on boss's desk; man dies lighting his farts in meth-lab explosion, etc.[2] These examples all emanate from *thevalleyreport.com*, which properly carries a disclaimer announcing its satiric intentions on its website.[3]

However, for journalism, the problem the fake news sites pose is not that the binary between truth and lies is unperceived by their readers; far more grievously, it is that the boundary is porous. The marks distinguishing the fake – kernels of verifiable truth, misquotes, fake attributions, fake sources, misrepresentations – presented on the fake sites are, albeit much more rarely, also found in mainstream journalism. Fake news routinises the comparatively rare lapses of the news but the news, unfortunately, is not above reproach.

Kernels of verifiable truth

As the catalogue of indicative scandals we have given shows, the press is not above reporting stories containing only kernels of truth, e.g. the 2002 *New York Times* story on Saddam Hussein's pursuit of nuclear weapons production capacity (see p. 10). But what is significant is that the fakers have made this their standard MO. Most of the fake political stories Buzzfeed noted are grounded in fact, e.g. 'Donald Trump sent his own plane to transport 200 stranded marines' – <hannity.com>. As presented, this is a lie (from Sean Hannity, a Fox News star); but marines were commercially flown on Trump's failed airline, Trump Shuttle, on one occasion in 1991.[4] Also in that year a young reporter in Brussels covering the European Union for the (London) *Daily Telegraph* filed a great story: 'Brussels bureaucrats have shown their legendary attention to detail by rejecting new specifications for condom dimensions'. The reporter, Boris Johnson, had not entirely made this up. The commission was properly concerned to maximise the protection condoms gave against the AIDS epidemic then raging by revising specifications in the light of the latest research. Johnson ignored all that and filed a story – far from the only one during his time at the EU HQ – that was, in essence, 'bullshit'.[5] The *Telegraph* published it anyway and, arguably, Johnson's inexorable climb to the door of No 10 Downing Street began.

Misquotes

The same is true of misquotations – rare in the press, common on the web. Quotations are normally selective, so seldom is speech reported in full, and on occasion one word can cause a scandal in the mainstream media. In 2018, for instance, the 23-year-old England soccer star, Raheem Sterling, had an AK-47 tattooed on his right shin. This provoked the usual sort of gratuitous sensationalist furore in the tabloids, so Sterling posted an explanation via Instagram:

> When I was 2 my father died from being gunned down to death I made a promise to myself I would never touch a gun in my life time, I shoot with my right foot so it has a deeper meaning N still unfinished.[6]

On the Sky Sports Channel this became: 'I made a promise to myself I would never touch a gun *again* in my lifetime' [emphasis added]. In the light of the trauma the young star was seeking to salve, the added 'again' caused him and his family enough stress to force the broadcasters to apologise.[7] It would seem reasonable to suppose that although such an apology was rare, similar reasons for similar editorial changes (never mind mere transcription mistakes) are not that uncommon, but they seldom come to mass attention as seriously distorting the story.

Not so with internet news fakery. It is saturated with egregious misquotes. During the 2016 US election campaign, Wikileaks posted a report of a speech Hilary Clinton had given at Goldman Sachs' New York HQ three years earlier:

> You know, I would like to see more successful business people run for office. I really would like to see that because I do think, you know … you [bankers] have a certain level of freedom. And there's that memorable phrase from a former member of the Senate: You can be maybe rented but never bought.[8]

Leave aside the status of the leak: on 17 October 2016 <therightists.com> website published a report of this with her saying: 'I Would Like To See People Like Donald Trump Run For Office;They're Honest And Can't Be Bought'. She did (if we trust Wikileaks) speak on the subject but the story is in essence a lie: no mention of Trump, and the bankers, after all, she felt could be 'rented'.[9]

Promulgation of stories from fake news sources

This is ubiquitous on the web, as Donald Trump – ignoring their bias in his favour – complained particularly loudly throughout the process which, in 2016, got him appointed President by the Electoral College. In September of that year, for example, news that 'Obama Signs Executive Order Banning the Pledge of Allegiance in Schools Nationwide' appeared on the <http://abcnews.com.co> website. The fact is that the <abcnews.com.co> site exemplifies a far from rare internet phenomenon in that it is deliberately designed to confuse. <abcnews.**go**.com> ('**go.com**' not just '**com.co**') is the actual site of the breaking news service of the American Broadcasting Company, originally founded as the NBC Blue Network of radio stations in 1927 and established, as a result of an FCC divestment order, as ABC in 1945. It is now owned by Disney. <abcnews.**com**.co>, on the other hand, is actually a species of Nocturnal but on the net that is disguised. The story appears, quite falsely, to emanate from a small Baptist church in Topeka, Kansas, but the perpetrator has yet to take down the lie; and nor have the lords of the internet have not removed it either.[10]

Fake attributions

Again, these are commonplace: 'Pope Backs Trump" – <WTOE5>. His Holiness, of course, did no such thing.[11] The perpetrators behind <WTOE5> have not been identified and the site was taken down within weeks of appearing but, according to the fact-checkers at BuzzFeed News, this posting was 'the biggest fake news hit of the 2016 Election'.

> [The story] improbably quoted the Pope as saying that the FBI's inability to prosecute Hillary Clinton for her emails led him to endorse Trump. The story also falsely declared that 'news outlets around the world' were reporting the endorsement.[12]

It was picked up and seen by 1.7 million Facebook users. And, because of the disconnect between content and promulgator which characterises the web, it was de facto anarchically 'unpublished' by any identified news-producing entity. Moreover, it was but one of the 750 stories BuzzFeed identified as emanating from 40 fake news sites during the election.

Misrepresentations

Fake news producers can merely play follow the leader on this. Spin of every kind has always been built into the fabric of journalism, especially of the tabloid variety. On 23 November 2015, 10 days after the *Daesh* jihadi attacks in Paris that took 130 lives and injured 400, Rupert Murdoch's *The* [London] *Sun* ran a telephone poll of 1,000 British Muslims and produced the splash: '**1 in 5 Brit Muslims' sympathy for jihadis**'. This was, in the paper's view, a 'wake-up call' and we can certainly agree. It was indeed alarming, although not so much regarding the loyalty of British Muslims as in its vivid illustration of the fact that distortion, rather than being an internet innovation, is a characteristic still widely deployed by the press itself. *The Sun* had asked:

> Which of the following statements is closest to your view?
> - I have a lot of sympathy with young Muslims who leave the UK to join fighters in Syria
> - I have some sympathy with young Muslims who leave the UK to join fighters in Syria
> - I have no sympathy with young Muslims who leave the UK to join fighters in Syria
> - Don't know

So, never mind that the question said nothing of jihadis, and never mind that the word 'sympathy' can mean 'support' or merely 'understanding', according to the dictionary (an ambiguity unknown to *The Sun's* subs, it would seem), the survey revealed that 80% of British Muslims either had no sympathy for, or didn't know what they thought about, young Muslim men who decided to enlist in this particular foreign cause. This reporting, given the context of the moment, constituted a distortion approaching the point of being outright bigotry. The real news was (one might argue) exactly how little support such actions had in the community. Even the UK press industry's toothless watchdog, the Independent Press Standards Organisation, found it misleading and ordered that its investigation be published in the paper.[13]

Unlike on the web, however, at least such a body was there to give such an order. Online fake news faces no controls of any kind, except the largely inept fumblings of bloated de facto web-owners, publishers who insist that they are only 'common carriers'. (This, a crucial factor in the fake news panic, is discussed in greater detail below, p. 150). But before we blame the internet, and/or Facebook's algorithms, we must keep a wider context in mind. And that means acknowledging the press's failings as having given hostages to fortune. Indeed, when it comes to ethically dubious and illegal (or potentially illegal) misdemeanours – phone-hacking, garbage-sifting, harassment, and the like – the (usually) better-resourced press goes where few internet fakers follow. All this must be acknowledged before we can hope to clean up the web's fetid news swamp.

That being said, a pre-21st century dossier of press mendacities and other misdemeanors would be fairly easy to assemble, but what would be remarkable is how few even the most comprehensive investigative cull of such scandals would yield, in comparison with the millions upon millions of news stories produced over the last half-millennium. Yet we should take little comfort from this as these rare *causes célèbres* merely distract from a consideration of journalism's real Achilles' heel. The roots of fake news have flourished for five centuries, but focusing on that scourge is to miss the point – as much as is spotlighting the presence of a few press bad apples (so to speak), which are anyway far fewer than most people probably think. This does not answer journalism's present trials and tribulations.

A central fact for us here is the disabling reality that, at a rhetorical level, to defend itself and to draw a distinction between itself and the faked, journalism in a sense drapes itself, implicitly or explicitly, in the lab-coats and gowns of the liberal professions and occupations. This is not, admittedly, by virtue of certification processes which create barriers to entry and – supposedly – assure 'standards':

> But journalism [writes Jay Rosen] is like the most honoured professions in other ways. It expects the individual practitioner and the practice as a whole to serve the general welfare … directly, through acts of journalism that amount to public service. If a professional is one who hears a calling in the opportunity for a career, then most journalists consider themselves professionals.[14]

Rosen, without a doubt, accurately represents what many journalists, especially in America, have been taught to believe, and have believed for a century. In 1914, Walter Williams, the journalist who had established the world's first higher education journalism department, at the University of Missouri, promulgated a 'Journalist Creed' which began: 'I believe in the profession of journalism'.[15] But the belief is delusional. Williams talks of journalists serving 'the public trust' and for Rosen they are 'serious people serving the public good'. It becomes easy to take an elevated view, as does Rosen's mentor James Carey, holding to the lofty ideal that 'journalism is usefully understood as another name for democracy'.[16] The press takes comfort from such opinions. In 2017, *The Washington Post*, for example, adopted as its masthead slogan: 'Democracy Dies in Darkness'. But this will not do as a defence against present woes.

We can agree as to the centrality of journalism as a species of 'public good', but do not hold with ill-founded and self-aggrandising visions of it as an 'honoured profession'. The issue, to be clear, is not one of misplaced esteem. It is not that journalism is either dishonorable or honorable in a received sense. Rather it is a question of a mis-categorisation which highlights its limitations. With respect to shared characteristics, it does not belong in the group of professions into which it is being placed. Nor does it mesh with an insistence on a quasi-constitutionality for its practice. The Rupert Murdochs of the press business give such elevated rhetoric a daily lie, and insisting on it merely provides ever more points of obvious weakness. Michael Schudson is correct to object that: 'Democracy does not necessarily produce journalism nor does journalism necessarily produce democracy'.[17] And he points out Carey's assertion's obvious ahistoricism – for example, those long centuries of newspapering in far from democratic western societies – including, of course, the colonial American provinces.[18]

As with democracy, so with the claim of matching the high occupational status of the 'honoured professions', and other valued occupations whose business it is to conform as closely as is possible representations of events with those events in the world – science, say, or law or, in its most practical aspects, philosophy's pursuit of truth and concern with ethics. Even if we limit ourselves to the presses and news platforms of the representative bourgeois democracies; even if we discount the prejudices of their owners and the pressures of the market, there are fundamental aspects of their processes which journalism does not – cannot – share with these callings. The reality of the news is that its ideological underpinnings are overlaid by the practicalities of news production, and these do not allow the scientific, legal, or philosophic procedures designed to produce objective knowledge in any coherent and consistent way. Practice in those spheres deploys protocols which, almost without exception, journalism simply does not.

Given the urgent need to defend journalism against the threats it faces, overstated, unsustainable claims as to journalism's commitment to a truth/objectivity idea befuddle our understanding, rendering, in Michael Schudson's view, the crucial analysis of what journalism actually does 'a task long overdue'.[19] He suggests that, instead of easily dismissed hyperbole, the business of the news can be thought of as a set of six functions which may or may not much overlap with democracy or, indeed, with the objectivity-seeking practices of the 'honoured' or valued professions or occupations. For him, journalism at various times in various places has worked:

- to provide information about what is not generally known;
- to investigate as guardians those who should be the guardians of public welfare;
- to be a public forum for the expression of ideas and opinions;
- to analyse the context in which events occur;
- to encourage 'social empathy' better to understand 'how the other half lives';[20] and
- to mobilise, in the name of partisanship, like-minded groups of the citizenry.[21]

And we can surely add that, in the bourgeois democracies, to maintain sufficient independence from any, including the state, who would constrain its freedoms under law, the press needs to be profitable (either financially or as an agreed public good warranting necessary unfettered support from the public purse). And to be that it needs to be a mass medium – a popular (in its most basic sense) medium. Hence its need to be entertaining – albeit often of a sobering variety of entertainment, not unlike a disturbing fiction in one medium or another. So we can add to the press's functions:

- to maintain itself as an enterprise;
- to be entertaining (i.e. in a sense, to be sufficiently popular).

The crisis provoked by the fake news panic might be ahistorical, ungrounded, and hysterical, but the light it shines on legitimate journalism's inevitable shortcomings vividly illuminates flaws long needing to be addressed. It is time to reboot the entire enterprise and, in this book's second part we propose beginning this process by mapping Schudson's (and our) functions against something other than hypothetical 'truth', or even the liberal art of history – journalism, after all, is admitted to be only its 'first rough draft'.[22] Rather, in the context of current panics, we need to explore how its procedures stack up against the protocols of science, law, and pertinent areas of philosophic inquiry, the better to understand why claiming objectivity, in the manner of other such 'professional' ideologies, is, as we've said, an Achilles' heel, and what instead really needs defending in the defence of journalism. This is not to prosecute a pretty pointless case against pretentious status-seeking. Rather it is to use an examination of the gap between these other arenas and the press in order to flesh out an agenda addressing journalism's real problems. To do this we need to offer what the philosopher Gilbert Ryle termed 'a thick description'[23] – that is (in essence) a description going beyond surface to involve context – of exactly how the activities of the press are not easily (or at all) meshed with Rosen's 'honoured professions'. Constructing our objections to the promise of journalistic objectivity as the press's central ideology, via the examination of the complex reasons why journalism does not belong to this group, is the focus of the second part of this book.

Notes

1 *The Onion* celebrated the 50th anniversary of the first moon landing (16 July 1969) with a splash: 'Real Buzz Aldrin spends 50th straight year on moon trying to signal Earth to warn Of imposter'. www.theonion.com/real-buzz-aldrin-spends-50th-straight-year-on-moon-tryi-1836538506 [accessed 20 July 2019].
2 Silverman, Craig & Jeremy Singer-Vine (2016). 'The true story behind the biggest fake news hit of the election', *BuzzFeed News*, December 16. www.buzzfeednews.com/article/craigsilverman/the-strangest-fake-news-empire [accessed 20 July 2016].
3 https://thevalleyreport.com/disclaimer/.
4 Kessler, Glenn (2016). 'Too good to check: Sean Hannity's tale of a Trump rescue', *The Washington Post*, 11 August. www.washingtonpost.com/news/fact-checker/wp/2016/08/11/too-good-to-check-sean-hannitys-tale-of-a-trump-rescue/?noredirect=on&utm_term=.978746692aa7 [accessed 20 July 2019].

5 Rankin, Jennifer & Jim Waterson (2019). 'The Brussels years: "He was the paramount of exaggeration and distortion and lies. He was a clown"', *The Guardian*, 15 July, p. 6.
6 Prenderville, Liam (2018). 'Tragic story behind death of Raheem Sterling's father as England star explains deeper meaning to gun tattoo', *Daily Mirror*, 29 May. www.mirror.co.uk/sport/football/news/tragic-story-behind-death-raheem-12618847 [accessed 30 April, 2020].
7 Anon (*The Independent*) (2018). 'Sky Sports apologise after misquoting Raheem Sterling over gun tattoo furore', *The Independent*. www.independent.co.uk/sport/football/world-cup/sky-sports-apology-raheem-sterling-gun-tattoo-england-world-cup-a8376851.html [accessed 20 July 2019].
8 Keith, Tamara (2016). 'WikiLeaks claims to release Hillary Clinton's Goldman Sachs transcripts', *National Public Radio*, 15 October. www.npr.org/2016/10/15/498085611/wikileaks-claims-to-release-hillary-clintons-goldman-sachs-transcripts [accessed 30 April, 2020].
9 Evon, Dan (2016). 'Claim: Did Hillary Clinton say "I would like to see people like Donald Trump run for office"? Rating: False', *Snopes*, 28 October. www.snopes.com/fact-check/people-like-donald-trump/ [accessed 20 July 2019]. < therightists.com > has been taken down.
10 http://abcnews.com.co/obama-signs-executive-order-declaring-investigation-of-election-results/ (it is still there) [accessed 20 July 2019].
11 Evon, Dan (2016). 'Claim; Pope Francis shocks world, endorses Donald Trump for President. Rating: False', *Snopes*, 10 July. www.snopes.com/fact-check/pope-francis-donald-trump-endorsement/ [accessed 20 July 2019].
12 Silverman, Craig & Jeremy Singer-Vine (2016) The true story behind the biggest fake news hit of the election, *BuzzFeed News*, December 16. www.buzzfeednews.com/article/craigsilverman/the-strangest-fake-news-empire [accessed 20 July 2016].
13 Nagesh, Ashita (2016). 'The Sun's British Muslim "jihadi sympathy" article was "misleading"'. *Metro*, 26 March. https://metro.co.uk/2016/03/26/the-suns-british-muslim-jihadi-sympathy-article-was-misleading-5776827/?ito=cbshare [accessed 20 July 2019].
14 Rosen, Jay (1999). *What Are Journalists For?* New Haven, CT.: Yale University Press, p. 1.
15 Farrar, Ronald (1998). *Walter Williams: Journalist to the World*. Columbia, MO: University of Missouri Press, p. 203.
16 Carey, James (1997). 'Afterword: The culture in question', in *James Carey: A Critical Reader* (Eve Stryker Munson & Catherine Warren, eds.). Minneapolis, MN: University of Minnesota Press, p. 332.
17 Schudson, Michael (2007). *Why Democracies Need An Unlovable Press*. Malden, MA: Polity, p. 12.
18 Schudson, Michael (2007). *Why Democracies Need An Unlovable Press*. Malden, MA: Polity, p.11; Mott, Frank (1962). *American Journalism: A History, 1690–1960*. New York: Macmillan.
19 Schudson, Michael (2007). *Why Democracies Need An Unlovable Press*. Malden, MA: Polity, p. 12.
20 Riis, Jacob A. (2011[1890]). 'Introduction: Framing the poor – The irresistibility of how the other half lives', in *How the Other Half Lives: Studies Among the Tenements of New York*. Boston: Bedford/St.Martin's.
21 Schudson, Michael (2007). *Why Democracies Need an Unloved Press*. Malden, MA: Polity, p. 12.

22 The thought is usually attributed to *Washington Post* publisher Phil Graham but has been traced back to a 1943 book review. Shafer, Jack (2010). 'Who said it first?', *Slate*, 30 August. https://slate.com/news-and-politics/2010/08/on-the-trail-of-the-question-who-first-said-or-wrote-that-journalism-is-the-first-rough-draft-of-history.html [accessed 28 August 2019].

23 Ryle, Gilbert (1968 [1949]). 'The thinking of thoughts: What is "*Le Penseur*" doing?', University Lectures No 18, University of Saskatchewan. http://lucy.ukc.ac.uk/CSACSIA/Vol14/Papers/ryle_1.html [accessed 7 November 2019].

Objecting to objectivity

7
FACT: 'HARD' SCIENCE

> 'What is behind a scientific text? … Inscriptions'
> *Bruno Latour (1947—)*
> *Philosopher*

The professor is waiting for us in his lab ready to assuage our doubts as to his finding that the drug naloxone inhibits, albeit temporarily, the effects of morphine. 'You doubt what I wrote?', he says. 'Let me show you'. We – 'obstinate dissenters' as Bruno Latour calls us in this, his classic explication of a fundamental scientific research practice – are led to an array in which there is a glass chamber filled with life-sustaining nutrients in which a scrap of tissue, attached to electrodes, is suspended. The tissue, the professor assures us, is 'the myenteric plexus-longitudinal muscle of a guinea pig illium' and it has been 'hooked-up' so its regular contractions drive the stylus of a physiograph. The professor first takes a syringe, then fills it with morphine which he injects into the flask. He repeats the process but with a syringe of naloxone.

The physiograph's zigzagging line declines but then recovers its prior vigor: naloxone is therefore clearly seen as an 'antagonist' of morphine.[1] *Quod erat demonstrandum.*

Latour's scientist proves his point with an inscription – the marks on the graph paper – and in this (Rosen is not wrong to claim) he duplicates the report of a journalist. A reporter, too, is – very often – equally concerned with providing as accurate a representation of the real as possible, on paper (or aurally/visually). The function of the scientist's investigation matches this; both seek to provide information, both can have potential impact on the public sphere,[2] and both can be concerned with context. And we, whether obstinate scientific dissenters or just plain readers, viewers, and/or listeners, confront in either case 'an "audio-visual" spectacle', as Latour terms his scientific example, of one sort or another.

The professor is the stereotypical lab-coated, 'honoured' professional whom Rosen appears to have in mind when he implies a consanguinity between science and journalism. Of course, the professor represents only one of a variety of scientist archetypes, not all of whom necessarily share his bench-research protocols. But the point here is that, when it comes to the fundamentals of the activity, there is actually not much in journalistic practice that meshes with the procedures of research in natural science. Three of Schudson's six journalistic functions – information, impact, and context – are shared but, closer inspection reveals, only rather superficially. Although all scientific researchers can of course be concerned with public morals, social empathy, and/or mobilising the populace – these are not the primary functions of their work. And, although their paymasters might be commercial, they are certainly not focused on making profits or attracting mass audiences (or at least, not in the way journalism is). They are not remotely in the entertainment business. Journalism shares the elements of description and the search for understanding but it entirely lacks hard natural science's predictive intentions. This is what fundamentally renders a claim of a science/journalism correspondence erroneous. The essential dissimilarity with such natural 'hard' science is simply that scientific research of the professor's kind crucially depends on repeatability and journalism does not so depend – nor does it want to: it is, after all, concerned with the news – the 'new' – not with exact repeatability.

The dissenter queries the professor's set-up, doubting, say, that the ilium muscle is what he says it is and so:

> [Another] guinea pig is placed on the table, under surgical floodlights, then anaesthetised, crucified and sliced open. The gut is sliced open, a tiny section is extracted, useless tissue peeled away, and the precious fragment is delicately hooked up between two electrodes and immersed in a nutrient fluid so as to be maintained alive.[3]

And back we go to the array, the injection, and the physiography, and the zigzagging stylus repeating its previous pattern. *QED*. And, in the west, for exactly as long as there have been newspapers (i.e. from the early 17th century), such repeatability has been an essential protocol of modern natural science's effort to represent reality accurately. It is a repeatability journalism cannot, and need not, match.

As Francis Bacon put it at the start of his template for scientific enterprise: '*Fiat experimentum diligenter*'. Making an experiment carefully (*diligenter*), rather than citing ancient authorities refracted through medieval schoolmen's texts, is at the heart of his 'new method' published in 1620:

- Ask a question, e.g. is there any warmth in moonlight?
- Consult any previous authorities on the question BUT (crucially) then –
- Test your hypothesis – no, there is no warmth – by doing a careful experiment: take a 'burning glass' (a convex lens) to focus the moon-rays and, as

experience tells you the warmth – if it were to exist– is too weak to be perceived sensorially, also take a thermometer. Place the thermometer under the lens.
- Analyse the data (you felt no heat and the mercury in the thermometer did not move) and so draw a conclusion (moonlight has no heat).
- Write up the result in a book (which may still be readily available 400 years later).[4]

Obstinate dissenters are invited to repeat the experiment.

Of course, prior to Bacon, there was already science, but, in essence, physics was Aristostle's; mathematics, Euclid's; medicine, Galen's, and so on. Observation was random, e.g. 'All animals possessing horns lack teeth in the upper jaw', noted Robert Grosseteste, 13th century theologian and proto-scientist, having seen a cow or two.[5] Post-Bacon, it is the obstinate dissenter's (or any more neutral investigator's) repetition of experiments that confirm hypotheses. Repetition is crucial. It is the essential protocol of Bacon's new way of reading 'the Book of Nature' – the procedure which underpins the scientific notion of 'objectivity'. Objectivity, then, is the mark of 'knowledge which bears no sense of the knowers'– the product of 'blind sight, seeing without interference, interpretation or intelligence'.[6]

And, of course, journalists, however 'diligent', do not (cannot) 'experiment' in this way and they are not blind-sighted. Even when they construct an 'array' (that is, for example, conduct an interview or, more contentiously, organise a 'sting') they usually go with whatever 'results' they initially produce. Their notebooks (or, these days, possibly the electronic equivalents) are not lab-books, with numbered pages time-dated, signed by the experimenter and counter-signed, without any interference or comment, by a colleague as having been 'seen and understood'. The unsigned notebooks of reporters, on the other hand, are repeatedly rewritten and edited by the investigator (reporter) and third (editorial) parties.

The implications of Bacon's 'new method' were to create – through inductive logic applied to explicating the consistency of repeated results – a specific concept of the scientific fact. After Bacon, the OED has: 'fact ... something that has occurred [1632]' – and can be shown, in identical circumstances, to occur again. Objectivity, then, becomes a prophylactic against the contaminations of subjectivity by 'looking only at the facts, setting aside personal preference or interest'.[7]

Despite the general reception of science over the last several centuries as being 'factual' in this way, there are, of course, a number of possible objections, starting with a major logical problem. To repeat experiment X to produce finding Y could well be to repeat an error. However, were one anomalous result to appear either at the first repetition, or thereafter at any point when repeating the experiment n times, the scientific fact being illustrated would fall. Of course, in reality, it would need more than one anomaly to have such a destructive outcome. Karl Popper's insight along these lines was to suggest that finding such anomalies was the exact purpose of repeating the exercise:

> It is not truisms which science unveils. Rather it is ... that we can learn, through our own critical investigations, that the world is utterly different from what we ever imagined until our imagination was fired by the refutation of our earlier theories.[8]

In Popper's view, the business of science was thus actively to seek such falsifications of established theories (what his fellow theoretician Thomas Kuhn called 'paradigms') better to establish facts.

Kuhn, on the other hand, took the view that what he called 'normal science' was not aimed at falsification, but was rather a 'mopping-up operation' designed to:

> force nature into the preformed and relatively inflexible box the paradigm supplies. No part of the aim of normal science is to call forth new sorts of phenomena; indeed those that do not fit in the box are often not seen at all.[9]

And when the mopping-up produces results that do not fit (as history shows it almost always will eventually), the paradigm is weakened until the point where the accumulation of anomalies causes a 'paradigm shift' – a 'scientific revolution'.

There has been much debate about the validity and rigour of both Popperian 'falsification' and Kuhnian 'shifts', but it is clear that the concerns these analyses address have little to do with the press. The only 'theory' journalists bring to bear is a 'lay' one which produces 'a proposition, which in a given context belongs to common sense'. Common sense is effectively a basis for understanding 'if and only if all competent users of the language involved agree that the proposition in the given context is true and that its negation is false.'[10] Although reporting the news might be seen as mopping up the unpredictable, it is no part of journalism's common-sense business to undercut:

> [t]hose plain, self-evident truths or conventional wisdom that one needed no sophistication to grasp and no proof to accept precisely because they accorded so well with the basic (common sense) intellectual capacities and experiences of the whole social body.[11]

Nor are the usual circumstances of reporting designed to produce anything other than what might be termed 'thin' descriptions. In the press, 'thickness' – context and detail – is the business of, for example, background boxes of contextual 'facts' or the work of dedicated investigative teams, both of which, by their existence, suggest such contextualsing is comparatively rare elsewhere in the news pages.[12] Moreover, for journalism, especially when in its most popular mode, taking on board the dangers of 'over-verification' (the very opposite of diligence) is likely to be the real threat to accuracy, not the production of facts to falsify initial data.

Science, of course, is also deeply concerned with humanity, but in ways distinct from journalism's approaches. We, scientists especially, have always found it difficult to resist seeing humanity in terms of the contrivances we develop – a sort of *mechanemorphism* seduces us. Shakespeare has the suicidal Hamlet sign off a love letter to Ophelia 'Thine evermore, most dear lady, whilst this **machine** is to him, Hamlet' [emphasis added], and la Mettre, in *L'homme Machine* (*Man A Machine*, 1748), carefully itemised just how 'mechanical' our bodily actions often are.[13] Watches, internal combustion engines, electrical devices have all served the mechanemorphic impulse (as when we think/speak of ourselves using terms/concepts such as our batteries running low, or of winding down, or of needing to recharge ourselves, etc.), but computing science has a particular mechanemorphic feel. The electromagnetic activity of the brain begs for it to be seen as an electrical device like any other (and when we speak of how our brains/minds are 'wired', for example, we can expect to be readily understood).

Conversely we also talk, anthropomorphically, of some machines exhibiting human-style 'intelligence'; implicitly therefore these are not that mechanical.[14] Thus *The First Draft of a Report on the EDVAC*, which outlined the contours of the earliest modern computer, already noted in 1945 that the valves/tubes in the device being built had, like biological neurons, the same 'all-or-none character, that is two states: quiescent and excited'.[15] In short order, as computers came online, what Charles Babbage had called in the 19th century the 'store' of his 'Analytic Engine' calculator became the computer's 'memory', its operational code a 'language' and the machine, in the popular parlance of the day, was an 'electronic' or 'robot brain'.[16] Its central processing unit even has a parent – the 'mother-board' – and the brain/CPU analogy suffuses (and confuses) contemporary understanding.

But if machines can have 'brains' which can be programmed, then so can the brains of mechanemorphic humans. The natural scientific project can be adapted to embrace more than prediction. It can also, using experimental 'hard' protocols, seek to impact – and, indeed, alter – predictive outcomes. As the 20th century dawned, for example, Ivan Pavlov was moving on from observing dogs in laboratory conditions (including surgically implanted devices to measure such things as salivation) to training the animals to respond in specific ways to specific stimulations,[17] By the First World War, the psychologist, John Watson, also began exploring what Pavlov had called the 'conditional' [or 'conditioned'] reflex' but with humans, not dogs. He called the approach 'behaviourism': 'Psychology as the behaviourist views it is a purely objective experimental branch of natural science. Its theoretical goal is the prediction and control of behaviour'[18] – a promise that retains its attractiveness in, for instance, some schools of business management.

In psychology, after the Second World War, B. F. Skinner was concerned with demonstrating how stimulus–response behaviours observed in the lab can be modified. Skinner worked in the name of 'order', in the service of the usual agenda of authoritarian dys/utopianism. In effect, his tradition of psychology invited the abandonment of any striving to understand mental states in situ, so to speak, in favour of controlled experimentation to effect behaviour modification. If you can train a pigeon to perform a task, as he did, you can train a human in the same way. He called it 'operant conditioning'.[19]

By the later 20th century, scientific investigations into the processes of human cognition involved, for example, producing EEGs (electroencephalograms) by festooning a person's scalp with the small metal disks of a couple of hundred electrodes to plot brainwaves. This is medically useful in detecting epilepsy and other disorders of the brain, but reading EEG print-outs better to understand human mental states in general is to invite, at best, classic causation/correlation confusions. And now we also have functional magnetic resonance imaging (fMRI) and positron emission tomography (PET), which can track blood flows within the brain – but all still offer no answers to the confusions.

Psychologists interested, for example, in the impact of media look to all 'emerging research in fields such as neuroscience' because of a belief that these give the researcher looking 'for indications of how, why and when media messages trigger individual and social change' -- insights beyond those to be gleaned, for example, from 'marketing and box office metrics'.[20] They do no such thing, of course. They are what they are: statistics – and their causation remains a black-box. Three-quarters of a century of attaching electrodes have yielded little evidence, say, to convincingly condition social policy. We can plot brain activity and stimulations but, in reality, we do not know what is being thought. This does not, however, deter the search for empirical, quantitative data as a key to understanding the mentality underlying human behaviour. Reporting of such experimental data has, however, fuelled media panics (e.g. approaches to social media platform 'use' which, essentially, assume all 'clicks' are meaningful, condition received current understanding of new media impact). Journalists, anyway, do not use EEG, fMRI, or PET as news-gathering tools. For all that the press, too often entirely uncritically, reports the findings of those who do, some might think it is rather to journalism's credit that this is obviously not like the work of journalists.

It is no wonder that the protocols of 'hard' (or harder) science, even when dealing with humans, in general have little to do with the daily practices of the news media.

Natural science does not need a laboratory bench, however. Even outside the lab, its observational protocols at best only superficially echo journalistic practice. Like journalists, ethologists, say, observe (in their case, only animal) behaviour, but their training to do this is (unsurprisingly) not really like that of a reporter.

Consider the following: Race Rocks Ecological Reserve was established on Vancouver Island in British Columbia in 1980. It is not a recreation site but a centre for ethological studies. New Race Rocks researchers are instructed as follows:

1. Preliminary Observations: Work in pairs for this exercise. Spend a few minutes observing the animal you have chosen for the study before you start the actual study ….
2. Collecting Data: You will be presenting the data in two forms: as an ethogram, and also as a time budget. An ethogram is a qualitative list of the behaviours observed, whereas a time budget is a quantitative table that gives the percentage of time the animal spends engaged in each form of behaviour. The ethogram

should be prepared prior to the time budget .... Once you have decided how long to observe one subject, stick to this time period. It will be tempting to shift to the individual that is most active at any given time, but this practice would skew the resulting time budget in the direction of that behaviour ....[21]

And so on.

Needless to say, although the production of information and, potentially, context for possible social impact are involved, the ethologist's purposes again do not easily mesh with the journalist's. Nikolaas Tinbergen was one of the trio of zoologists who won the Nobel Prize in 1973 for establishing this as a distinct area of science – the others were Konrad Lorenz and Karl von Frisch. Tinbergen suggested there were, à la Aristotle's 'causes', four basic questions underlying this sort of *diligenter* observationalism, leading to (usually) distinct sets of findings:

- What are the stimuli that elicit the response? – i.e. causation (mechanism).
- How does the behaviour change with age? – i.e. development (ontogeny).
- How does the behaviour impact on the animal's chances of survival and reproduction? – i.e. function (adaptation).
- How does the behaviour compare with similar behaviour in related species? – i.e. evolutionary (phylogeny).

Only the first of these bears any direct comparison with news-gathering.

We the public, though, are fascinated by animal behaviour and accounts of no area of scientific enquiry are as popular as those of ethologists (not that the word itself is generally in circulation). Lorenz's 1949 description of animal intelligence (published in English as *King Solomon's Ring* in 1952) is still in print. As a consequence of its popularity, his concept of 'imprinting' (the rapid learning process of the imitative new-born animal), for example, is generally understood.[22] Tinbergen himself collaborated on a series of wildlife films – one of which won the Prix Italia documentary film prize.[23] But the behaviour generally recorded in such films (e.g. in David Attenborough's brilliantly photographed explorations of the natural world), although informed by ethology, are a consequence of happenstance rather than sustained observation. The point for journalism, then, is that exactly – as with the popular wildlife documentary – such happenstance is a prime driver of the films (and the news), whereas ethological protocols are specifically designed to avoid its contaminations.

Human, as well as animal, behaviour is susceptible to investigation following the ethological model. Tinbergen, Lorenz, and von Fisch's Nobel prize was, after all, for 'physiology or medicine'. (Tinbergen, for example, became concerned with autistic children.[24]). After all, studying human behaviour is, obviously, ultimately to study the behaviour of an animal, and even without medical implications such work can have considerable social impact. Take this classic of behavioural psychology, Albert Bandura's ethologically-influenced Pavlovian Bobo Doll experiment of 1961. (We quote this at length because few research papers have had more influence in

116 Objecting to objectivity

this area. It is the foundational document apparently scientifically establishing that violent behaviour in children is learned through imitation.)

The Bobo Doll, the toy at the centre of this demonstration, was an inflatable 'bounce-back' punching bag, styled as a traditionally made-up and costumed male clown.

Subjects
The subjects were 36 boys and 36 girls enrolled in the Stanford University Nursery School. They ranged in age from 37 to 69 months, with a mean age of 52 months....

Experimental Design
... Half the experimental subjects were exposed to aggressive models [adults] and half were exposed to models that were subdued and nonaggressive in their behavior ....

After having settled the subject in his corner, the experimenter escorted the model to the opposite corner of the room which contained a small table and chair, a tinker toy set, a mallet, and a 5-foot inflated Bobo doll ....

With subjects in the *nonaggressive condition,* the model assembled the tinker toys in a quiet subdued manner totally ignoring the Bobo doll ....

In contrast, with subjects in the *aggressive condition,* the model began by assembling the tinker toys but after approximately a minute had elapsed, the model turned to the Bobo doll and spent the remainder of the period aggressing toward it.

Experimental Conditions
... At the end of 10 minutes, the experimenter entered the room, informed the subject that he would now go to another game room, and bid the model goodbye.

Test for Delayed Imitation
The experimental room contained a variety of toys. The aggressive toys included a 3-foot Bobo doll ....

Complete Imitation of Models' Behaviour
Subjects in the aggression condition reproduced a good deal of physical and verbal aggressive behaviour resembling that of the models ... subjects in the nonaggressive and control groups ... exhibited virtually no imitative aggression.[25]

Young children watching violent behaviour imitate it – *QED.*

But this experiment is not only a classic of behaviourist psychology, it also classically illustrates all the dangers of the experimental method. Bandura, in this instance, was reporting on an unprecedented situation: the 'models' were strangers in the nursery, their behaviour uncharacteristic of adults in that setting; the 'subjects' were unrepresentative (primarily four-year-old scions of Stanford university staff and faculty); and, above all, the object of the violence was a toy designed to be hit. Moreover, the procedure when repeated has produced significantly different results, e.g. prior familiarity with toys made to be bopped was found to increase aggressive imitative behaviours five-fold.[26] In sum, despite the surface clarity of such empirical studies, psychology's pretentions, in and out of the lab, to be a hard science 'of the mind' were (albeit controversially) dismissed by Kuhn as being in a 'pre-paradigm' state and thus not a 'real' science. The real significance of this particular behaviourist example is that it has been persistently and, it would seem, universally misread (not Bandura's fault, of course) as involving children being exposed to television screen violence. Never mind that no screens were involved, the Bobo Doll has sustained a moral panic about malignant media impacts for now nearly three-quarters of a century. Such causation claims lie deep beneath the fake news media panic.

But leave media as a subject of scientific investigation aside. For journalists, the interventionism involved in such experiments is not unknown – investigations into corruption, for example, can involve setting-up stings, but this is not an everyday journalistic procedure and the extrapolation of paradigms from what is discovered is no part of it. The positivist grounding of such social science, with its supposedly enhanced 'objectivity', therefore cannot be nearly so strenuously claimed by journalism.

Notes

1 Latour, Bruno (1987). *La Science en action*. Paris Gallimard [trans (anon) as: (1987) *Science in Action: How to Follow Scientists and Engineers Through Society*.] Cambridge, MA: Harvard University Press, pp. 64–72.
2 Latour was writing more than three decades ago but naloxone, the drug in his example, is used to treat opioid (pain-killer/heroin) overdoses, no small matter of social concern given that we are now in the midst of an 'opioid crisis'.
3 Latour, Bruno (1987). *Science in Action*. Cambridge, MA: Harvard University Press, p. 66. In general Latour's scepticism probing the still then usually uninterrogated authority of science unsurprisingly occasioned a backlash, e.g. Amsterdamska, Olga (1990). 'Surely you are joking, Monsieur Latour!', *Science, Technology, & Human Values*, 15:4, pp. 495–504.
4 Bacon, Francis (1826 [1620]). *Novum Organum* (Book II). (*The Works of Frances Bacon*, Vol VIII.) London: C&J Rivington *et al.*, p. 91).
5 Crombie, Alistair (1953). *Robert Grosseteste and the Origins of Experimental Science, 1100–1700*. Oxford: Oxford University Press.
6 Daston, Lorraine & Peter Galison (2007). *Objectivity*. Cambridge, MA: MIT Press, p. 17.
7 Williams, Raymond (1976). *Keywords*. London: Fontana, p. 312.
8 Popper, Karl (1959). *The Logic of Scientific Discovery*. London: Hutchinson, p. 431.
9 Kuhn, Thomas (1962). *The Structure of Scientific Revolutions*. Chicago, IL: University of Chicago Press, p. 24.
10 Smedslund, Jan (1986). 'How stable is common sense psychology and can it be transcended? Reply to Valsiner', *Scandinavian Journal of Psychology*, March. https://doi.org/10.1111/j.1467-9450.1986.tb01191.x [accessed 2 August 2019].

11 Rosenfeld, Sophia (2014). *Common Sense: A Political History*. Cambridge, MA: Harvard University Press, p. 23.
12 The use of a rectangular box for this purpose – at first, in US papers, indicated by 'dots' (known as 'benday dots') – was developed in the 1880s by Ben Henry Day Jn (whose father had founded *The New York Sun*). Investigative units (e.g. in the UK, *The Sunday Times* 'Insight' team or, in the US, *The Boston Globe* 'Spotlight' team) date from the 1960s.
13 Offray de La Mettrie, Julien (1748). *L'homme Machine*. Leyden: Luzac.
14 See *Journal of Consciousness Studies, passim*
15 von Neumann, John (1945). 'The first draft of a report on the EDVAC'. University of Pennsyvania, Moore School of Electrical Engineering, June 30. (EDVAC = Electronic Discrete Variable Automatic Computer).
16 Winston, Brian (1986). *Misunderstanding Media*. Cambridge, MA: Harvard University Press, p. 169.
17 Pavlov, Ivan (1925). *Twenty Years of Objective Study of the Higher Nervous Activity of Animals*. Moscow: State Publication.
18 Watson, John (1913). 'Psychology as the behaviorist views it', *Psychological Review*, 20, p. 163.
19 Skinner, Burrhus Frederic (1948). 'Superstition in the pigeon', *Journal of Experimental Psychology*, 38:2, pp. 168–172.
20 Anon [Harmony Institute] (n/d). 'About Us'. New York: Harmony Institute. http://harmony-institute.org/about-us/ [accessed 24 February 2015].
21 Fletcher, Gary (2006). 'Ethological Assignment, Jan 3'. www.racerocks.ca/the-ethology-assignment/ [accessed 2 August 2019].
22 Lorenz, Konrad (1961). *King Solomon's Ring* (Marjorie Kerr Wilson, trans). , London: Methuen. In the decades after the Second World War, Lorenz cut an avuncular figure, the fact that he joined the Nazi Party after the 1938 Anschluss of Germany and Austria being generally unknown. His eventual partial explanation of this caused the removal of one honorary degree but the Nobel Prize was left in place. His fellow awardee Karl von Fisch, on the other hand, was accused by the Nazis of practicing 'Jewish Science' for his work decoding the 'dancing' behaviour of bees. Tinbergen was a prisoner of the Nazis during the war and his experience of atrocities confirmed him as a committed atheist.
23 *Signals for Survival*, Hugh Falkus, UK, 1969.
24 e.g. Tinbergen, Nikolaas & E. A. Tinbergen (1986). *Autistic Children: New Hope for a Cure*. London: Routledge.
25 Bandura, Albert, Dorothea Ross & Sheila Ross (1961). 'Transmission of aggression through imitation of aggressive models', *Journal of Abnormal and Social Psychology*, 63, pp. 575–582.
26 Kniverton, Bromley & Geoffrey Stevenson (1970). 'The effect of pre-experience on imitation of an aggressive film model', *British Journal of Social & Clinical Psychology*, 9:1, pp. 88–99.

8
FACT: 'THICK' DESCRIPTIONS

> 'Cultural analysis is intrinsically incomplete'
> *Clifford Geertz (1926–2006)*
> *Anthropologist*

Not all psychologists, it must be said, expose themselves to the practical challenges of empiricism or the existential difficulties of mechanemorphism. Psychology is not limited to making people jump through hoops or sticking electrodes on their heads – it has another, 'soft' therapeutic side which, in essence, spotlights subjectivity and proceeds by conversation. Talking to people – witnesses, experts – is also an essential part of journalism but, again, the correspondence is only superficial.

When the prime 20th century exponent of this alternative 'soft' approach, Sigmund Freud, died in 1939, W. H. Auden, in his eulogy, simply noted:

> He wasn't clever at all: he merely told
> the unhappy Present to recite the Past.[1]

Freud was an 'honoured' medical doctor – a neurologist – but his techniques for the curing of the mind's ills did not require such formal hard-science qualifications.[2] Now a degree in psychology is usually a state licensing requirement, but those offering 'the talking cure' are not generally licensed as doctors of medicine.[3] Freud's base assumption was that the causes of mental illness were buried in the unconscious mind, and that the psychodynamics of bringing repressed conflicts to the attention of consciousness enables sufferers better to confront and combat the issues disturbing them. In conversation, analysts minimise their role, merely prompting the patient to free-associate (though not all traditions of talk-based psychotherapy remain entirely uniform in their application of this principle). This opens up the possibility of catharsis and cure.

Without prejudice as to psychology's (or, indeed, psychiatry's) efficacy as treatment, on the basis of patterns in what his patients told him, Freud also articulated a topographical theory of the mind, mapping different levels of consciousness and unconsciousness and labelling their various characteristics. All this, though, was dismissed by Popper as unscientific, because it was resistant to falsification. But, as evidenced by language, Freud's vision is nevertheless deeply embedded in western thinking – from 'ego' to 'neurotic', 'libido', 'denial', 'repressed', and 'cathartic'; from 'Freudian slip' to 'anal personality', we use his ideas, and his terms for them, to think and speak about others and about ourselves. To the poet, Freud was a critical figure in understanding the human condition whose death meant:

> One rational voice is dumb. Over his grave
> the household of Impulse mourns one dearly loved.[4]

Whether a science or not, psychoanalysis comes close to journalistic practice only in this matter of conversation, but reading too much into this resemblance is unhelpful. The news-interview is not an open-ended affair, nor is its substance to be kept secret, and its purpose is almost never concerned with the inner-life of the interviewee, even, in truth, when reaction to events is being sought. Moreover, unlike the pursuit of a therapeutic agenda by the psychologist, reporters make use of the agenda-setting power of questioner solely in order to obtain information useful to the production of news, often to the extent of ignoring responses that do not fit their predetermined lines of enquiry.

Anyway, in the aftermath of catastrophes and horrors natural or anthropic, journalists approach survivors and witnesses with little indication that the insights of psychology are known to them. They do not adjust their questioning, say, in line with trauma-focused cognitive behavioural therapy (CBT) or any other technique used to treat post-traumatic stress disorder. To do so is not among their functions.

In sum, in reality, journalists are not like therapists, even though they talk to people to find out about them, just as they are not like ethologists, even though they too document behaviour. They are not like experimenters, even though they (occasionally) create artificial circumstances in order to record the results (e.g. 'stings'). Fundamentally, even though they seek to observe and record, in order to find out previously unknown 'facts' about the world, they are simply not like scientists, especially 'hard' scientists.

Journalism protocols most closely echo those of the descriptive, 'soft', social sciences – anthropology and sociology (and their sub-disciplines). The scientific nature of these rests on the late 18th century concept of positivism – in essence, the production of 'facts', grounded in perception, explained by reason and logic in the Baconian mode. Such a positivist attitude was initially propounded as a fruitful alternative approach to understanding society in general, in contrast to metaphysics or theology. However, the (apparently) invariant 'objective' observations of science proper actually escape these 'soft' social sciences, even when they follow – or seek to follow – 'hard' observational protocols or the strictness of the 'hard' sciences' empiricism.

In its various forms, anthropology – social (and its subsets: visual, cultural, or linguistic) – is a species of ethological inquiry into individual human behaviour and into the nature of societies. The study of patterns of behaviour is the business of social anthropology; the production of cultural meaning that of cultural anthropology; and linguistic anthropology focuses on language's impact on social life. Anthropology's claim on science is that it deals with 'thick description'. The anthropologist Clifford Geertz was the first to apply the term in this way, in reference to his own work, borrowing it from the philosopher Gilbert Ryle. For him, it described the necessary quality in anthropology's central procedure – fieldwork, essentially in the form of careful observation and recording. This is, of course, exactly what reporters do, but, both because of time-constraints and context, doing this 'thickly' is a luxury seldom afforded them.

Geertz's seminal example of what he was after is contained in his classic de facto sports report on cock-fights in Bali. It begins:

> Early in April of 1958, my wife and I arrived, malarial and diffident, in a Balinese village we intended, as anthropologists, to study. A small place, about five hundred people, and relatively remote, it was its own world. We were intruders, professional ones, and the villagers dealt with us as Balinese seem always to deal with people not part of their life who yet press themselves upon them: as though we were not there. For them, and to a degree for ourselves, we were nonpersons, spectres, invisible men [sic] ... My wife and I were still very much in the gust of wind stage, a most frustrating, and even, as you soon begin to doubt whether you are really real after all, unnerving one, when, ten days or so after our arrival, a large cockfight was held in the public square to raise money for a new school.[5]

In 'Deep Play: Notes on the Balinese Cockfight', the description he gives of this event is 20,000 words long.

Participant observation is 'the systematic description of events, behaviours, and artifacts in the social setting chosen for study'.[6] It is a 'process of learning through exposure to or involvement in the day-to-day or routine activities of participants in the research setting'[7] As an anthropologist, Geertz – technically a 'participant observer' – was to gather detailed information on over 50 (never better than semi-legal) fights, detailing everything from the betting structures of the crowds to the relationships of the cocks' owners. And as a participant observer at the fights he attended, Geertz came to understand that they had considerable symbolic value as the animals substitute for their owners, who gain (or lose) social prestige with the outcome of the fight. (Notably, the word 'cock' has the same double-meaning in Balinese as it does in English – male genitalia and rooster).

This transforms the encounters into a dangerous game, especially when the owners are village faction leaders, the odds are even and the stakes very high. A species of cognitive dissonance (the self-delusion that justifies stupid or contradictory behaviours) informs the gambling. To explain this, Geertz borrows Jeremy Bentham's concept of 'deep play' – play putting at risk so much money and status that it is always especially fraught to engage in it:

> Every people, the proverb has it, loves its own form of violence. The cockfight is the Balinese reflection on theirs: on its look, its uses, its force, its fascination. Drawing on almost every level of Balinese experience, it brings together themes – animal savagery, male narcissism, opponent gambling, status rivalry, mass excitement, blood sacrifice whose main connection is their involvement with rage and the fear of rage, and, binding them into a set of rules which at once contains them and allows them play, builds a symbolic structure in which, over and over again, the reality of their inner affiliation can be intelligibly felt.[8]

Geertz the anthropologist is a particularly attractive figure to support the Rosen concept of journalism as an honoured profession because, length aside, this classic anthropological report reads (almost in its entirety) as a brilliant piece of reporting. When it (rarely) doesn't, it is being specifically 'scientific'. Geertz tells us the Balinese terms used at the cockfights, but otherwise he eschews the technical language of anthropology – agnate, phratry, gens, etc. – in favour of common (in the sense of being widely comprehensible; not, sadly, that of being ubiquitous) lucidity and elegance. And his subjectivity, a crucial element giving the report's context, can be read as a sober version of the subjectivising Hunter S. Thompson and the 'Gonzo Journalism' approach, as well as some other explicitly subjective niche species of long-form journalism (e.g. Wolfe's 'New' journalism, some types of personal and so-called literary journalism). But in this Geertz is an exceptional figure, and anthropology does not necessarily provide journalism with a role model. For one thing, journalists, investigative reporters aside, seldom are able to match his thoroughness or astuteness (or length). Nor are reporters, unlike anthropologists, necessarily attendees at the events they cover. More, they uncover events as much by interview and the examination of aftermaths as they do by being their own witnesses.

The importation of the constructs of structuralism – that observed practices, phenomena and activities are significations of underlying mental/social constructions – distances anthropology yet further from journalism. Journalists have enough trouble at a surface level, understanding what they see or are told, never mind probing such evidence for these kinds of deeper meanings. Claude Lévi-Strauss, for instance, delineates the gap between the actual (apparently random) physical placement of structures in a South American Indigenous village and various different accounts, from, for instance, male or female villagers, as to how they are organised. They see the scattered huts, etc., logically laid out in clearly (but in each case differently) divided sub-divisions, concentric circles, moieties, etc.[9] Again, Lévi-Strauss produces a detailed triangular diagram to explain how various cultures differently conceive of food as being raw, cooked, or rotten.[10] Fellow social anthropologist Edmund Leach comments, tongue in cheek, that on being presented with this structuralist insight, some 'might begin to suspect that the whole argument was an elaborate academic joke'.[11] It is fair to say that were those readers journalists they would, indeed, likely find it so and report it as such.

Nor are anthropologists in other ways necessarily positive role models for journalists. Until recently, anthropology has been primarily concerned with the 'other', particularly the world's 370 million Indigenous people,[12] often seeing them, however sympathetically, as primitives without history, living in the 'stone-age', etc., and, at best, romantically considering them as offering us lessons on how to be in the world without destroying it. This type of (mythical, patronising) construction has arguably become more prevalent in some places, as representations of a looming, largely western-engendered environmental catastrophe grow in prominence and clarity. Not for nothing did the great French ethnographer Jean Rouch call anthropology 'the eldest daughter of colonialism'.[13] In avoiding this inheritance, the discipline has broadened its scope to embrace concerns with western culture, but, no more than with behavioural psychology are its protocols readily capable of journalistic emulation, or, indeed, necessarily worthy of it. Participant observation, after all, is no guarantee of 'thickness'. Reports in this mode could be as lacking context as any tabloid news story, and the prior understanding the anthropologist brings to any society under investigation can function to narrow vision so that what was noted 'scientifically' was only what accorded with predetermined ideas.

In the 1960s, the Yanomami of the Amazon were among the largest unacculturated (at least in the eyes of the colonisers) groups in South America – some 40,000 strong, living in a complex network of over 200 villages, sustained by hunting and cultivating 'gardens' cleared in the rainforest. The anthropologist Napoleon Chagnon was not alone in choosing them for his fieldwork. However his conception of them, after repeated sojourns in the 1960s, as *A Fierce People* (the title of his popular, and popularising, ethnographic account), has been seriously challenged. Other anthropologists who have subsequently spent considerable time living with the Yanomami have found them to be not at all 'fierce', although, as in any human community, on rare occasions there is strife. But for the most part they dwell communally, intimately sharing shelters, with a commendable minimum of conflict. How are we to evaluate these different takes?

The Ax Fight is a complex film made in 1971 by Chagnon and Timothy Asch, a leading ethnographic cinematographer, in a Yanomami village in Venezuela, and, in contrast to Geertzian insights, it vividly illuminates the partiality ('thinness'?) of reports from even 'trained' western ethnographers.[14] In its 30 minutes, it repeatedly presents images of a face-off and fight between some men, egged on by some women. At first, the ten-minute, 400 ft reel is shown uncut and unexplained, as it came from the camera. This footage is then annotated, explicated with captions and commentary, and is finally shown cut according to established editing norms. We are assured in an early caption that: 'Large Yanomamö [sic] villages are volatile and the slightest provocation can start a violent outburst'. Towards the end there is also an anthropological caption card entitled 'SIMPLIFIED STUCTURE OF THE CONFLICT IN TERMS OF MARRIAGE AND DESCENT'. This diagrams the cause of the fight as a conflict between three agnate lineages.

Despite its exhaustive nature, *The Ax Fight* fails as a thick description in the Geertzian sense. Rather, it highlights how tenuous are the protocols being deployed as 'scientific'. The film is a bonanza for any 'obstinate dissenter'. The commentating western voices and the captions are firm where the visual evidence is ambiguous – 'blows' are mentioned, for example, when only one is seen. Or action is unexplained – there are amused bystanders. The language of the commentary, too, is biased in support of the alleged fierceness, e.g. thin sticks become 'clubs'. Claims are made which are, for any obstinate dissenter, actually unsupported. People are said to be 'trembling with anger' which is not self-evident – although there is a lot of yelling. The actual moment of the attacks, one of which fells a villager, are unseen, and although there is a still of him lying on the ground, on film we see only that he has recovered sufficiently to be sitting up.[15] On screen, there is no general melee and the conflict is stabilised when one of three agnate leaders, unarmed and with only a band of vegetation round one upper arm to signify his status, merely approaches the angry parties.

Overall, it is easy to read the conflict quite differently, seeing it as an exemplary imposition of order on a tense situation, rather than as an example of 'fierceness'. And although there are many machetes in evidence, none are used. The axes themselves, which are deployed, are turned blunt side forward. But, crucially, there is more: we now know that Chagnon had brought the axes to the village, although he has denied that this contributed to the tension. The axe fight was, then, at a minimum, seriously impacted by an unmentioned American action.[16]

Nevertheless, despite this fairly fatal ethical flaw, Chagnon does signpost a crucial distinction in ethnographic filmmaking and in the practice of anthropology generally, which affects its appositeness as a model for journalism. Richard Sorenson classes as 'Cinema Research Records for the study of nonrecurring or exceptional phenomena'[17] what Chagnon is actually initially doing in *The Ax Fight* – raw footage explained without editing. Sorenson himself had worked on the Papua New Guinea/Indonesia border in the 1960s, producing a series of films detailing, activity by activity, the life of the Fore in this unedited 'record footage' mode.[18]

Needless to say these films, whatever their status as 'field-notes', do not otherwise rank as full ethnographies, but are the materials from which such are drawn. Anthropology's usual procedure involves taking down notes, initially, for the purpose of 'writing them up' later. With visual anthropology, filming is the note-taking, and the 'writing up' involves the narrativising of such footage according to the (western, dramatic) norms of, in essence, documentary film-making. Sorenson calls them 'demonstrative films'. These constitute the archive of ethnographic movie classics, and all too many of them buy their accessibility with the distortions demanded by narrative norms; in their protocols they end up being indistinguishable from the documentary. And documentary's shaping of footage is, like the writing-up of field notes, closer to what unscientific journalists do with their (usually untriangulated) notes. Journalism has no equivalent of publishing its unedited ('raw'?) versions of recorded footage.

Geertz suggests that 'thick description' requires seeing that '[t]he culture of a people is an ensemble of texts, themselves ensembles, which the anthropologist strains to read over the shoulders of those to whom they properly belong'.[19] The functions of journalism, however, generally do not embrace this concept of obtaining information by a species of stealth. On the contrary, it is usually entirely open about the fact that extracting it is the underlying purpose of the exercise – and this perhaps constitutes the greatest obstacle to journalism claiming the status of anthropological protocols for its own procedures.

'People,' Clifford Geertz observed, with much justice, 'keep asking how anthropology is different from sociology, and everybody gets nervous'.[20] Sociology, too, is very much concerned with assembling 'texts', straining to understand the underlying structures of society, and sharing anthropology's 'over the shoulder' approach. It is when counting quantifiable phenomena that it comes closest to the 'hard' sciences and/or the 'harder' social sciences, and it is with such counting that it comes closest to being echoed, albeit only usually in certain spheres of reporting, by the press.

At the outset of such official data harvesting, in the 1830s say, the aggregated crime statistics the French state had begun to assemble from court records suggested to the mathematician Adolphe Quételet a 'remarkable constancy'. He noticed that 'the same crimes appear annually in the same order, drawing down on their perpetrators the same punishments, in the same proportions'. He saw this 'propensity to commit crimes at certain ages' as 'a singular fact' which he had uncovered in the process of elaborating, via a project involving the extensive measurements of individuals, a general statistical description of *l'Homme moyen*'s physique.[21] He thought the crime statistics were obviously of considerable significance:

> We might even predict annually how many individuals will stain their hands with the blood of their fellow-men, how many will be forgers, how many will deal in poison, pretty nearly in the same way as we may foretell the annual births and deaths.[22]

These last being statistics which had been long (if patchily) kept.[23]

The seductive appeals of 19th century positivism's possible applications were not limited to criminology. Positivist counting protocols can produce data to measure issues of social concern (description) which can then be used as a rationale for policies with which to address them (prediction with a view to control). They can also follow up, assessing the efficacy of such policies (description again). None of this is reflected in journalism's functions.

Nevertheless, here is the moment when journalism comes closest to ('soft') social science.

Across the channel, Henry Mayhew, a journalist and contemporary of Quételet's, was also engaged in considering statistics, both officially published ones and also the products of his own 'counting'. In the protocols he used can be clearly seen models for later social scientists' research. To study in the 'thickest' detail possible the nature of work and poverty in the London of the late 1840s, he interviewed a vast array of people, putting their individual accounts into the context of a general picture of their conditions. These he obtained, for instance, by calling meetings. On December 3 1848, he gathered 1,000 woollen 'slop' workers (jackets, coats, etc.) together to inform him of the general terms of their labour. Ten days later it was the tailors ... and so on.[24] He would take the known mileage of London's streets and divide it by the best assessment of the number plying a certain trade, in order to obtain a measure of the physical density of the activity. And so on. His ambition was to be scientific, if only in a descriptive sense.

This was anyway a somewhat unlikely focus for Mayhew, among other things a co-founder of the satiric magazine *Punch*, but he was far from being alone in his interest in the conditions of the working- and under-classes. The times were fraught, not least because of the impact of rapid industrialisation, and 1848 itself had been a 'Year of Revolutions' in continental Europe. It was also one of Chartist unrest in Britain. Government commissions of inquiry (usually involving many 'barristers of not less than five-years' standing') were not uncommon and one, investigating the conditions of hand-loom weavers nationally, having begun in 1838 had since broadened its scope to consider the overall economic condition of the family. Mayhew, though, was the first, as 'Metropolitan Commissioner' for *The Morning Chronicle*, to inquire into the question of poverty itself.[25] He did so with the help of closely supervised assistants (including a photographer[26]), but for all that his title might have sounded official, it was nothing more, really, than his byline as a journalist.

From October 1848 the poorest Londoners spoke, via Mayhew's pen, first weekly in the 82 essays he filed to the liberal *Chronicle*, 10,000 words at a time, and then in pamphlets (and eventually collected volumes) to the tune of a couple of million words – occupation by occupation, individual by individual. And they spoke vividly:

> the tumult of the thousand different cries of the eager dealers, all shouting at the top of their voices, at one and the same time, is almost bewildering. 'So-old again', roars one. 'Chestnuts all'ot, a penny a score', bawls another. 'An 'aypenny a skin, blacking', squeaks a boy. 'Buy, buy, buy, buy, buy– bu-u-uy!' cries the butcher. 'Half-quire of paper for a penny', bellows the street stationer ... 'Penny a lot, fine russets', calls the apple woman: and so the Babel goes on.[27]

Such general descriptions were grounded in the structured information he gathered about these street activities, and more stable trades. They were further illustrated by first-person accounts of individual lives, such as Edward Albert, a crippled sailor of colour, born in Kingston, Jamaica. 'It is an English place, sir' (he tells Mayhew), 'so I am counted not a foreigner. I'm different from them Lascars'.[28] His main source of income is as a crossing sweeper:

> Sometime I might get two shilling a day at my crossing, sometimes one shilling and sixpence, sometimes I don't take above sixpence. The most I ever made in one day is three shillings and sixpence but that's very seldom. I'm a very steady man and I don't drink what money I get; and if I had the means to get something to do, I'd keep off the streets.[29]

Despite the quality of these oral histories, such was the speed of production that what is left is often closer to field-notes than it is to formally written-up accounts. And Mayhew was at pains to ensure, by consulting with neighbours and fellow workers, as well as with other middle-class persons who were concerning themselves with the plight of the poor, that such representatives were indeed representative. His modern editor Eileen Yeo quotes a letter he wrote: 'I seek for no extreme cases'.[30] Nevertheless, all this care does not buy journalism the honoured status Jay Rosen wants for it.

In the bourgeois democracies, achieving 'thick' descriptions using Mayhew's protocols requires a commitment of personnel and resources which has not been often forthcoming in the press, at least in a sustained way. Mayhew himself has been dismissed as 'no more than a gifted journalist, with an undisciplined zest for collecting facts about the poor and interesting characters among the poor' – 'offering little more than a panorama of poverty'.[31] He was descriptive but not predictive, much less overtly directed at specific policy developments. In short, it was, of course, not natural science, but, by this view, neither was it an early example of social science.

This, though, is more than a little unfair. It is not that Mayhew was no proto-sociologist; on the contrary, he was that. The time and effort of his work has been more reflected in sociological research protocols than in press practice, at least until recently. The Pulitzer prize, for instance, was slow to acknowledge some reporting as 'No Edition' journalism (which indicated, in essence, longer preparation times). It only recognised 'Investigative Journalism' as a stand-alone category in 1985. Today, as often as not, major investigations – the Wikileaks exposés, say – require a combined multi-national press effort to fund and process. The appearance of websites such as the Bureau of Investigative Journalism, founded in 2010, compensates in part for the pressures on full-scale, permanent investigative units in individual newspaper offices, and among broadcasters. But the existence of the Bureau and its rivals speaks, in effect, to a general failure of mainstream press institutions and the limited nature of Mayhew's practice as a model.

Nevertheless, his work did make contributions to the practice of journalism, for instance to the development of the interview which was being introduced as a journalistic tool around the time in which he was researching. There is also the exposure element – the tearing down of 'veils and vizards' – which speaks to a time-honoured journalistic tradition, and the Schudsonian functions of journalism. His exposés can be seen, perhaps, as precursors of the stunts of the 'New Journalism' that emerged towards the end of the 19th century.[32] But 'the Yellow Press' scarce brought honour, and 'muck-raking', as the investigative aspect of these stunts was termed, did not necessarily demonstrate 'thickness' so much as sensationalism. It is no wonder that journalism, investigative or not, has never achieved the respectability accorded to sociology, and that Mayhew's collected work, *London Labour and the London Poor*,[33] has not been received as an example of what the founder (conventionally) of modern sociology, Émile Durkheim, required of his new 'distinct and autonomous science'.

Durkheim insisted that it 'extend the scope of scientific rationalism to cover human behaviour by demonstrating, in the light of the past, it is capable of being reduced to causes and effects'.[34] For him this constituted a positivist enterprise. Still the de facto injunction remained in place: *fiat experimentum diligenter* (or diligently discover quantitative alternatives) to demonstrate a social fact: 'What has been called our positivism is but a consequence of this rationalism'.[35] It is no wonder then that he begins his seminal text, *The Rules of Sociological Method,* quoting Quételet, and that an early work demonstrates, for example, the greater propensity to commit suicide among Protestants as compared with Catholics and Jews, a social fact gleaned from the French death records.[36]

Mayhew (and journalism) should not feel too bad about this, as the positivist sociological imagination rather ran away with itself in its search for social facts. Take, somewhat at random, sociologist Melvyn Defleur's demonstration (1951–1954) that in small, rural American communities, children were major agents for the dissemination of public information. Leaflets were dropped onto a number of villages in Washington State and then sociologists investigated how and from whom adults heard about the leaflets' contents. The finding was that 'as transmitters of the leaflet via *pass-on diffusion*, children were more active in more segments of the population than were adults'.[37] The reader can again be forgiven for thinking *pass-on diffusion* was another example of an 'elaborate academic joke', but the project (designated 'Paul Revere' by its military sponsors) was far from whimsy. Carried out during the 1950s at the height of the Cold War, it was intended to explore how official communications could be distributed following the complete destruction of all public information systems in a nuclear exchange. The leaflets were 'a medium of the last resort'.[38]

As positivism was refined in order to embrace a need to understand as well as to describe, it came to require that social facts be subject to the protocols of the harder sciences – replicability, reliability, and validity – and that such matters as observer bias be better accounted for. Sociology to some extent increasingly came to emphasise 'quantitative research', bolstering its claims to be a science. But, by the same token, this distances it from the press, for all that there is, on occasion, a superficial correspondence. Be that as it may, we are now a long way from science and the protocols of diligent experimentation. For all that there are now here, with sociology, correspondences closer than with other recognised sciences, the press is not essentially limited to the provision of 'thick' descriptions of society, and its functions, information provision aside, remain distinct.

It remains the case that attempts to buy some notion of 'respectability' for journalism with a general reference to the sciences, by arguing for similarly 'honoured' status, is to pursue a chimera. For not only is everyday journalistic practice almost inevitably defeated by the standards of even the 'softest' of scientific protocols, science itself is not what it used to be – even at its most Baconian, never mind in the hands of technicist, positivist social scientists. The Baconian vision was that 'The products of science are not tainted by human desires, goals, capabilities or experience … They do not depend on contingent social and ethical values, nor on the individual bias of a scientist.'[39] But even that is no longer quite the case:

> The close examinations of scientific practice that philosophers of science have undertaken in the past fifty years have shown, however, that … [t]he prospects for a science providing a non-perspectival 'view from nowhere' or for proceeding in a way uninformed by human goals and values are fairly slim.[40]

The bottom line remains: journalists eschew the protocols of science, 'hard' or 'soft', attainable or otherwise. The accuracy of the representations their protocols produce are of a different order. Claiming honoured professional status in the face of such difference is to distract from the crucial functions of the press, which can be exercised without this accolade. Making such a claim is to open a can of worms and be eaten by them – a situation arguably in progress, with the 'fake news' attacks. Claiming any consanguinity with the sciences, like other claims to various flavours of objectivity, is, as we have been arguing, to give a hostage to fortune. There are others --

Notes

1 Auden, W. H (1940). 'In memory of Sigmund Freud', in *Another Time*. New York: Random House.
2 The prescription of medication, etc., to alleviate mental illness is psychiatry's specific business. Psychiatrists are medically qualified specialists whose claim for 'honoured' status is grounded in the natural 'hard' sciences.
3 e.g. the International Psychoanalytic Association added oversight of training to the usual academic remit of conferences and publications in 1924.
4 Auden, W. H (1940). 'In memory of Sigmund Freud', in *Another Time*. New York: Random House.
5 Geertz, Clifford (1958). 'Deep play: Notes on the Balinese cockfight', *Daedalus* 86:1, p. 56
6 Marshall, Catherine & Gretchen Rossman (1995). *Designing Qualitative Research*. London: Sage Publications, p. 79.
7 Schensul, Stephen, Jean Schensul & Margaret LeCompte (1999). *Essential Ethnographic Methods: Observations, Interviews, and Questionnaires*. Walnut Creek, CA: AltaMira Press, p. 91.

8 Geertz, Clifford (1958). 'Deep play: Notes on the Balinese cockfight', *Daedalus*, 86:1, p. 84.
9 Lévi-Strauss, Claude (1966 [1962]). *The Savage Mind* (anon., trans.). Chicago, IL: University of Chicago Press, p. 34.
10 Lévi-Strauss, Claude (1966.) 'The culinary triangle', *The Partisan Review* 33, Autumn, pp. 586–596.
11 Leach, Edmund (1989 [1970]]. *Claude Lévi-Strauss*. Chicago, IL: University of Chicago Press, p. 24.
12 According to the United Nations (but without any full definition of Indigeneity). www.un.org/en/events/indigenousday/ [accessed 26 October 2019].
13 Eaton, Mike (ed.) (1979). *Anthropology – Reality – Cinema*. London: BFI, p. 26.
14 *The Ax Fight*, Napoleon Changon/ Timothy Asch, USA/Venezuela, 1975.
15 Sandall, Roger (1978), 'More ethnic than graphic and often remarkably long', *Sight and Sound*, 47:4, Winter, p. 219.
16 Ferguson, Brian (2002). 'Darkness in El Dorado: Comments on the Working Paper 2.4 of the AAA El Dorado Task Force: Involvement in Yanomami political affairs'. http://anthroniche.com/darkness_documents/0100.htm [accessed 27 August 2018].
17 Sorenson, Richard (1967). 'Cinema Research Records for the study of nonrecurring or exceptional phenomena', *Current Anthropology*, 8:5, December, p. 443.
18 e.g. *South Fore: Children IV: Waisa village, Eastern Highlands, East New Guinea, December 16, 1963*; Sorenson, Richard (1976). *The Edge of the Forest: Land, Childhood and Change in a New Guinea Protoagricultural Society*. Washington, DC: Smithsonian Institution Press, pp. 260–261.
19 Geertz, Clifford (1973). *The Interpretation of Cultures*. New York: Basic Books, p. 3.
20 Olson, Gary (interviewer) (1991). 'Clifford Geertz on ethnography and social construction', *Journal of Advanced Composition* 11.2. http://hypergeertz.jku.at/GeertzTexts/Olson_Interview.htm [accessed 13 September 2019].
21 Quételet's work suggested a whole useful science – anthropometry. In the form of ergonomics, it has influenced, for example, the chair in which you (probably) sit reading this.
22 Quételet, Adolphe (1835). *Sur l'homme et le développement des ses faultés, ou, Essay de physique sociale*. Paris: Bachelier. Republished in English: (R. Knox, trans., T. Smibert ed.) (2013[1842]). *A treatise on man and the development of his faculties*. Cambridge: Cambridge University Press, pp. 6–7.
23 e.g. In 1558, Thomas Cromwell ordered baptism, marriage and burials be noted in England, parish by parish. In London, these last became weekly printed 'Bills of Mortality' with the slang phrase 'within the Bills of Mortality' eventually standing for the city itself.
24 Mayhew, Henry (1971 [1849–50]). *The Unknown Mayhew, Selections from the 'Morning Chronicle' 1849–50* (E. P. Thompson, Eileen Yeo, eds). Talgarth, Brecon: The Merlin Press, pp. 24, 50.
25 Mayhew, Henry (1971 [1849–50]). *The Unknown Mayhew, Selections from the 'Morning Chronicle' 1849–50* (E. P. Thompson, Eileen Yeo, eds). Talgarth, Brecon: The Merlin Press, pp. 52, 54.
26 Richard Beard's daguerreotypes (now lost) were printed as engravings.
27 Mayhew, Henry (2008 [1851–53)]). *London Labour and the London Poor* (selc. Rosemary O'Day & David Englander). London: Wordsworth, p. 419.
28 Sailors from British-ruled India and elsewhere in the East crewing East Indiaman vessels.
29 Mayhew, Henry (1973). *The Unknown Mayhew: Selections from the* Morning Chronicle *1869-50*. Eileen Yeo, ed.). Harmondsworth, Middx: Penguin, p. 78.
30 Mayhew, Henry (1973). *The Unknown Mayhew: Selections from the* Morning Chronicle *1869–50* (Eileen Yeo, ed.). Harmondsworth, Middx: Penguin, p. 59.

31 qt in: Mayhew, Henry (1973). *The Unknown Mayhew: Selections from the* Morning Chronicle *1869–50* (Eileen Yeo, ed.). Harmondsworth, Middx: Penguin, pp. 56, 78.
32 The term was revived to indicate the subjective American journalism of the 1960/70s.
33 Mayhew, Henry *et al.* (1852–1861). *London Labour and the London Poor.* IV volumes. London: *various*. (Reprinted [1968–1983]): New York: Dover.
34 Durkheim, Émile (1950 [1895]). *The Rules of Sociological Method.* New York: The Free Press, p. 145.
35 Durkheim, Émile (2001). 'Letters to Marcel Mauss' in *Critical Assessments of Leading Sociologists 1.* London: Routledge, p. 27.
36 Durkheim, Émile (1951[1897]). *Suicide: A Study in Sociology.* New York: The Free Press.
37 Defleur, Melvyn & Otto Larsen (1958). *The Flow of Information: An Experiment in Mass Communication.* New York: Harper.
38 Defleur, Melvyn (1987). 'Introduction', *in* Defluer, Melvyn & Otto Larsen, *The Flow of Information: An Experiment in Mass Communication.* New York: Routledge, pp. viii, 35–57.
39 Reiss, Julian & Jan Sprenger (2017). 'Scientific Objectivity', in Edward N. Zalta (ed.), *The Stanford Encyclopedia of Philosophy.* Palo Alto, CA: Stanford University Press. https://plato.stanford.edu/archives/win2017/entries/scientific-objectivity/ [accessed 7 November 2019].
40 Reiss, Julian & Ian Sprenger (2017). 'Scientific Objectivity', in Edward N. Zalta (ed.), *The Stanford Encyclopedia of Philosophy.* Palo Alto, CA: Stanford University Press. https://plato.stanford.edu/archives/win2017/entries/scientific-objectivity/ [accessed 10 September 2019].

9

JUDGEMENT: THE LEGAL MINDSET

> 'To collect all the proofs on both sides; to compare them'
> *Jeremy Bentham (1748–1832)*
> *Philosopher*

'I swear by almighty God' (or 'I solemnly and sincerely declare and affirm') 'that the evidence I shall give shall be the truth, the whole truth and nothing but the truth' are words unlikely to be addressed to a journalist; and, if they are, they will not have the same force they have if uttered in a court of law. The law, like science, is another honoured profession whose practices do not quite mesh with those of journalism.

The law, though, is crucial to journalism. It guarantees the press's right to speak and ours to hear. In the western representative democracies, this safeguard is a facet of the essential, legally protected, right of free expression. It is the law plus journalism which gives meaning to the assertion that (to paraphrase Jefferson) where the press is free and everyone is able to read, all is safe. This, though, is no absolute, even for the press, and prior to this century, newer forms of media, as they have come on stream, have enjoyed lesser degrees of more highly regulated freedom.

But, within the general liberty to speak or publish or broadcast or post, the law controls and regulates conduct. Journalism, of course, is still subject to the law. Its practice has to conform to the general duty of care to others which governs all societal interactions. Its activities render it particularly liable to actions for defamation, although, a critical matter fuelling the current fake news panic, this has not been quite the case when it comes to the internet, an issue to which we shall return (see p. 150).

But first, the question of the honoured profession.

The hostages journalism gives to fortune when making any degree of claim of shared protocols with the 'honoured' professions turns, when it comes to the law, most obviously on the matter of evidence. But there, as with the similarities of procedures in the social sciences, journalism's consanguinity is superficial.

Throughout recorded history there have always been judges, of one kind or another, and a fundamental ancient charge on them (albeit with certain exceptions), before coming to any verdict, has been 'hearing the other side' – *audi alterem partem*. Proving a truth in this process was, however, a persistent challenge for law. In Europe, more than a millennium ago, legal processes intended to discover the truth of a case initially relied very much more on the closeness of communities and the then-effective threat of eternal damnation for perjury, than they did on any concept of elusive 'facts'. (Even the word itself was unknown in English before the mid-16th century.)

In order to make our point, then, regarding the mismatch between law and journalism, we will consider (with apologies for the narrowness of the focus) the example of the common law and how it is reflected (or not) in Anglophone press practices. This will also serve to indicate a template for considering the other main western legal tradition – what the utilitarian legal philosopher and reformer Jeremy Bentham called 'Rome-bred law' – and the presses within its jurisdictions.

At Common Law, criminal cases and, unless documents (preferably under seal) were at hand, civil disputes, were as much resolved by the evaluation of the parties' social status and reputation as by any other probative (truth-producing) procedures, e.g. the testimony of witnesses.[1] The word of a knight, for example, was, on its face, worthier than that of a villein who might be required to find others to vouchsafe his testimony; and, given the threat of hell-fire for liars, he might find it hard to assemble such 'compurgators' in the numbers required by the court. But, beyond that, in all cases of doubt, the resolution was easily to hand (although, it would seem – outside of witch-crazes and the like – not that often used): trial by ordeal would access the all-seeing, all-knowing mind of the Almighty, revealing a *judicium Dei* – God's judgement. Survive the cauldron, the poison, or the dunking, or have your champion best the other side's champion, etc., and you were clearly either innocent or in the right.

As the centuries passed, within the writ of the common law, the compurgators slowly morphed into a modern jury who were no longer legitimated by what they knew of the parties, but rather by their independence of them. They were to determine facts while the judge minded the applicability of the law and pronounced on the final outcome. For Bentham: 'In jury-trial, the grand features of excellence are – interrogation by parties on both sides –examination vivâ [*sic*]voce – consequent exclusion, to a considerable degree, of the faculties of mendacious invention and suggestion'.[2] The jury's lack of expertise and the opaqueness of their reasoning weighed against the advantages of this independence, and the law slowly evolved complex rules to address this, including ones governing the presentation of evidence at trial. These were ostensibly to contain these inherent weaknesses but, as they often involved endless fees, they were as much to line the pockets of the entity Bentham called 'Judge and Co':

134 Objecting to objectivity

> From the very first ... they took upon themselves – these experienced and learned judges – to determine what *evidence* should, and what should *not*, be presented to the cognizance of these their unexperienced and unlearned assessors: – but the *evidence* once presented to them, by these unexperienced and unlearned assessors it was, that the *judgment* on it was to be formed and pronounced[3] [emphasis in original].

What juries were told by witnesses was, in effect, adjunct to the process. The burden of proof did not necessarily lie with prosecutors. Prisoners in criminal proceedings could not give evidence on their own behalf. As defendants, they were deemed too partisan to be able to attest; and there were real problems about hearsay, to the point where it was excluded completely, not least because the source of the information was not under oath (although the witness to what they said was). The result was: '*Delay* ... *Vexation* ... *Expense*'.[4]

Bentham's centrality in fostering the 19th century's reform of 'Judge & Co' has lately been questioned[5] but, with or without him, 'grand features of excellence' were liberated until all 'logically probative evidence' had to be heard, 'unless a clear ground of policy of law excludes it' (e.g. matters of national security or – still – hearsay).[6] Even then exclusion became, as Bentham had argued was necessary, a matter of 'cautionary instruction' to determine whether 'prejudicial potential outweighed probative value', rather than mandated rules to do so. The result of this reform process, long achieved at this fundamental level, has been to ensure that: '[t]oday there are almost no priority rules, no rules of weight or probative force, and hardly any rules about capacity of witnesses or corroboration'.[7]

What we have now is a situation of 'free proof'. As William Twinning points out: 'all of us nearly all of the time (except in law and evidence-based medicine) live in a world of free proof, that is, free from rules of admissibility or weight or quantum or priority'.[8] This is certainly true of journalists. Even at law, now in place is a largely 'natural' system, which brings it close to the everyday with a minimum of specific rules for the admission of evidence. So it is no wonder that at this 'natural' level, the evidence-gathering of journalists is of a piece with legal processes. Nevertheless, the comparison is inexact in a number of regards.

Already by the 13th century figures had appeared in England's courts with specialist legal knowledge who, for a price, could be hired by persons needing their services. Some could be deputed to act on a principal's behalf – attorneys and solicitors – in attending to all such requirements, e.g. conveyancing. Others, *narratores* who were to become 'serjeants-at-law', could specifically help clients present their cases in court. These arranged themselves, by analogy with the colleges of Oxford and Cambridge, into secular 'Inns of Court' in London, eventually hierarchised with benchers, readers, and a class of apprentices known as barristers.[9] And these last came to operate a monopoly on advocacy in the higher courts.

The press's production process, however, in separating the reporting and editorial functions, is not easily reflected in the tripartite legal division of advocate, jury, and judge that resulted from these developments. The journalist cannot play all three roles, but what she does impinges on them all, if only to a certain extent. So, with advocacy, there is certainly a correspondence between the legal interrogatory and the journalistic interview, as both operate in the realm of free proof. Both require, as Bentham demanded:

> Answers, impromptuary – called forth without *time* allowed for mendacity-assisting invention or recollection
> – questions put *singly*
> – questions deduced from and *grounded on the answer*[10] [emphasis in original].

While legal questioning might match that of the journalist, with the legal advocate, that they are contracted spokespeople renders the process distinct – as does the constrained circumstances of those being questioned. The journalist is no courtroom interrogator acting *on behalf* of a client, and the relationship between the questioned and the questioner is completely different. Moreover, with journalism, two sides are not necessary, although for a time in the USA, the FCC required stations to allow any person criticised a right of reply. This 'Fairness Doctrine' was abandoned in 1987. Of course, some news formats, particularly in the realm of essentially two-party political environments, do ape such a procedure, albeit superficially, since there can be no intention of producing a binding 'verdict', and, without the bench's heavy controlling hand, the interviewer (i.e. the reporter,) is not bound by Bentham's desiderata. Anyway, those interviewed by the press are not necessarily represented by third parties; and when they are – in the coverage of celebrity, say – these advisors tend to be observers rather than quoted participants.

The principle of hearing the other side also makes the lawyers – advocates and judges – different. They function in a forum which takes *audi alterem partem* as a necessity:

> In relation to any supposed matter of fact, evidence being delivered on one side of a cause, *counter-evidence* is any evidence delivered in relation to the same supposed matter of fact on *the other* side: if more parties than two with conflicting interests, on *any other* side[11] [emphasis in original].

Ideally journalism shares this as a journalistic protocol, but it is not an essential one. 'Counter evidence' (aka 'alternative facts'), for the press, can all too easily mean 'over-verification' – 'the ruin of many a good news-story', in the opinion of Gordon-Bennett, Jr. A note in the coverage, to say an opportunity to comment by a second party was declined, is often sufficient to enable publishing, and even that is not always needed.

In effect, the requirement to hear the other side produces another common law 'grand feature of excellence', also not necessarily reflected in journalistic practice – cross-examination; that is, whereby the advocate of one party interrogates the argument presented by the other (in criminal cases, the state), including the questioning of defendants and their witnesses in an 'impromptuary' manner. This process of cross-examination, boosters of the common law claim, 'is beyond any doubt the greatest legal engine ever invented for the discovery of truth'.[12] It is 'the surest test of truth and a better surety than the oath'[13] (especially now in our relatively godless age). And it is a procedure not by any means available to the press, even in its cross-checking, triangulating mode.

Finally, the press can, and certainly does, sit in judgement, but here the difference lies in the direct power of judges to impose sanctions; the press can only articulate judgement as opinion. And this means that the journalist – reporter/editor – does not match the judge's role in that verdicts of any kind rest ultimately not with them but with their publics. So journalists are not quite jurors either, since their understanding is not the end of a matter, but rather merely (in objective theory, at least) facilitates an account being put into the public sphere before a jury (as it were) of their readers, listeners and viewers. The journalists' conclusions, should they reach any, lack the impact of a legal verdict. But, if there is demonstrably damaging impact upon publication on the parties being reported, then the journalist becomes a defendant in any legal action seeking redress for that damage.

Despite these mismatches, in journalism's search for professional respectability an analogy with the law proved most seductive. It did not turn on the closest of legal roles – that of the court reporter whose main tool, shorthand, was shared with the press reporter.[14] Rather, as Gordon Bennett's father, James Sn, interviewing the bordello-keeper in 1835, illustrates, the claim suggests a far greater correspondence. In crossing the police-line, Gordon Bennett Sn asserted he was doing no more than the 'courts and juries and justices' in looking after public morals (see p. 54). He was, of course, actually in the process of selling sensationalism, not seeking justice, but be that as it may.

Journalism interacts with the law in a variety of ways, aside from the one's procedures influencing (or not) the protocols of the other. The law legitimates it. Article 19 of the UN's Universal Declaration of Human Rights, 1948:

> Everyone has the right to freedom of opinion and expression; this right includes freedom to hold opinions without interference and to seek, receive and impart information and ideas through any media and regardless of frontiers.

It is profoundly to misunderstand the right, however, to insist, as is these days commonly done by semi-literate spewers of digital hatred and bigotry (and, to all effects and purposes, the capitalist net-maestros who give them platform), that the right is in some way absolute, when it is quite clear that it is not. And moreover, its exercise involves a fundamental problem.

All rights entail a responsibility to the rest of society, but we commit no crime or occasion no civil hurt when we assert our rights to life, liberty, personal security, freedom from slavery or torture, due process, work, and education, or to justice or to a living wage or to be left in peace, etc. We can, though, cause harm, (and even commit a crime,) when we speak – certainly on occasion to individuals and less directly perhaps to society in general. Free expression as a legal right can, therefore, be at odds with the general legal requirement that no harm be done, or no crime be committed: 'the Harm Principle'. In play, then, is an antinomy – a contradiction – of both principles (which is a matter of moral philosophy to which we shall return, see p. 140) and black-letter law. The antinomy pits doing no harm, the essential requirement of an ordered society, against a right without which no other rights can be guaranteed. As has been often noted, life and liberty and all the rest are easily abridged and abused if none are allowed to speak or to hear of such maltreatments. And herein lies the heart of both the press's irrefutable case (in a democracy) to be free, and the dangers to society of letting it be so. The result is that, as far as the law is concerned:

> Free speech does not mean free speech: it means speech hedged in by all the laws against defamation, blasphemy, sedition and so forth. It means freedom governed by law.'[15]

Within the law, free speech – including that of journalists – has to be exercised with a duty not to commit or transgress this set of torts and crimes. These might say little or nothing specific about the press but, to add another layer of complexity onto the practice of journalism, the black-letter clarity of the right is seriously blurred by their uncertain and dynamic definitions. Traditionally, the citizenry (including, of course, journalists) need pay heed to obscenity, defamation, etc., but none of these were (or are) at all stable. Penalties for infringement have, over the centuries, proved far easier to establish than have definitions of the offences in question.

Obscene material, for instance, was that which exhibited 'a tendency to deprave and corrupt'.[16] The 'tendency' was enough, and has remained so since the bench first glossed the offence in this way in 1868. The demonstration of negative outcomes in the world was not necessary, and the 'tendency' to produce such outcomes alone was and is, officially, the sufficient condition of obscenity. Current official guidance, however, is that:

> real caution must be exercised when assessing the tendency to deprave or corrupt ... That is particularly so because whilst they may well be construed to be 'repulsive', 'filthy', 'loathsome' or 'lewd', and so fall under ordinary language to be classified as obscene, that will not suffice for obscenity under the [Obscene Publications (1959)] Act.[17]

And throughout all these long years, as far as the law was concerned, the best it could offer by way of working definition was that, in effect, you (the jury) will know what matter might induce such depravity and corruption if you should glimpse it.

As for sedition, intention would suffice again, irrespective of outcome. In the UK, 'Seditious Intention' was:

to bring into hatred or contempt, or to excite disaffection against the person of Her Majesty ... the government and constitution ... or otherwise than by lawful means, the alteration of any matter in Church or State by law established ... or to raise discontent or disaffection among her majesty's subjects, or promote feelings of ill-will or hostility between different class of subjects.[18]

But no discontented, disaffected citizen need be produced for the offence to be proved. Nothing, perhaps, better illustrates Jefferson's observation that all governments, even those supposedly of liberal representative democracies, 'have propensities to command at will the liberty ... of their constituents' (see p. 46). Even in the republic he helped found, despite the constitutional protection of free speech, sedition, especially in time of 'clear and present danger' (such as war, or periodic 'Red Scare' panics), could just as easily be used to send an oppositional speaker to prison as in any other jurisdiction.[19]

With blasphemy, there were no issues of danger, depravity, civil disorder or the like: 'speaking ill of sacred matters' was enough on its face. Jefferson had already pointed out, in the 18th century, that: 'It does me no injury for my neighbor to say there are twenty gods, or no gods. It neither picks my pocket nor breaks my leg'.[20] Nevertheless, blasphemous utterance was unprotected by law, although, in the west, which deities were protected (apart from the Christian God) could be contentious.

Defamation is as inexactly defined as obscenity, sedition, and blasphemy. In the 19th century, defaming matter was that which, again, 'tended' to bring persons into 'hatred, ridicule or contempt'.[21] In the 20th century, this was glossed as that which 'lowered a person [] in the estimation of right-thinking members of society'.[22] Nevertheless, despite the vagueness of 'the estimation of right-thinking members of society', defamation is far more focused than are these other unprotected areas. It is an utterance's attacking specific named legal personages that is the issue here, and not any ill-defined, unnamed, and supposedly damaged potential receivers. The distinction between slander – defamatory utterances – and libel – defamation in writing – is that slander (alone of these offences) required actual proof of harm. It needs identifiable complainants demonstrating identifiable damage. For journalists, libel, not slander (obviously), is the central legal concern. And the law takes the view that all media, including the stage and other spoken forms (e.g. broadcasting) follow the press. All such media utterances, should they be challenged at law, are classed as libellous, not slanderous. With libel, the damage was assumed upon publication but, unlike with obscenity, etc., it is the business of the court to assess its actual extent and consequences for the people and entities named – though in some circumstances internal harms can be attested to.

Where the writ of the common law runs, most of the above, defamation apart, is now dead-letter law – laws lying in abeyance – or is moving that way. Such desuetude – outdatedness – suggests that the lapse of time without any actions renders the offences unenforceable – but the laws remain. And note how desuetude works: buried within sedition was 'exciting disaffection against the person of Her

Majesty'[23] and those around the throne etc., i.e. the ancient and medieval offence of lèse-majesté. The last trial for that in Britain had been in 1715 but in 1737 it was used as a basis for censoring stage plays.[24]

Rhetorically referencing lèse-majesté, the Prime Minster Robert Walpole (who, by the way, in essence used money from taxing newspapers in order secretly to bribe supportive, toadying editors) brought in a licensing system for spoken theatrical performances to prevent figures of authority, e.g. His Highness George II (but also himself, etc.), from being lampooned on stage. This naked censorship required prior textual approval for any presentation and was operated through the office of the Lord Chamberlain, the court official historically responsible for, among other things, royal entertainments. The act also required that venues for public theatrical performances be licensed. Arguing fruitlessly against the legislation as the thin end of the wedge, the Earl of Chesterfield said:

> [I]t will prove a most arbitrary Restraint on the Liberty of the stage; and, I fear, it tends towards a Restraint on the Liberty of the Press, which will be a long Stride towards the destruction of Liberty itself.[25]

The censorship apparatus was not removed until 1968, and the specific offense lingered until 2010 – 295 years after the last case.[26] With blasphemy, there had been only two cases since 1922,[27] but the offence was nonetheless not removed until 2008.[28] The last sedition case in the UK was heard in 1947, but the law was abolished only in 2015. Its purpose, though, is still being met with, for example, elements of public order legislation. Formal removal seems to be a rather haphazard business.

What usually fosters dead-letter law are amorphous changes in social attitudes. Alexander Hamilton had argued that freedoms (such as that of the press) 'altogether depend on public opinion, and on the general spirit of the people and of the Government'.[29] He thought, wrongly (?), that the First Amendment to the US Constitution would be 'impracticable' as a protection for the press without this 'spirit' (call it what you will) being manifested, but there is truth in his view that public opinion plays a role in the defence of free speech. Western publics have exhibited levels of tolerance for pornographic materials which cast doubt on the efficacy of obscenity legislation, for example.[30] And, clearly, the largely (at best) agnostic populations of the Global North have come to support Jefferson's view of the ineffectualness of blasphemy laws as well. The democratic instincts of the public can also be detected in the deep suspicion in which it holds any expansive definition of sedition which criminalises every utterance in opposition to the state. It is public opinion far more than the law that finds this offensive to the right of free expression and the operation of a healthy democracy. But this does not mean that, everywhere, desuetude is any bar to smart lawyers who continue to reach for the old offences. In the early 1990s, for example, some of them brought a case that Salman Rushdie's *The Satanic Verses* was seditious, when their initial attempts to brand it blasphemous failed.[31]

The 'spirit' defending free speech to which Alexander Hamilton referred is, however, no absolute protection. In a number of European democracies, for example, it is still sedition to offer contempt to visiting foreign heads of state. And everywhere new legislation – public order acts, which can include the criminalisation of 'hate' or 'racist' speech – include prohibitions against incitement. The entire question of the bounds of protected expression has been constantly reformulated. And even within the Anglosphere there are quite profound differences of practice. The protections of the First Amendment, for example, despite Hamilton's low opinion of it, carry a force unparalleled in UK courts. It has worked, distinct from the UK and many other jurisdictions, to prevent legislation against 'hate' or 'racist' speech. It has also strengthened journalism's hand in ways elsewhere unknown. For instance, in America it is not enough for a journalist to be caught libelling officials; US courts will require proof of malicious intent.[32]

In the laws of a free society, it might be thought that failures to exercise proper care must always require victims, probative causation and measurable damage in order to justify incurring sanctions. But, as we have indicated, this has not been quite the case with these offences. Dynamic uncertainties in these areas chill the fundamental right to free expression.

Already in 1769, the great English jurisprudent, William Blackstone, had formulated a rule to resolve the antinomy between free expression and the Harm Principle:

> The liberty of the press is indeed essential to the nature of a free state; but this consists in laying no *previous* restraints on publications, and not in freedom from censure for criminal matter when published.[33]

Blackstone insisted that there be no restraints on laying 'sentiments … before the public', but that if these proved to be at law 'improper, mischievous, or illegal'[34] then consequences would ensue. The 'no prior restraint' rule, in effect, brings only one certainty with it – 'Publish and be damned', as the Duke of Wellington put it to the publisher of an ex-mistress, who, in 1824, was asking for hush money in return for removing his love letters from her text. Publication – an act enabling the actual or possible sighting of offending materials by third parties – appears to be the only readily determinable issue under any of these heads. Otherwise, we are back with the dynamics of 'improper, mischievous, or illegal' expression, i.e. the fuzziness of the definitions, the usual anonymity (if not hypotheticality) of the supposedly damaged and, crucially, the authorities' legal license to act preventatively (e.g. on 'intentions'), all of which have a chilling effect on the right of free speech. In reality, cumulatively, restraints can approach levels of control unacceptable in a democratic society.

In Britain, Blackstone's rule was blatantly abandoned in his own time, as we have seen, by misusing the offence of lèse-majesté to exercise prior restraint over the medium of theatre. But it is not just a matter of taking a preventative view of possible damage. By the 21st century the rule had also become 'badly eroded in other areas of media law'.[35] Blackstone had said a speaker 'must take the consequences of his [sic] own temerity'[36] – even, it turns out, when there are no consequences. Overall, with issues of free expression, despite the (not as firm as it might be) rule against prior restraint, prevention and punishment for speech on its face has been a norm within the law, encouraged, as much as anything, by popular (but actually not proven) assumptions about the power of media effects. Perhaps this was inevitable given that the social sciences, after all, have been little help in determining such impacts, the fundamentally unsafe finding of media sociology being too unsafe to be of much use in court.

Finding 'victims', in the mass of the population receiving media messages, of the impact of a specific communication, is nigh on impossible, as the inconclusive outcomes of over a century of media sociology research demonstrate. For one thing, causation is always a thorny business. How, among the myriad messages and influences swarming in the social sphere, can a single message, or even a theme, or meme, be established as causing a given effect? Demonstrating such causation, certainly in direct enough a manner to raise legal concerns, is vexed. Apart from isolating impact, can coincidence ever be discounted? Can other contaminating factors not as much or more condition outcomes? Far simpler just to assume effect, and proceed without any need for victims, or probative causation.

So it is that actions for obscenity never required actual persons to present themselves, claiming, even without further evidence, that they had been depraved and corrupted by their encounter with the offending material. As tends to be the case with moral panics around all other kinds of media effects – including, for example, the idea of people being tricked by fake news into changing their votes (see p. 180) – the assumption is always that the 'harm' is being done to unspecified others, and even the idea of seeking evidence to support this 'common sense' assumption is seldom raised. The apogee of this necessarily curious approach was reached a century or so after the 'tendency to deprave' test was introduced. In 1962, two booksellers were charged with selling obscene materials to officers of the London Metropolitan Obscene Publications Squad:

> The officers conceded that pornography had ceased to arouse any feelings in them whatsoever. The prosecution's argument that the pictures were 'inherently obscene' and tended by their very nature to corrupt all viewers was rejected.[37]

The same can be true of incitement to riot, that part of sedition now covered by public order legislation. However, an invitation to break the peace (especially, it would seem, when published on the web) is sufficient to establish guilt, even if the 'incitement' goes unnoticed or ignored. Judges remain as ready as ever to convict without any persons influenced by the criminal communication actually presenting themselves.[38]

During the summer disturbances of 2011 in England, a Facebook page, 'RIOT IN THE TOON', appealed to those clicking onto the page to be in the Dundee city centre on the evening of 17 August: 'Only join if yir actually gonna come – if anyone has guns bring them down to this – kill some daftys'. According to Alison Munroe, Dundee's Sheriff, who heard the case, the 221 people who visited the site, by merely clicking, actually 'said they would attend the riot event in Dundee'.

But they did not, and the four responsible for the post did nothing either. No crowd gathered and, in fact, there were no riots anywhere in Scotland. Nevertheless, the page's administrators, including two Scottish teenagers – one a 16-year-old, the other 19 –were each sentenced to three years in prison. Even given that the younger one had some form – he had been involved in a disturbance the previous summer, and had served a sentence in a youth offenders institution – this judgement is, arguably … is 'extreme' even the word? What were the consequences of their 'temerity'? How was the Harm Principle demonstrated? Sheriff Munro held that the post constituted: 'one of the worst breaches of the peace that I have ever had to deal with'. But, unless one is clearly in the grip of serious technicist delusions, the only breach was the 221 clicks. And none of those clicking were reported in the press as even giving evidence.[39]

This case also speaks to the question of probative causation and this has, it can be noted, nothing to do with technology. There were riots in towns and cities across England, and their underlying causes (not to be confused with the singular incident which sparked them) were complex, numerous, and disputed, as is more or less always the case with large-scale civil unrest.

The clearer focus of defamation does require that there always be a 'victim', a plaintiff, and assuming a causal relationship between act and harm is, self-evidently, more reasonable. But here the problems lie in the matter of the nature of damage. Only slander, which is not a major problem for the press, requires probative proof of actual damage and with libel there can also be provable economic damage, as when a published untruth causes loss of current or future earnings or of earning capacity. Otherwise, the sensitivity of western societies to the possibilities of internal hurts, on the rise since the 18th century, becomes actionable as 'pain and suffering'. Such damage can exhibit external, verifiable symptoms – everything from lack of energy to sexual dysfunction to sleep disturbances, etc. – but it can also be only internally attested to: anguish, anxiety, and emotional distress. Personal humiliation – 'damage to reputation' – is enough although 'it is an abstract concept that has no equivalent in money or money's worth [with the result that] those who throw sticks and stones that break bones can be better off in law than those who project hurtful words that leave no permanent mark'.[40]

What is significant is that, because of the law's inattention, none of this much applies to the net, if it does so at all. Paradoxically, at the same time, its supposed hypodermic needle-like effects are the cause of the current media panic – a panic made worse because the danger is thought to be uncontrollable.

Notes

1. Plucknett, Theodore (1956). *Concise History of the Common Law*. Boston, MA: Little, Brown & Co, p. 436.
2. Bentham, Jeremy (1843). 'An introductory view of the rationale of evidence: For the use of non-lawyers as well as lawyers' in *The Works of Jeremy Bentham, Vol 6* (John Bowring, ed.). Edinburgh: William Tait. https://oll.libertyfund.org/titles/bentham-the-works-of-jeremy-bentham-vol-6#lf0872-06_head_005 [accessed 13 December 2019].
3. Bentham, Jeremy (1843). 'An introductory view of the rationale of evidence: For the use of non-lawyers as well as lawyers' in *The Works of Jeremy Bentham, Vol 6* (John Bowring, ed.). Edinburgh: William Tait. https://oll.libertyfund.org/titles/bentham-the-works-of-jeremy-bentham-vol-6#lf0872-06_head_005 [accessed 13 December 2019].
4. Ibid.
5. Twining, William (2019). 'Bentham's theory of evidence: Setting a context', *Journal of Bentham Studies*, 18:1, pp. 20–37.
6. Thayer, J. (1898). *A Preliminary Treatise on Evidence at the Common Law*. Boston, MA: Little, Brown & Co, Boston, p. 530.
7. Twinning, Willian (2019). 'Bentham's theory of evidence: Setting a context', *Journal of Bentham Studies*, 18:1, p. 28.
8. Ibid.
9. Plucknett, Theodore (1956). *Concise History of the Common Law*. Boston, pp.216–227.
10. Bentham, Jeremy (1843). 'An introductory view of the rationale of evidence: For the use of non-lawyers as well as lawyers' in *The Works of Jeremy Bentham, Vol 6* (John Bowring, ed.). Edinburgh: William Tait. https://oll.libertyfund.org/titles/bentham-the-works-of-jeremy-bentham-vol-6#lf0872-06_head_005 [accessed 13 December 2019].
11. Bentham, Jeremy (1843) 'An introductory view of the rationale of evidence: For the use of non-lawyers as well as lawyers' in *The Works of Jeremy Bentham, Vol 6* (John Bowring, ed.). Edinburgh: William Tait. https://oll.libertyfund.org/titles/bentham-the-works-of-jeremy-bentham-vol-6#lf0872-06_head_005 [accessed 13 December 2019]. The phrase (as 'alt. facts') was then coined in 2017 by Kellyanne Conway, Trump's legal counsel, for which she was widely ridiculed by the (as it were) 'failing … @nytimes … etc.' press.
12. Wigmore, John (1974). *Evidence in Trials at Common Law* (James H. Chabourn, ed.). Boston, MA: Little, Brown & Co., § 1367.
13. qt in Wellman, Francis (1904). *The Art of Cross-Examination*. London: The Macmillan Co., p. 6.
14. Shorthand (or 'short-writing') systems allowing for the accurate transcription of speech in real time had been known from antiquity and Anglophone systems were well established by the 18th century. Pitman's was introduced in 1837, one of the plethora of developments and inventions to secure widespread diffusion in response to the emerging modern capitalist system.
15. *James v Australia* [1936] AC578, [1936] 2 All ER 1449 (cited in Robertson, Geoffrey & Andrew Nichol (2006). *Media Law*. Harmondsworth, Middx: Penguin, p. 2).
16. *R v Hicklin* (1868). LQ 3 QB 360.
17. *Legal Guidance, Sexual offences*. Revised: January 2019. www.cps.gov.uk/legal-guidance/obscene-publications#b02 [accessed 28 December 2019].
18. Stephens, James (1950 [1887]). *Digest of the Criminal Law* (cited in Robertson, Geoffrey & Andrew Nichol (2006). *Media Law*. Harmondsworth, Middx: Penguin, p. 672).
19. *Schenck v United States* (1919). 249 U.S. 47.
20. Jefferson, Thomas (1787[1782]). *Notes on the State of Virginia*. London: John Stockdale.

21 *Parmiter v. Coupland*, (1840). 6 M&W 105.
22 *Sim v. Strech*, (1936). All ER 1237 (HL).
23 e.g. *Burns v. Rawnsley* [1949] HCA 45; 79 CLR 101; [1949] ALR 817.
24 *Licensing Act* (1737). 10 Geo.II, c. 28.
25 Chesterfield, Earl of (Philip Stanhope) (1737). 'Journal of the proceedings and debates in the last session of Parliament', *London Magazine*, 14 August.
26 *Criminal Justice and Licensing (Scotland) Act* (2010).
27 *R. v. Lemon* (1979). AC 617, 664; see also: *Whitehouse v. Lemon* (1979). 2 WLR 281; *Gay News Ltd and Lemon v. United Kingdom* (1982). 5 EHRR 123.
28 *Criminal Justice and Immigration Act* (2008) 5:79.
29 Hamilton, Alexander (1788). *The Federalist*, 84, 28 May. https://founders.archives.gov/documents/Hamilton/01-04-02-0247 [accessed 14 May 2007].
30 This is without prejudice to the criminality involved in its production (e.g. the abuse of minors and others) and the illegal reception of same.
31 The case was dismissed (Robertson, Geoffrey & Andrew Nichol (2008). *Media Law*. Harmondsworth, Middx: Penguin, p. 673).
32 *New York Times Co. v. Sullivan* (1964). 376 U.S. 254.
33 Blackstone, William (1979 [1769]). *Commentaries on the Laws of England: A Facsimile of the First Edition of 1765–1769, Vol. 4*. Chicago, IL: University of Chicago Press, p. 151.
34 Ibid.
35 Robertson, Geoffrey & Andrew Nichol (2008). *Media Law*. Harmondsworth, Middx: Penguin, p. 25.
36 Ibid.
37 *R v Clayton & Halsey* (1962). 1 Q.B. 163.
38 This is of a different order from the preventative actions taken by the authorities to foil acts of terrorism being prepared in secret.
39 *BBC News: Tayside and Central Scotland* (2011). 'Dundee teenagers locked up for Facebook riot threats', 12 December. www.bbc.co.uk/news/uk-scotland-tayside-central-16144640 [accessed 31 December 2019]; Carrell, Severin (2011). 'Pair jailed for trying to start a riot in Dundee via Facebook', *The Guardian*, 13 December, p. 16; Davies, Caroline (2012). 'Rioters' appeal hearings to start next week', *The Guardian*, 22 September, p. 17.
   Robertson, Geoffrey & Andrew Nichol (2006). *Media Law*. Harmondsworth, Middx: Penguin, pp. 96, 180, 178).
40 *R v Hicklin* (1868). LQ 3 QB 360.

10
JUDGEMENT: THE FINE PRINT

> 'No provider ... shall be treated as the publisher'
> *Section 230, Communications Decency Act (1996)*
> *47 U.S.C. § 230*

Journalists might proceed in their day-to-day activities in ways that only superficially resemble the practices of lawyers, but the press for which they work consists of legal entities with all the rights and duties that that status entails. Those rights and duties have suffered something of a sea-change with the rise of the internet. The legal basis for a journalist's work is root and branch challenged by the comparative lawlessness of the web – a lack of constraint which has clearly given fake news its head. This chapter, then, will address how, legally, the internet has come to stand in such contrast to all previous media. The change turns in essence on the upturning of traditional common law thinking contained in the fine print of a piece of American legislation.

In practice, as Blackstone explained, 'the liberty of the press properly understood is by no means infringed or violated'[1] by the imposition of checks and bounds. Without prejudice as to the nature of media harms – what they might be and whether they can be determined as arising from media activity – press 'freedom' has actually always been effectively constrained – and not just by specific actionable limitations. For one thing, de facto 'Freedom of the Press' was for centuries 'guaranteed only to those who own one'.[2]

The argument that the general law was a sufficient restraint on free expression did not prevent presses from being licensed and what they produced being taxed. In the 16th century, the philosopher John Locke was in no doubt about the inappropriateness of these further impositions:

> Everyone being answerable for the books he [*sic*] publishes, prints or sells containing anything seditious or against the law makes this[3] or any other act for the restraint of printing very needless.[4]

It didn't wash and the struggle to remove what came to be termed, in the eventually successful campaign against them, 'the taxes on knowledge', went on for a century and a half; and, furthermore, it was not until the incorporation of the European Convention on Human Rights (the ECHR) into British law via the passage of a Human Rights Act, more than 400 years after Locke, that the UK press acquired statutory protection.[5] The Americans did better. The First Amendment to the Constitution – 'Congress shall make no law … abridging the freedom of speech, or of the press' – was enacted in 1791.

It can be no surprise, then, that with the other legacy media – the stage, film, and broadcasting – even owning the outlet did not allow you to escape controls. Licensing and regulation was far more firmly imposed, even in the democracies where supposedly free speech was protected. As we have seen, it took the British theatre 237 years to get rid of prior censorship (see p. 139). When it came to film, never mind the First Amendment, the initial judgement in American law was that the movies 'were a business pure and simple … not to be regarded … as part of the press of the country or as organs of opinion'.[6] (After all, cinema had played no role in the Revolution. Not once in his life did Thomas Jefferson say a word about movies being important to democracy.) Everywhere films were licensed for exhibition and soon classified as to their suitability for different audiences.

Broadcasting was even more tightly controlled. Thus, the tenth article of the European Charter on Human Rights echoes the UN Charter:

> Everyone has the right to freedom of expression. This right shall include freedom to hold opinions and to receive and impart information and ideas without interference by public authority and regardless of frontiers.

But it adds a crucial caveat: 'This Article **shall not prevent States from requiring the licensing** of broadcasting, television or cinema enterprises' [emphasis added]. And this merely reflected what had become the de facto practice, the rhetoric of free expression notwithstanding. After all, the technology of radio had its roots deep in the military-industrial complex of the late 19th century (see p. 72). Such a background encouraged an official mindset which did not view radio communication as a platform for free expression, even after it emerged as a mass medium after the First World War. Moreover, unlike press buildings, theatres, and cinemas, it had rapidly become clear that nobody was free even to build, equip, and switch on a radio station transmitter, as its operation required the use of a common natural resource: bandwidth. Without regulation, signals would talk over each other producing a cacophony which only the state could legitimately untangle by regulation, allocating specific wavelengths.

Of course, there was a distinction between this necessary allocative function and direct control of signal content – censorship – but this was nowhere acknowledged. On the contrary, as the ECHR Article 10 makes clear, all media but the press can be regulated in these ways.

The tradition of press freedom in the democracies inhibits the state's interfering proclivities, but only goes so far. And the law is easily surprised by technological developments. States are encouraged in this by the received, uninterrogated assumption that each new mode and platform produces irresistibly powerful media, from which susceptible publics need to be protected.

In the 19th century, the French conception of intellectual property rights could not initially come to terms with the then new technology of photography – a totally mechanised mode of image creation; the law – *le droit*, according to the legal theoretician Bernard Edelman, was *saisi* – seized/captured – *par le photographe*.[7] Across the channel, though, this development had not confused the common law. Initially copyright simply belonged to the owner of the photographic plate, whoever pressed the shutter, etc., however, the French tradition of protecting artistic works through ideas of intellectual property rejected such materialism. But this pointed to the solution: the French law simply declared that the person who pressed the shutter was, after all, an artist. The potential technological disruption to legal practice was tamed (and the new and booming business of photography was made safe for capitalist exploitation).

And if the law was confused by photography it has, this century, shown itself to be utterly confounded by the latest digital technologies. Given the hegemonic power of technological determinism as an explanation of how the world works, it is scarcely surprising that, today, the apparent ineffectualness of the law to control the internet and/or the companies that exploit its revenue-generating potential, is unquestioningly attributed to its all-pervasive (and therefore uncontainable) technological base. The anti-social activities sustained by the World Wide Web are seen as unavoidable, a price to be paid for all the manifest advantages it brings. The law, though, has seemed rather impotent thus far; but, just as photographers were legally re-classified as artists to bring them into line, so, simply, the web can, to some extent, be controlled by re-classifying (at least some) service providers as publishers.

The act of publishing is foundational to the process of assigning legal responsibilities for the content of expression; but most of the law and regulation we have just outlined has not been applied to the control of the net, basically because online providers, unlike the purveyors of media information for the past half-millennium, are held not to be publishers. Instead, the online platforms are, de facto, considered in law to be a species of common carrier. No more than a postal delivery person can they be held responsible for what they convey. But to believe the technology is responsible for this state of affairs is, arguably, to fall prey to the very worst technicist delusion.

The specific legal character of the concept of the common carrier is rooted in centuries-old notions of official messages, such as royal dispatches, as being afforded special protections. And in the protocols governing the inviolate, sealed, medieval royal dispatch is the idea of a privacy of communications that is, obviously, very different from the public nature of, say, a social media post. In the former case, the carrier cannot know of the contents and therefore cannot be held responsible for them. The democratisation of this system into postal services accessible by all cemented this idea. Envelopes were not to be opened without prima facie legal cause, and, as they came on stream, those operating terrestrial telegram and telephone services, and then satellite distribution facilities, were also so regarded by law and by society. But were contents open to a mass of receivers, as with a newspaper, for example, rather than to single individuals, then identifiable originators could be held to account as publishers. There was, in the early days of the World Wide Web's meteoric rise, some uncertainty as to where different web-based and/or web-access-providing businesses belonged, in terms of such legal distinctions.

In October 1994, Prodigy (a now defunct internet service provider) allowed an anonymous person to post a claim on its *Money Talk* website that a Long Island, NY, brokerage house was guilty of a criminal fraud in connection with an IPO (Initial Public share Offering) his company was handling. The claim was libelous, but Prodigy argued before the New York State Supreme Court that they were not the publishers and could not therefore be held liable for the post.[8]

Already in 1991, a lower New York court had held CompuServe, the first internet service provider, to be a distributer – i.e. a common carrier – rather than a publisher of posted disputatious matters concerning two firms involved in a row about trade competition.[9] But, the court held, had CompuServe operated any form of editorial control, it would have known – as, say, any newspaper would know – of the content and would then have been liable in the traditional way. As it did not exercise any oversight, it could not be held liable. In effect, this was to judge that no longer did the maxim *ignorantia juris non excusat* quite hold (see *Leviticus* 5:17). Now, if you were an internet service provider, ignorance of what you were enabling allowed you effectively to get away with ignorance of the law itself as an excuse, a defence even concerning the law of libel. The common-sense distinction, that, say, a letter-carrier had normally sight only of envelopes, whereas these materials were all openly visible on screen, did not apparently inform this judgement. It created a legal absurdity, a triumph of a species of 'no-nothingism', deeply infected by technicist purblindness. In effect, it legitimated a clear abuse of the right of free speech. (This is not to say that the web's capacity for anonymous communication and socialising is without value, for example to members of marginalised and/or stigmatised communities of various kinds. The point here is that the weighing of such issues one against the other, and perhaps of considering the construction of a more nuanced legal framework, has, at least until recently, gone largely unconsidered.)

The *Prodigy* case turned on whether or not it could be presumed to have known the libelous nature of the anonymous post's content. The court found that as Prodigy did publicise content guidelines which were re-enforced by editorial oversight and screening software which blocked obscene language, it was liable for the libel: 'Prodigy's conscious choice, to gain the benefits of editorial control, has opened it up to a greater liability than CompuServe and other computer networks that make no such choice.'[10] Prodigy, after all, was a publisher.[11]

Washington was in the throes of revising six decades worth of Federal telecommunication legislation, as well as addressing such new factors as those raised by *Prodigy*, when a Democratic congressman with an impeccable progressive record sat down to lunch with a Republican colleague who had served in the Reagan White House. Both were (unsurprisingly) lawyers. The Democrat, Ron Wyden, then represented Portland, Oregon (aka 'Silicon Forest'), one of America's most liberal districts, while the Republican, Chris Cox, represented the very much not-liberal district of Orange County, California – though it too was something of a tech hub. They were equally concerned at the chilling effect, as they saw it, of the decision in *Prodigy* on the rapidly expanding Internet Service Provider (ISP) industry – as were lobbyists for that industry itself.

Technicist enthusiasms were then at a peak and the technology was, more or less, universally perceived as an unmitigated good. This was, after all, the time of Barlow's *Declaration of the Independence of Cyberspace* (see p. 86). Such positions implied simply taking speech-without-consequence-no-matter-what as a given, and damage was merely a necessary consequence of freedom of expression. Such rhetoric has persisted and, indeed, expanded. The 'cyberfreedom' delusion (a 90s name for a 90s myth) now embraces a claim that access to the net – already available to an estimated 46% of the world's population (depending to some extent on how you figure it) – ought to be a human right.[12] Given that the quarter of humanity who lack sanitation might have a need for more pressing rights, this determination seems, on its face, to be rather insultingly irrelevant. In the lands with ubiquitous bathrooms, as the century turned, the right was frequently becoming confused with the privilege of anonymous speech, without much thought for the consequences. The technicists were accepting a situation where, for example, a libellous, anonymous post which leads and directs a lynch-mob, virtual or otherwise, to somebody's home, is *effectively* to be considered nobody's responsibility under the law. Exactly this occurred in 2013 in the aftermath of the Boston Marathon bombing when Reddit, a social news aggregator, established a 'Find Boston Bombers' thread which misidentified a number of innocents, including one 17-year-old boy in particular who then suffered extensive online abuse. Reddit 'apologised'.[13]

'Cyber'-enthusiasm also insisted that the nature of the internet itself, rather than its content, necessitated its exceptional legal status. The user-base was too enormous for anybody to be able to control anything to do with subject matter, ever. The requirement that platform providers, as publishers, should be responsible for any unsigned, untriangulated post which, under existing law, on its face, might be illegal, was deemed necessarily insurmountable. Proposals involving any control whatsoever were readily dismissed as the babbling of hardcore reactionaries, authoritarians, or, at best, those just too old and out of touch to understand this brave new world. Anyway, the clincher was the self-evidently crucial importance of the internet as a key driver of the world's economy. Obviously then, it could not and should not be constrained. The decision in *Prodigy* was, simply, not viable.

And so, for the 1996 *Telecommunications Act,* Representatives Wyden and Cox framed a bipartisan clause in *Title V* (itself commonly known as the *Communications Decency Act (CDA)*). Efforts towards the criminalisation of online pornography being the most eye-catching aspect of this legislation, *Section 230* – the 26-word outcome of their collaboration – was not much noticed:

> No provider or user of an interactive computer service shall be treated as the publisher or speaker of any information provided by another information content provider.[14]

In 1997, the other part of the CDA, attempting to outlaw internet porn, was overturned by the Supreme Court as being offensive to the First Amendment,[15] but *Section 230*, dubbed the 'First Amendment Clause', was left (and is still) in place. Case-law confusion was removed – the legislation meant that, de facto, *CompuServe* held, *Prodigy* was 'distinguished' (i.e. discarded) – and the unique legal status of (what we were all still enjoying calling) cyberspace, compared with all previous media technologies, was confirmed. Mark Zuckerberg was 12 years old at the time, but these 26 words wrote his birthright into law.

After centuries of weighing the Harm Principle against free media-expression, the balance was tipped. The defamation law was, to a large extent, neutered for the new technology of the net, in a way quite distinct from how previous innovations had been treated and constrained. The argument is made that whatever its negatives, the internet deserves this unprecedented freedom because of its unprecedented value to humanity, but this is self-serving. Locke had argued special legal constraints on the press were unnecessary because it was controlled by the general law and, despite the myriad ways that principle has been subverted and abridged over the centuries – especially in connection with new media – it has held well enough for the western press to have exercised its functions effectively. On more than one occasion it has done so magnificently.

In exactly the same way, there is no reason to suppose that, were the internet service providers to be considered publishers, they would be less able to operate profitable platforms still enabling free expression than are any other publishers. Even as we acknowledge the unprecedented scale of the requisite task of controlling them, we should also be cognisant of the availability of both the unprecedented technological tools the technology provides and the nearly unimaginable wealth that is available to deploy them. Unlike the postal carrier, the lords of the net already exercise the capacity to inspect, edit, censor, process, and ultimately sell our unfathomably complex data-profiles via the information they somehow purport merely to 'carry', making billions and billionaires in the process. Obviously they also have the capacity for taking on some of the responsibility for the other externalities of their business models. We do not wish to downplay the complexities of the legal and technical issues involved, but it is important, in getting a clear view of the landscape in which we now find ourselves, that we consider alternative perspectives to those popular constructions of the internet which essentially categorise the idea of any regulation of Web 2.0 as something unthinkable.

Liebling's notion of a free press being available only to millionaires does need re-evaluation in the light of this technology. Now one-to-many channels of communication are widely available and, in the name of democracy, must be welcomed. To be clear, it also offers uncounted social, cultural, economic, you-name-it benefits. But there is an argument to be pondered: the legacy-media millionaire's freedom was limited for a reason. It is proving clearly anarchic not at least to consider imposing some of the same limitations on the digi-media billionaire who profits from the (libelous? crime-inciting? ... maybe even hate-speech-speaking?) bigot and his blog. There is less than no reason not to at least give some thought to the idea that if we were to make an effort, it is perhaps not beyond us to drain *some* of this bathwater without throwing out the baby (in this case, the value and vibrancy of Web 2.0).

Doing this does require dismissing out of hand the argument that the internet's user-base is too enormous for anybody ever to be able to control anything to do with content. This is, arguably, technicist nonsense. Consider, for example, the reports of algorithmic surveys of, say, unfathomably large cancer-imaging datasets to better detect disease than can individual medical practitioners. Although the problems are of course very different, such uses of large-scale data analysis – at a level far beyond pulling out a bigot's printed rants – give one pause.

Voices claiming insurmountable technical problems have also long suggested that regulation, were it to be effective, will result in a dystopian, cyber-authoritarian internet. Such worries about censorship are, of course, merited, but this prompts two questions. The first is, why would this be necessarily so? We made newspapers subject to laws such as libel without turning them into state propaganda engines. And, as a further example, film censorship has not precluded the establishment of a vibrant film industry and culture. Secondly, confusingly, cognitive dissonance also allows those who worry that internet freedom is always under 'threat' to draw on frightening stories of the ways in which undemocratic states such as China have utilised it as a tool of state control, without noticing the contradiction. If China can constrain or censor net content (however effectively or ineffectively they do it) in line with the norms of Chinese cultural assumptions about personal freedom, why can't we do the same in the west, in line with ours? The computing power that enables the net to exist can be applied to containing the providers' activities as publishers, so they remain within the law. Content control (or its inhibition at least) is not impossible, and need not produce authoritarian over-reach (though obviously we would need to remain ever-mindful of the possibility, much as we do with regard to current restrictions on all other media).

We can imagine that our present circumstance might well come to be thought of as an electronic equivalent of the medieval city's open sewers. Indeed, one day scholars may wonder how we let such a situation continue for so long. The internet's social problems are, after all, in no way determined by technology. It is the law's ineptitude in holding the key players to account – perhaps unthinkingly supported by a public in the grip of a technicist delusion, that the path of the unregulated internet leads to digital utopia – that is primarily responsible. It is not digital affordances themselves that have given otherwise unprotected or even merely disapproved-of speech its license – among it, fake news. The right to publish fake news, an act which has never been on its face illegal, is not created by the technology, but it is much encouraged and flourishes by it. The sewers that run through this purported digital Eden are beginning to clog with effluent (fake news, say) and the sludge and solid waste of what is truly evil speech. Society is, however, perhaps slowly starting to exhibit signs of the will to correct at least some aspects of this. The effluents in the sewer are now being noticed more and more. Government after government – not all necessarily undemocratic – are moving against the (usually American) giants of the web.

So far, legislative actions in the democracies have tended to be reactive and specific. For example: within three weeks of the March 2019 attack on a New Zealand mosque which left 51 dead at the hands of a white supremacist, the Australian Federal Parliament made it an offence, punishable by fine and/or prison, for a internet provider to 'share … *Abhorrent Violent Material on the Net*'.[16] In October 2019, in a precedent-setting judgement, the European Court of Justice mandated that EU national jurisdictions could legally order companies such as Facebook to block access to 'information [deemed unlawful] worldwide within the framework of the relevant international law'.[17] Of course, while such moves demonstrate an escape from technicist enchantments, they still cleave to older, highly questionable 'hypodermic needle' assumptions about media power. Nevertheless, that level of misunderstanding is preferable. Whatever the impact of media messages, or lack thereof, in a civilised society we cannot lose sight of the need for there to be legally responsible parties for what is published. Technicism has been supporting the denial of this principle, and that is what must be rethought.

That we might be on the brink of such rethinking is signalled by the recent actions of some of the major players of Web 2.0. What appears to be most significant is that the knee-jerk freedom of speech rhetoric and obstinate uncooperativeness of the web-companies, faced with growing hostility, has been weakening. In March 2019, for instance, Mark Zuckerberg himself signed an op-ed in *The Washington Post*. He said:

> I believe we need a more active role for governments and regulators. By updating the rules for the Internet, we can preserve what's best about it — the freedom for people to express themselves and for entrepreneurs to build new things — while also protecting society from broader harms.[18]

Zuckerberg went on to remind us of a PR move his company had made some four months earlier:

> Lawmakers often tell me we have too much power over speech, and frankly I agree. I've come to believe that we shouldn't make so many important

decisions about speech on our own. So we're creating an *independent body* so people can appeal our decisions [emphasis added].

So, thank you, Mr Zuckerberg: *an independent body!* Are you also selling the Brooklyn Bridge?

Facebook still does not get it. As one website put it, the plan was nothing less than '[a] step toward a Facebook Supreme Court'.[19] This clear-sighted comment indicates the degree to which the corporate culture Zuckerberg has created finds it hard to understand that there is a Supreme Court already, and Facebook is already subject to it – and subject to the supreme courts of all the countries in which it does business. Still, at least we are now starting to hear acknowledgments from their owners that this business and others like it are causing problems in the world which might be mitigated by oversight. We will finally know Zuckerberg and his fellows are serious if and when they ever get round to calling for the repeal, or at least reform, of *Section 230*, however good it may have been to their bank accounts. *Section 230*, if only in its total lack of nuance or complexity, scarcely represents an honourable achievement for the law. At 168 characters, it ought to be seen as the tweet that broke the internet.

Notes

1. Blackstone, William (1979 [1769]). Commentaries on the Laws of England: A Facsimile of the First Edition of 1765–1769, vol 4. Chicago, IL: University of Chicago Press, p. 151.
2. Liebling, A. J.(1964). *The Press*. New York: Pantheon, pp. 30–31.
3. Locke was arguing against extending 'An Act for preventing the frequent Abuses in printing seditious treasonable and unlicensed Books and Pamphlets and for regulating of Printing and Printing Presses' which had been repeatedly renewed since its first enactment in 1662 (14 Car. II. c. 33).
4. King, Peter (1829). *The Life of John Locke*. London: Henry Colburn, p. 208.
5. *Human Rights Act* c. 42 (1998). It is ironic that the general hostility of the right-wing UK newspapers to Europe has included endless attacks on the HRA, seemingly oblivious of this.
6. *Mutual Film Corporation v. Ohio Industrial Commission*, 236 U.S. 230 (1915).
7. Edelman, Bernard (2001). *Le droit saisi par la photographie*. Paris: Flamarrion. (1979: *Ownership of the Image: Elements for a Marxist Theory of Law*, trans. Elizabeth Kingdom, London: Routledge & Kegan Paul, pp. 44–49).
8. *Stratton Oakmont, Inc. v. Prodigy Services, Inc.*, 23 Media L. Rep. 1794 (N.Y. Sup. Ct. 1995).
9. *Cubby, Inc. v. CompuServe Inc.*, 776 F. Supp. 135 (S.D.N.Y. 1991).
10. *Stratton Oakmont, Inc. v. Prodigy Services, Inc.*, 1995 WL 323710, 1995 N.Y. Misc. LEXIS 229, 23 Media L. Rep. 1794 (N.Y. Sup. Ct. May 26, 1995).
11. Nothing to do with the libel, seven years after the case, the Stratton Oakmont directors were imprisoned for fraud and the firm closed.
12. La Rue, Frank (2011).'Conclusions and recommendations', *Report of the Special Rapporteur on the promotion and protection of the right to freedom of opinion and expression*. Human Rights Council, Seventeenth session Agenda item 3, United Nations General Assembly, 16 May.
13. Levenson, Eric (2015). 'Reddit's find Boston bombers thread moderator is full of regrets', *Boston* [on-line site of *The Boston Globe*], April 11. www.boston.com/culture/movies/2015/04/11/reddits-find-boston-bombers-thread-moderator-is-full-of-regrets [accessed 31 January 2020].

14 *Telecommunications Act* (1996). Title 5 §230, Pub. LA. No. 104-104, 110 Stat.
15 *Reno v. American Civil Liberties Union*, 521 U.S. 844 (1997).
16 The Parliament of the Commonwealth of Australia: *Criminal Code Amendment (Sharing of Abhorrent Violent Material) Act*, 2019. No. 38, 2019.
17 Bowcott, Gwen (2019). 'Facebook ruling gives EU states power to take down content globally', *The Guardian*, 4 October, p. 12.
18 Zuckerberg, Mark (2019). 'Mark Zuckerberg: The Internet needs new rules. Let's start in these four areas'. *The Washington Post,* 29 March. www.washingtonpost.com/opinions/mark-zuckerberg-the-internet-needs-new-rules-lets-start-in-these-four-areas/2019/03/29/9e6f0504-521a-11e9-a3f7-78b7525a8d5f_story.html [accessed 31 January 2020].
19 Newton, Casey (2018). 'Facebook will create an independent oversight group to review content moderation appeals'. *The Verge*, November 15. www.theverge.com/2018/11/15/18097219/facebook-independent-oversight-supreme-court-content-moderation [accessed 31 January 2020].

11
TRUTH: THE PHILOSOPHICAL APPROACH

> 'Journalism by nature is reactive and practical'
> Bill Kovac (1932–) & Tom Rosenstiel (1956–)
> *Journalists*

The challenges of new media further strain journalism's interactions, symbolic and otherwise, with the honoured professions, as the protocols that have governed its own practice – its claim of objectivity – seem so readily ignored and/or sidelined by the affordances of the internet. Despite this, however, journalism still has its crucial role to play. And so, in terms of a search for firmer foundations, philosophy's 'honoured' pursuit of truth is of considerable relevance: what can it teach us about journalism?

Journalism and philosophy do not initially appear to have much in common, perhaps representing, or at least being seen as representing, respectively, the practical versus the abstract, the specific versus the general, the timely versus the timeless, etc. It would nonetheless seem reasonable to address the thought that if journalists are concerned with the limits of what can be confirmed, proved, known, there may be some value in considering how their approaches and understandings relate to the theories and practices of philosophy's longstanding investigation of the nature of knowledge itself, and the role of truth within that. That being said, even the most sober list of journalism desiderata – such as that found in the 2001 report of the Neiman Foundation for Journalism at Harvard, which we mentioned on page 2 – admits that:

> Journalism by nature is reactive and practical rather than philosophical and introspective. The serious literature by journalists thinking through such issues is not rich, and what little there is, most journalists have not read.[1]

The authors of the report, senior pressmen Bill Kovach and Tom Rosenstiel, acknowledge that there could be something of a problem here. As journalists go about their knowledge-creation work, Kovach and Rosenstiel believe that '[j]ournalism's first obligation is to tell the truth'.[2] Knowing what that is, however, is no straightforward matter. They cannot take much comfort from the clarity of the lexicographers who offer definitions of 'truth' such as 'a state of being in accord with fact or reality', both the latter being terms as vexed as truth itself. It is no wonder then that Kovach and Rosenstiel admit that when it comes to the central need for truth:

> there is absolute unanimity and also utter confusion: Everyone agrees journalists must tell the truth. Yet people are fuddled about what 'the truth' means … Truth, it seems, is too complicated for us to pursue. Or perhaps it doesn't exist, since we are all subjective individuals.[3]

A philosopher might well call this conclusion little more than 'a reflex against deceptiveness'.[4]

Truth, as it has perplexed philosophy for millennia, is a can of worms journalists avoid opening largely by taking it, in effect, as read. It is not lies: i.e. things they know themselves to have invented from whole cloth. They simply proceed on the basis of Bertrand Russell's and G. E. Moore's 'correspondence theory': that truth corresponds 'to, or with, a fact' … in fact (as it were) that it is related to reality in some way.[5] And that will have to do. The nuances of the philosophic thinking in such a theory are not their concern. Nor is the contrasting 'coherence theory' — that any truth is actually a proposition which, in essence, consists of other propositions rather than corresponding in some way with external reality.[6] And as for Charles Peirce's 'pragmatism' — that, in essence, all philosophical concepts should be tested via scientific experimentation — we have explained above (Chapter 7) how such protocols do not mesh with journalism's practices.[7]

Though philosophy is not much of a help as a guide to everyday journalistic activity, it comes closest with Nietzschean 'relativism'. Nietzsche thought that truth

> is only a world-exposition [i.e. description] and world-arrangement (according to us, if I may say so!) and NOT a world-explanation; but in so far as it is based on belief in the senses, it is regarded as more, and for a long time to come must be regarded as more — namely, as an explanation. It has eyes and fingers of its own, it has ocular evidence and palpableness of its own: this operates fascinatingly, persuasively, and CONVINCINGLY … What is clear, what is 'explained'? Only that which can be seen and felt.[8]

Nietzsche, in effect, here agrees with Marx: 'Philosophers have only interpreted the world, in various ways'[9] — just as journalists only look at it — with little practical impact. The situation, therefore, is generally much as Terry Pratchett described it, as being the case in *Discworld*, when journalists confront a philosopher 'talking in philosophy', they usually listen 'in gibberish'.[10]

However, if truth, whatever else it is or isn't, is journalism's first obligation, then a lack of agreement and/or understanding of it would seem to suggest that the press has a serious problem. At a bedrock ideological level it means that journalists, as a body, lack a coherent, shared idea of a concept which they themselves consider to be crucial. That's obviously bad enough, but as a matter of practice the issue produces a particularly thorny double-bind, in that journalism's nature renders the (re)presentation of 'truth' extremely difficult, while at the same time exacerbating the demand for it. And, generally speaking, journalists eschew reaching for epistemology, the most obvious paddle available to help them navigate this creek, because (see above) to do so simply befuddles.

It is perhaps not an absolute rule, but there can be little question but that the protocols of honoured philosophy, unlike those of science and the law, are not something journalism anyway aspires to emulate. As we have noted, these other aspirations tend to present journalism with challenges, if not downright impossibilities. Scientific and legal protocols, despite the shared purpose of creating information, are largely beyond journalism's reach and are also certainly not essential to it. But, however ineffectually, the ideological and practical processes of science and law are, as we have seen above, nevertheless – and however faintly – echoed. Not so philosophy. It is not considered as having a superior methodology to inform practice, and professional theories of journalism are even less informed by its protocols.

By journalism's lights, emulating the philosopher would anyway be by no means an unambiguous good. In western (especially Anglophone) popular culture, the stereotypical notion is of philosophers worrying about truly knowing, for example, if they are really awake because '[i]t is a question of fact, whether the perceptions of the senses be produced by external objects',[11] it is fair to say such Cartesian issues – or, indeed, any seemingly 'abstract' philosophical theories – are seldom the topic of conversation at the bars where journalists stereotypically gather. By contrast, journalism aims at more than mere interpretation: 'The news is the material that people use to learn and think about the world beyond themselves, the most important quality is that it be useable and reliable.'[12] And so, it can be proudly (?) claimed that 'journalism by nature is not so much 'philosophical and introspective' as it is 'reactive and *practical*' [emphasis added].

Moral philosophy on the other hand, in the form of ethics, is of commendable concern to journalists, although it is not unfair to assert that ethical issues raised by their practice will tend to be treated as pragmatically as possible. This is not to say that ethical behaviour is in any way vouchsafed by journalism's interest in the moral dimension of its effect in and on the world. Neither should we assume that journalism and philosophy's interests in ethics are coextensive. The further reaches of the philosophy of ethics are of as little concern to journalism as is epistemology. The 19th century Kantian concept of the Categorical Imperative, or subsequent 20th century investigations of Logical Positivism, are ignored, but 18th century

Utilitarian Ethics do remain, however overtly unacknowledged, as much an influence on journalism's practice as they are on the law (see p. 137).

Utilitarian Ethics offers a philosophical antidote to uncertainty in one area of being – that of how we treat other persons: how, for example, a journalist treats those upon whom she reports and also, albeit with less clarity, how her work impacts on those who absorb it. Ethical precepts to avoid causing harm can be distinguished from their legal framework to suggest directly broad rules for governing proper moral behaviour in the world. The Enlightenment philosopher Frances Hutchinson formulated the grounds for this as: 'that Action is best, which procures the greatest Happiness for the greatest Numbers; and, that, at worst, which, in like manner, occasions Misery'.[13] This basic value judgement became, in the 19th century, the basis for John Stuart Mills' 'Harm Principle' which locates ethical behaviour in the injunction: 'Do no Harm'.[14] Moral Philosophy, however, almost from the moment of its articulation, subjected this approach to a critique grounded in its lack of nuance. Nevertheless, a general acceptance of its persuasiveness is undeniable. It reflects, after all, the even more pressing biblical obligation that 'whatsoever ye would that men [sic] should do to you, do ye even so to them'.[15]

Moral Philosophy's critique and its other approaches are, again, pretty unlikely to be discussed in that hypothetical bar. Unlike epistemology, however, de facto ethical utilitarianism is a serious concern (or, sometimes, the subject of excessive know-nothing guilty dismissal) for the press. We shall come back to this, but first, just because journalism doesn't seem much interested in how philosophy's ideas of truth relate to its practices, that doesn't mean that we shouldn't be.

Journalism cannot and does not actually avoid the epistemological 'problem' of truth. The bottom line is, as we have said, that the news relates to a kind of de facto truth, **a** truth about the world rather than **the** truth. But it can be argued, with no hint of disingenuousness, that inasmuch as journalism is a practical pursuit, more abstract and/or absolute conceptions of truth in fact have little to do with it. In 1922, Walter Lippman, the authoritative journalist whose high conception of his calling continues to influence especially the American press, famously declared:

> news and truth are not the same thing, and must be clearly distinguished. The function of the press is to signalize a truth, the function of truth is to bring to light hidden facts, to see them in relation to each other, and make a picture on which men [sic] can act. Only in those points, where social conditions take recognizable and measurable shape, do the body of truth and the body of news coincide.[16]

For journalism, then, 'truth' is rather *sui generis* – **a** truth, not **the** truth, which is fair enough. Kovach and Rosenstiel call this 'journalistic truth', suggesting that it involves 'more than mere accuracy … It is a sorting-out process that develops between the initial story and the interaction among the public, newsmakers, and journalists over time'.[17] One problem with this is that such a qualified/complicated 'journalistic truth' is not really how they sell the product to the public. Instead they still insist that the 'first principle of journalism' is 'its disinterested pursuit of truth' and that that 'is ultimately what sets it apart from all other forms of communications'.[18] Journalists might not know what 'truth' is and Lippmann might say it is not necessarily the news, but they nevertheless claim 'disinterestedly' to pursue it.

To do this, as a consequence of their allergic reaction to epistemology and their need to be, in some way, useful, 'truth' – **a** truth, 'journalistic truth' – becomes glossed as 'objectivity'. The term first appears in connection with journalism in 1911, in the same year as the trade's arrival on the US college campus as a degree-worthy subject.[19] Being objective was a central factor in the drive towards professionalism, constructing the journalist 'as an impartial mass-informer'.[20] For Jay Rosen, objectivity is a 'public philosophy' which is 'one of the identifying features of journalism in the United States and perhaps the major contribution American journalism has made to the rest of the world'.[21]

But, beware (perhaps) of Americans bearing gifts: objectivity is just another philosophical can of worms and journalists are just as confused about it as they are about truth. For the lexicographers, objectivity is a journey while truth is a state, meaning that the former is defined as the process of reaching a state of truth (whatever that is) through a process independent of individual subjectivity arising from perception, emotions, or imagination. And in philosophy too, it stands in a binary opposition with subjectivity, and is seen to be most achieved in the case of 'knowledge which bears no sense of the knowers', as, ideally, with science.

Specifically, scientific objectivity comes from proceeding 'blind' – seeing 'without interference, interpretation, or intelligence', as we have indicated above (see p. 111). Philosophers have also been concerned with objectivity outside of science and within the humanities, primarily in history. There it presents a problem because the 'knower', the historian, denied repeatability and incapable of completeness, is – as it were – 'contaminated' (as is the journalist), by subjectivity. Journalism may be 'the first rough draft of history',[22] but, leaving historiography and its problems behind, it is more comfortable with – although still severely challenged by – legal approaches to the question of knowability than it is with the techniques of the historian. But for journalism reaching for objectivity is a process, in essence is a way of avoiding the conundrum posed by truth, a state of being related to fact. The objective journalist might not know exactly where they are going (truth) but they know, by denying self, how they are getting there (objectivity).

Perhaps we can note at this point that the claim of professionalism shared with other 'honoured' spheres of activity is, as expected, proving to be a tad hubristic. Given that journalists do not usually deploy legalistic protocols to weigh probabilities, equity escapes them. Science, too: without repeatability and many of the other means of triangulation, is also largely beyond them. And philosophically, as with truth, so with objectivity. For Steve Knowlton, '[o]bjectivity is one of the most troubling yet most fascinating concepts in journalism. Most professionals hold to it

160 Objecting to objectivity

(by that name or some other) at least as an idea to strive for'.[23] But there are press critics who:

> treat a belief in objectivity with the condescension they would have for an adult who swears by the tooth fairy – as generally harmless enough unless taken to extremes, but so far beyond the pale as to make serious discussion a laughable waste of time.[24]

And, we can note, it does no more than beg the question to admit, as Rosen does, that '[o]f course, no one can be really objective but we can try to be fair'.[25] The British National Union of Journalists also avoids 'truth' as an objective but instead 'strives to ensure that information disseminated is honestly conveyed, accurate and fair' without acknowledging the uncertainties of these terms. 'Honesty' does not suggest a need for triangulation; 'accuracy' does not require balance; and fairness, which does, involves uncovering all sides of a story 'without' according to the lexicographers, 'favouritism or discrimination', i.e. being, to all intents and purposes, unobtainable.[26]

Others add that 'true objectivity as a goal is unattainable' but use terms which are also, upon examination, just as vexed, e.g. nonpartisanship. This sounds promising:

> in so far as it is defined as keeping personal political preferences (if the reporter has any) out of news stories, [it] is quite possible.[27]

But surely a reporter's subjective political awareness (even glossed over as 'preferences') cannot in fact be readily 'kept out' (nor is it desirable to do so, but that is a separate issue with which we shall conclude, see p. 199). As with all the other such terms – balance, neutrality, impartiality, etc. – the assumption here is that people, intrinsically subjective, can be good journalists by pretending not to be. The problem persists whatever the term. Objectivity ties practitioners up in knots.

By law, BBC objectivity is glossed not just as 'impartiality' but 'due impartiality'. In 2019, management felt it had reason (a single complaint) to censure one of its journalists (of colour), Naga Munchetty, for expressing a view that Trump was racist when, that summer, he told four congresswomen of colour (three of whom were born in the US, the fourth having come to the US as a child) to 'go back and help fix the totally broken and crime-infested places from which they came'.[28] The BBC's Editorial Content Unit – its internal thought police – was reduced to determining how many angels dance on the head of a pin:

> The BBC's editorial guidelines do require due impartiality, but the Editorial Complaints Unit's ruling is clear that Naga Munchetty was perfectly entitled to give a personal response to the phrase 'go back to your own country' .... She understandably feels strongly on this issue, and there was nothing wrong with her talking about her own experiences of racism .... However, our editorial guidelines do not allow for journalists to then give their opinions

about the individual making the remarks or their motives for doing so – in this case President Trump – and it was for this reason that the complaint was partially upheld.[29]

The absurdity of this decision was instantly recognised in a public backlash. The Corporation reversed it at the personal intervention of the Director General, Lord Hall.

But, objectivity (however defined) is held to be critical for a press which wishes to make any claim of integrity. In the Munchetty affair, an ex-chair of the BBC's Board of Governors, Lord Grade, announced that: '[T]he BBC's impartiality is sacrosanct. Naga Munchetty strayed into an area of comment and opinion, when she should have stuck to branding the President's tweet as racist …'[30] So, OK to call the tweet racist, but not the tweeter. OK to censure the female person of colour but not, as it turns out, her white male co-presenter who prompted her remark and was also named in the one complaint.[31] OK for Munchetty to talk about her personal experience of, and reaction to, racism but not to name persons causing her distress. All in the name of impartiality?

The objectivity claim, whatever it is called, is, as it has been from the outset, a very large worm in journalism's bud. In the past half-century and more, the press's vulnerability to ever more strident charges of bias and distortion has been grounded in the unconvincing nature of its counter-claim of a quasi-scientific or legalistic objectivity. Crucially, the press is mandated, among other things, to monitor the powerful – a purpose often called the watchdog function of journalism. A claimed but not delivered objectivity undermines the press's capacity to do this. It feeds its critics. Already by1964, Dwight Eisenhower, the former Republican president, was dismissing, to the general applause of his party's activists, as 'sensation seeking columnists and commentators' any who queried his party's line.[32] The hostility to the press which his successor Trump so readily exploits has been a long time suppurating. And this is the most pressing reason why dealing with objectivity in the 21st century requires something stronger than, as happens in some journalistic quarters, glibly denying that journalism claims to be objective, and treating those who say it does with condescension. To do so is certainly no laughable waste of time – if it ever was.

For Steve Knowlton, what amounts to objectivity has always been present. It might not have been recognised with this term, or always delivered, but it was a given of *newes* – the Galbertian sobriety seen, say, in Pecke's adjective-less report of the execution of Charles I, as opposed to the *strange newes* of witches and wonders which characterised the popular newsbooks. Press objectivity's marks – plain prose, sober contents, leaked documents, identified sources, corrected errors, etc. – can all be found in print well prior to its identification as a distinct journalistic protocol. When exactly that identification occurred has been a matter of dispute, but clearly, in the Anglophone sphere at least, the press's circumstances began to change significantly, at the very least laying the groundwork for future shifts, towards the end of the 18th century.

At the turn of the 19th, during the Jacksonian era, the American press, with its reliance on public subventions and private bribes, was 'opinionated, politically biased, one-sided, argumentative and frequently strident' in its explicit partisanship.[33] It was far from claiming objectivity. By the 1830s, however, there was an accelerating movement away from such partisanship, fuelled not only by growth in advertising revenues but also by street distribution. The new titles then appearing – Day's *Sun*, Gordon Bennett's *Herald* and their peers, the direct ancestors of our tabloids, were sold at the knockdown price of a single cent per copy. The 'elite' partisan papers cost six cents a day, well beyond what was affordable for the increasingly literate mass. According to Dan Schiller, objectivity then enters into public consciousness as a distinct mark of 'better journalism' – 'free of the insidious obligations born by the Elite Press'.[34]

Nevertheless, at this time, the word itself – 'objectivity' (which was first noticed in the language in 1803) – was not heard, and its value to journalism was by no means a given. It could lead, some newspaper editors thought, to nothing more than 'gagged ... neutrality', a poor replacement for the vigour of their own overtly personal approaches. In 1841, Horace Greeley, best remembered for the exhortation 'Go west, young man!', began publishing *The New-York Tribune* because: 'My leading idea was the establishment of a journal removed alike from servile partisanship on the one hand and from gagged ... neutrality on the other'.[35] This was not universally accepted as an ambition. It took time to take hold, but a simulacrum of 'neutrality' (all too easily also known as 'objectivity') came to prevail:

> objectivity seemed a natural and progressive ideology for an aspiring occupational group at a moment when science was God, efficiency was cherished, and increasingly prominent elites judged partisanship a vestige of the tribal 19th century.[36]

'The notion that journalism should be politically neutral, nonpartisan, professional, even "objective", did not emerge until the 20th century', McChesney notes,[37] though, of course, it did not emerge from nowhere, without antecedent and yet somehow miraculously full-grown. (That isn't how ideologies work.)

Objectivity – the word – first comes to appear in connection with journalism in 1911, i.e. at roughly the same time as the establishment of the first US university journalism schools, as previously noted. This is also around the same time that sociology began to theorise the nature of professionalism in general. Michael Schudson, in contrast to Schiller, suggests that it was now that this belief in objectivity took a firmer hold. It was grounded in the assumed possibility of a separation between facts – 'assertions about the world open to independent validation' – and values – 'an individual's conscious or unconscious preferences for what the world should be'.[38] Objectivity became a matter of clearly distinguishing one from the other, and recognising this became a key element in determining professionalism.

Throughout the middle decades of the 20th century, the vexed philosophical question of subjectivity was simply set aside, not to be contemplated until the coming of the second New Journalism wave in the 1960s/70s. The first, in the late 19th century, had been bound up with sensational 'muckraking' investigations and 'stunts', and was scarcely concerned with subjectivities, the focus of the term's second iteration.[39] The highly personalised reporting of this New Journalism involved implicit and explicit rejection of the idea of objectivity, and revealed the fragility of trying to avoid its impossibilities by using other terms, e.g. 'fairness', 'balance', and the rest.

Writing about objectivity in the late 1970s, Schudson could see it as an obfuscating 'distortion'. And by the 1990s even its most avid defenders knew there was a problem, for all that they still believed that the concept could be championed:

> With all its flaws [objectivity] still expresses certain deeply held and legitimate values: the notion of a disinterested truth, the wish to separate doing journalism from doing politics, the principled attempt to restrain your own biases, looking at things from the other person's perspective. These are important values for all of us, and particularly for journalists.[40]

Jay Rosen was insisting that: 'You can't just wave [these values] away by saying "objectivity is a myth"'. But, we would argue, neither can you defend an impossible, paradoxical, even nonsensical ideology simply by saying 'These values are important'.

Notes

1 Nieman Reports (2001). *Essays About 'The Elements of Journalism'*, 55:2. https://nieman-reports.org/wp-content/uploads/2014/07/Special2001.pdf [accessed 9 July 2019].
2 Ibid.
3 Ibid.
4 Williams, Bernard (2002). *Truth and Truthfulness*. Princeton, NJ: Princeton University Press, p. 1.
5 David, Marian (2016). 'The correspondence theory of truth', *The Stanford Encyclopedia of Philosophy*. https://plato.stanford.edu/archives/fall2016/entries/truth-correspondence/ [accessed 23 January 2020].
6 Young, James (2018). 'The coherence theory of truth', *The Stanford Encyclopedia of Philosophy*. https://plato.stanford.edu/archives/fall2018/entries/truth-coherence/ [accessed 23 January 2020].
7 Legg, Catherine & Christopher Hookway (2019). 'Pragmatism', *The Stanford Encyclopedia of Philosophy*. https://plato.stanford.edu/archives/spr2019/entries/pragmatism/ [accessed 23 January 2020].
8 Nietzsche, Friedrich (1886). *Jenseits von Gut und Böse: Vorspiel einer Philosophie der Zukunft*. Leipzig: C.G. Naumann, trans; Kaufmann, Walter (1966). *Beyond Good and Evil: Prelude to a Philosophy of the Future*. New York: Vintage), § 14.
9 Marx, Karl, (1969 [1845]). *Theses on Feuerbach*. Moscow: Progress Publishers. www.marxists.org/archive/marx/works/1845/theses/theses.htm [accessed 14 September 2019].
10 Pratchett, Terry (1993). *Small Gods*. London: Corgi, p. 281.

11 Hume, David (1748). *An Enquiry Concerning Human Understanding*. London: A. Millar, p. 237.
12 Nieman Reports (2001). *Essays About 'The Elements of Journalism'*, 55:2. https://niemanreports.org/wp-content/uploads/2014/07/Special2001.pdf [accessed 9 July 2019].
13 Hutcheson, Francis (1726). *An Inquiry into the Original of Our Ideas of Beauty and Virtue*. London: J. Darbay *et al*, p. 177.
14 Mill, John Stuart (1859). *On Liberty*. London: John W. Parker and Son, p. 28.
15 Matthew 7:12 (KJV).
16 Lippman, Walter (1922). *Public Opinion*. New York: Harcort Brace, & Company, p. 385.
17 Nieman Reports (2001). *Essays About 'The Elements of Journalism'*, 55:2, p. 7. https://niemanreports.org/wp-content/uploads/2014/07/Special2001.pdf [accessed 9 July 2019].
18 Ibid.
19 Maras, Steven (2013). *Objectivity in Journalism*. London: Polity, p. 38.
20 Ward, Stephen (2004). *The Invention of Journalism Ethics: The Path to Objectivity and Beyond*. Montreal: McGill-Queen's University Press, p. 33.
21 Rosen, Jay (1993). 'Beyond objectivity', *Nieman Reports*, 47, Winter, p. 48.
22 Needless to say, the origin of this phrase is in much dispute. Usually attributed to *Washington Post* publisher Philip Graham sometime in the 1980, it actually appeared in print in 1943 (Shafer, Jack, 2010. 'Who said it first?: Journalism is the "first rough draft of history'. *Slate*, 30 August. https://slate.com/news-and-politics/2010/08/on-the-trail-of-the-question-who-first-said-or-wrote-that-journalism-is-the-first-rough-draft-of-history.html [accessed 17 September 2019].
23 Knowlton, Steven (2005). 'Introduction: A history of journalistic objectivity' in *Fair & Balanced: A History of Journalistic Objectivity* (Steven Knowlton & Karen Knowlton, eds.). Northport, AL: Vision Press. p. 3.
24 Knowlton, Stephen (2005). 'Introduction: A history of journalistic objectivity' in *Fair and Balanced: A History of Journalistic Objectivity* (Steven Knowlton & Karen Knowlton, eds.). Northport, AL: Vision Press, p. 3.
25 Rosen, Jay (1993). 'Beyond objectivity' *Nieman Reports*, 47, Winter, p. 48.
26 Anon (NUJ) (2013). *NUJ code of conduct*. www.nuj.org.uk/about/nuj-code/ [accessed 7 November 2019].
27 Mindich, David (1998). *Just the Facts: How 'Objectivity' Came to Define American Journalism*. New York: New York University Press, p. 41.
28 BBC (2019). *Trump's tweet: What did he say and why's he being criticised?* www.bbc.co.uk/newsround/49004860 [accessed 15 November 2019].
29 Anon (BBC Media Centre) (2019). 'ECU ruling on BBC Breakfast'. www.bbc.co.uk/mediacentre/statements/ecu-breakfast-trump [accessed 10 October 2019].
30 Richard Spillett (2019). 'Former BBC chairman MICHAEL GRADE sees trouble on the horizon following the Naga Munchetty "racism" scandal'. *MailOnline*, 2 October. www.dailymail.co.uk/news/article-7524817/Lord-Grade-says-corporation-RIGHT-criticise-Naga-Munchetty.html [accessed 9 October 2019].
31 This was initially disputed. David Jordan, head of the ECU, said the white male person was not mentioned; however BBC News reported that he was. Anon (BBC NEWS) (2019). 'Original Naga Munchetty complaint also mentioned Dan Walker'. www.bbc.co.uk/news/entertainment-arts-49876929 [accessed 9 October 2019].
32 Knowlton, Stephen (2005). 'Into the 1960s and into the Crucible' in *Fair and Balanced: A History of Journalistic Objectivity* (Steven Knowlton & Karen Knowlton, eds.). Northport, AL: Vision Press, p. 221.

33 Baldasty, Gerald (2011). 'American political parties and the press'. *American Journalism History Reader* (B. Brennan & H. Hardt, eds.) New York: Routledge, p. 278.
34 Schiller, Daniel (1981). *Objectivity and the News: The Public and the Rise of Commercial Journalism*. Philadelphia, PA: University of Pennsylvania Press, p. 53.
35 Greely, Horace (1868). *Recollections of a Busy Life*. New York: J B Ford & Co, p. 137.
36 Schudson, Micheal (2001) 'The objectivity norm in American journalism'. *Journalism*, 2:2, pp. 162–163.
37 McChesney, Robert (2003). 'The problem of journalism: A political economic contribution to an explanation of the crisis in contemporary US journalism', *Journalism Studies*, 4:3, p. 300.
38 Schudson, Michael (1978). *Discovering the News: A Social History of American Newspapers*. New York, Basic, p. 16.
39 Although a certain self-reflexivity did appear in muckraking episodes and stings. See *The Maiden Tribute of Modern Babylon*.
40 Rosen, Jay (1993). 'Beyond objectivity'. *Neiman Reports,* 47:4, Winter, qt in Rosen, Jay (1999). *What are Journalists For?* New Haven, CT: Yale p. 214.

12
TRUTH: MORAL PHILOSOPHY

> 'Clear and verifiable links between cause and effect are still lacking'
> *Sophia Ignatidou (in 2019)*
> *Researcher/Journalist*

Despite its disavowal of epistemological concerns, and what (usually partisan) detractors allege, journalism does not similarly neglect the study of ethics/morality:

> It should be apparent that the belief in objectivity in journalism [] is not just a claim about what kind of knowledge is reliable. It is also a moral philosophy, a declaration of what kind of thinking one should engage in, in making moral decisions.[1]

University J-Schools have made courses on ethics a commonplace and journalists, many of them, are to be commended for taking moral issues seriously. But this is not just – or, to be candid, even – a question of telling the truth (however that is defined) because truth-telling has always been – from the very earliest news publications of centuries past – optional, a marketing ploy, not a substantive quality. Of course, the press has been served by truthfulness but, equally, it has as often been served just by purveying what sells – what attracts attention. Asserting truth, for the pioneering news-book and sheet printers, was their new product's USP, and adopting it as a selling-point did not always – or even often – mean actually telling the truth (or anything resembling it). The business of treating truth as brand is fake news's longest, deepest taproot.

So, to say again, it is the case that, historically, journalists have always, in practice, leaned more to Pontius Pilate's cynicism than George Washington's fabled inability to tell a lie. At a minimum, awareness of over-verification's potentially stultifying effect on output is likely to condition conduct and content. Ethically, of course, it is easy to condemn such mendacity or, more usually, flexibility, in reporting externally verifiable facts, but in practice so doing blunts the press's ability to perform its positive social functions. Moreover, even if clearly defined, truth cannot be insisted upon without a de facto repressive apparatus to enforce obedience. And a free press cannot tolerate that.

Given that, in the Anglophone sphere at least, journalism's announced predilection is for the practical, morality then involves adopting the fundamental utilitarian ethical position as the basis of proper behaviour, i.e. 'Do No Harm'. As compared with the pursuit of truth, this is comparatively straightforward, but the entanglements of the fakery taproot, again, render it dense. As we have pointed out (see p. 136), exercising the right of free expression, alone of the UN Rights, can be a crime. Freedom presents an 'antinomy', a contradiction which muddies the possible ethical dimensions of the problem, as is, for example, perfectly illustrated by *The War of the Worlds* incident (see p. 70).

It is no basis for invalidation but, as we have noted, the sociologists who wrote up their pioneering impact study on the reception of this programme as causing harm – that is, widespread panic – acutely needed a dramatic project to secure research funding from the broadcasters, or that the other players, the network, the press, and Welles all had a vested interest in hyping the programme's impact. But conclusions as to mass media impact (including that of the press) remained elusive. The exercise simply crudely spotlights the potency of received understanding of media effects.

In the half-century from the 1930s, the 'hypodermic needle' model was refined first into a 'Two-Step Flow' concept suggesting that, rather than direct individual impacts, people were influenced by 'opinion-leaders', that is: their family, friends, or colleagues who were seen as experts (in some sense) on, say, sport or politics or whatever. Media impact needed to be measured and assessed against this group rather than all message-receivers, as it was the opinion formers who absorbed, and were influenced by, the media directly.[2] Certainly, researchers found people listened to their fellows in this way, but that still left the question of media effect on their 'informed' interlocutors open. This, however, proved equally resistant to producing any agreed understanding of media influence and ultimately a 'Null Effects Hypothesis' or 'Re-enforcement Theory' emerged which, in essence, gave up on 'scientifically' demonstrating impact at all.[3] Instead, the autonomy of the receiver to resist hegemonic media message meanings came to be stressed in a 'Uses and Gratifications' model.[4] By the 1980s, a 'Cultivation Process' limited this de facto alternative focus by arguing that there were, after all, 'heavy' users in the mass of receivers, especially among the lower orders, who were, after all, susceptible to injections of understanding and opinion from the media.[5] The theories have thus proliferated but the evidence remains so unsafe that in 1996, a senior British researcher in this tradition, Sonia Livingstone, could conclude that '[d]espite the volume of research, the debate about media effects remains unresolved'.[6]

And it still is – and the reason is that we have been trying to measure something we have not properly defined. Obviously, we start with the understanding that

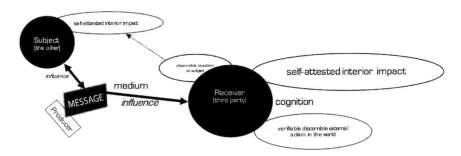

FIGURE 1 Media effects

we are dealing with influence, the influence media has on society; but 'influence' has a double aspect. It is both 'the power to have an effect on people or things, or a person or thing that is able to do this' (CED). Dismissing the second meaning, we can then think of effect as 'impact:' 'the force or action of one object hitting another' (CED). But this must be mapped on the communication process (see Figure 1). The media message producer has two lines of influence in the message-medium-receiver model of communication. One effect-line, actually a two-way street, runs between the producer and the subject. The other line, usually a one-way street despite the recent introduction of a measure of 'interactivity', essentially runs from the producer to the receiver.

And this – the one-way street – is where the focus of media effects research has lain. The impact can be internally registered by the receiver or it can produce an externally verifiable, discernible response from them but we fail to map this difference in the nature of their reaction. Media panics are as easily grounded in what people tell researchers as they are in what researchers see people actually doing. Our beglamoured technicist language exacerbates the problem – to describe 'clicks' as 'engagements', for example. Measuring them as significant is naïf. Analysing audience or readers' reports of distress, anger, empathy, or any other emotion at best unpacks but one factor among many in determining mindsets. For example, online civic activities come to cover signing online [petitions], sharing, uploading comments – but direct action (going on a demo, sending a donation) is not in view.[7]

This is why we take a position downplaying media power. This is not to marginalise the crucial importance of influence but it is to suggest that, when it comes to determining and regulating that power, concerning impacts should primarily be those which produce discernible effects in the world and, despite the endless brouhaha about media misfeasance, there is actually very little evidence of such measurable consequences to hand. Clear evidence of harm can seldom be seen.

The most salient example of clarity is evidenced by the reporting of suicides. Psychologists have gathered data to demonstrate a 'Werther Effect'[8] – a correlation between media coverage of suicide and increased suicide rates. 'Copycatting' – following media reports, especially of specific circumstances – has reached a point where, in a number of countries, guidance is available to journalists advising how such news can be reported in order to minimise the chances of copycat effects.[9] A particularly compelling study, done in Vienna in the late 1980s, supported the Werther Effect hypothesis and, subsequent to the local press agreeing to reduce its coverage, further monitoring of the reporting by the psychologists revealed a significant reduction in the rate of incidents.[10]

There are less compelling studies investigating a correlation between post-traumatic stress disorder (PTSD) and media reports of atrocities and natural disasters, etc., specifically on television.[11] The results are, broadly, unsurprising. The more direct involvement with the event – e.g. losing a loved one or directly helping the rescue effort during the 9/11 Twin Towers attack, say – the more likely were symptoms of PTSD arising from watching reports of it.[12] Secondary PTSD, i.e. PTSD attributable directly to television viewing among otherwise uninvolved viewers, was not demonstrated, although a study of Israeli students following attacks in which they were not involved did offer a variety of self-reported symptoms of clinical anxiety.[13] The media, generally then, appears as an aggravating agent for those watchers already impacted; but the psychologists do no better than the media sociologists when it comes to evidence of impact among those not involved. As for the Israeli students, common sense suggests that the threat of being called to arms following any rise in tension, as well as other direct dangers, rather than images of any specific incident, are the likelier prime source of stress.

Common sense is arguably similarly illuminating when applied to a US study following Hurricane Sandy in 2013, which found a greater level of distress among the quarter of its 1,000 respondents who had used social media as well as mainstream television to gain news of the disaster.[14] The researchers seemed ready to ascribe a possible technicist explanation of their finding, attributing greater impact to social media; but perhaps it is just as likely that people seeking further information on the new platforms were more concerned (and more susceptible to worry about extreme weather) than were the others?

It is, indeed, possible to reverse the gaze here. Instead of looking for evidence of media impact, the shared characteristics of the subjects of these studies offer an explanation for the results. A susceptibility hypothesis suggests that direct evidence of media apparently causing clinical mental distress or socio-/psychopathic behaviour is actually more evidence of prior distress or pathologies than it is of media power. But, however deviant these behaviours and however few in number, the question of press constraint can be brought forward for debate in these instances. The question becomes how many serious measurable harms – e.g. suicides – need to be registered to suggest constraining free speech? It would seem, given the current state of our understanding of the consequences of reporting suicide, a self-imposed (as it must be for a free press) limitation on reporting is clearly warranted.

This equally suggests that other groups of susceptible consumers might also be similarly impacted – 'terrorists', say – and warrant the same self-denying reporting ordinance on the part of the press. 'Small Outrage – Not Many Dead' on an inside page is perhaps unthinkable but it would undeniably reduce the supply of the oxygen of publicity to the perpetrators of terror, and perhaps weaken the possibility of copycatting. However, such arguments are always fraught. For all that a sort of 'Werther Effect' is far from being unimaginable in this instance, it is also clear from our knowledge of these perpetrators that the influence of offline as well as online peers, community opinion leaders, and even, for example, the membership of certain types of clubs, are significant factors, unrelated to the media. Reducing coverage of itself would be no prophylactic.

There is another instance of what could well be a 'Werther effect'. The anti-MMR vaccination campaign waged in the early years of this century by sections of the press and still continued on various dedicated disinformation websites has apparently negatively impacted take-up of the preventative vaccine. Without question, the incidence of measles, a disease nearly eradicated in the north, has reached epidemic proportions globally. According to the WHO, currently 10 million cases and some 142,000 deaths are registered.[15] Causation is easily attributed to the Anti-Vaxxers – but, as ever, it is not that simple. Much of the outbreak has to do with circumstances in particular communities and has nothing to do with the media. Civil strife and a lack of vaccines account for the 4,500 registered child deaths in the Congo, for example.[16] Nevertheless, in the UK – declared by the WHO to be measles-free in 2017 – there were 991 reported cases the following year. The 95% take-up of the first dose – MMR protection requires two injections – fell to 87.4% with the second. A 'Werther Effect' of disinformation on susceptible parents is clearly implicated.

It is reasonable to suppose that vaccination, always in danger of being perceived hostilely because of its counter-intuitive nature (give the disease to prevent the disease), would be of heightened concern to susceptible parents. It would seem from the plethora of official health sites dedicated to them that they were already turning to the net for legitimate official parenting advice. However, the case for impact here still has to be contrasted with the norm: with only averagely susceptible audiences, such effect is not so easily noticed, and less straightforwardly established at the level of probative cause. Pro-social stand-alone media health campaign communications are largely ineffective unless backed up by further sanctions (e.g. the illegality of smoking in public).[17] The general conclusion has to be that behaviour change triggering impacts reflect as much, or more, the susceptibility of the receiver than the power of the media.

It becomes clearer that, for the most part, news consumers are not that susceptible, and do not display behaviour change or – if they do – then, leaving these exceptional cases behind, an irrelevancy hypothesis comes into play. This suggests that, when susceptibility is not increased, demonstrated non-socially transgressive behaviour change – ads moving consumers from one brand of coffee to another, say – speak to the comparative irrelevance of the behaviour in question. Nevertheless, the world advertising spend of $562 billion demonstrates the value of such communications to those spending this money.[18] And within these billions lie charity spends which are clearly effective in producing far from irrelevant pro-social outcomes. But evidence that direct causation occurs in general is lacking.

However, as a society in the grip of technicist illusions, we seem very willing to believe in media power – indeed, loath to acknowledge at the level of general understanding that the hypodermic needle model is largely illusory. Rather, technology is currently once more being hyped. The new immersive interactive technologies, for example, are asserted as having increased empathetic pro-social affordances, but, thus far, it is the same old story of rhetorical claims being unsupported by any real evidence.[19]

And all this is why we seem to be in the grip of a media panic about improper media meddling in electoral politics. Following the votes which put Trump in the White House and prompted the UK to begin the process of leaving the EU, there was a flurry of investigations into improper foreign influences on the voting processes involved. It was seductive to attribute to social media the efficacy of traditional brown envelopes stuffed with cash as corrupters of elections; but there is, despite the brouhaha, no more proof of such effects than a century of media sociology has provided about the power of older media to cause socially significant changes in behaviour. In September, 2019, Chatham House published a 44-page research paper surveying in some detail *EU–US Cooperation on Tackling Disinformation* (aka fake news). The nearest it got to evidence of direct effects was to conclude that:

> Regrettably, clear and verifiable links between cause and effect are still lacking in disinformation research. The effectiveness of present approaches such as prioritizing transparency have to be properly audited, too, as without appropriate oversight and enforcement mechanisms, transparency can become a red herring.[20]

New communication technology, then, seems to be much of a piece with older techniques of political communication. A 2018 survey of 49 field experiments into voting influences in the US, for example, found campaign advertising had 'an average effect of zero in general elections'[21] (see p. 180). To recall one notorious 1990s post-election splash in Rupert Murdoch's London *Sun* – '**IT'S THE SUN WOT WON IT**'. It wasn't.

In short, it is possible to argue that media impacts the mass of population to change their behaviour at best in non-deviant ways and, charity-support excepted, on matters of comparative unimportance. This could easily be a matter of profound economic significance but it is no basis for hysteria. It is also, contrary to common belief, the case that evidence of even self-attested changes of opinion are equally difficult to pin-point. Classically:

> The media provide the materials for responding to experience and these accumulate over time in a long-term process of socialisation. The effects of the media on the individual are not only indirect, they may have happened long ago, certainly in the past.[22]

172 Objecting to objectivity

This is, of course, of immense significance but, against the noise of the social sphere, it has seldom been specifically demonstrated.

An exception is Greg Philo's experiment inviting subjects to act as journalists, writing up reports which were then mapped against their announced sources of news. This established a clear correlation between their understanding of a situation and what the sources they habitually used had reported about it, obviously reflecting causation.[23] But, even if we accept this conditioning possibility, it nevertheless still exists in the context of social noise and cannot be entirely isolated. It has to be a re-enforcing factor and, whatever its degree of influence, as far as ethical responsibility goes, for all that it may show a 'doing', it does not necessarily reveal a 'harm'.

And anyway, what exactly constitutes a 'harm', if it is not externally verifiable, discernible damage? The Jeffersonian breaking of a leg or robbing of a pocket is as tricky to define as what 'doing' really means here. What ethical responsibility can the journalist have for any consumer's self-attested interior responses? Where is the ethical harm involved in causing, say, annoyance or angst, upset or anger, discomfort or distress?

During the long European 18th century to 1815, there was a rise of sensitivity to the feelings of others[24] which has continued to expand its scope into our own time – and, of course, this must be held an unquestionable good. We started to empathise with the less fortunate, avoid patriarchal bigotry and now insist on a tolerance of the 'others' increasingly in our midst (or at least we started to do this more than we had previously). Above all, we have become concerned at giving offence – even, as we have seen, to the point of suggesting that doing so might be an actionable tort.[25] Be that as it may, against the need for free communications, what are these 'harms'?

Even though the changing attitude towards the possibility of emotional damage has influenced legal processes, albeit minimally, these outcomes (including causing offense) remain unactionable. Given the crucial importance of free expression, it cannot be the case that the production of news ought to be constrained by a sensitivity to the possible emotional responses of news consumers. This has to be a matter for them as autonomous individuals in a (comparatively) free society, and for the journalist's own moral sensibility. Purveying fake news is also therefore a matter of conscience for the press, if fakery of itself cannot be demonstrated to be recognisably damaging. Revealing lying actors, who wanted to distort understanding and cause damaging results, is not the same as proving that they were effective in their intentions. As Ben Jonson had it, readers can 'ha' their pleasure in believing lies that are made for them' and no harm done.[26]

For journalists travelling the two-way street, interacting directly with those on whom they are reporting, the ethical challenge to do no harm is far clearer, because it involves what the philosopher Emmanuel Levinas insists is the essential ethical moment – the encounter between the self and another person – *la rapport de face à face*.[27] The news consumer, however, is not quite the same as Levinas's *l'autre* – the other. They are a more distant third person, *la troisième personage*, connected by the one-way street, and to whom therefore a lesser ethical duty of care is owed. There is no face-to-face element.

When it comes to *l'autre* – the subjects directly involved – the difficulties around the harm principle dissolve in the sense that both causation and impact are far clearer and more long-lived. Being in the news can easily be a life-impacting event and for the journalists putting people there clear ethical standards are required. But, again, situations are not always clear cut. The influence is a two-way street and *l'autre* can put themselves potentially in harm's way, deliberately confusing the journalist's duty of care. Take celebrity, a phenomenon symbiotically linked to the functions of the press.

In February, 1599, the clown Will Kempe, a partner – a 'sharer' – in the Globe Theatre left the company (possibly because he spoke 'more than is set down', Shakespeare's complaint about comic actors in *Hamlet*).[28] Kempe set off to secure his future with a media stunt. He danced all the way from London to Norwich and chronicled his adventures in a news-book: *Kemps nine dais vvonder ... written by himselfe to fatiesfie his friends* but published to be sold in a shop 'at the weſt doore of Saint Paules Church'.[29] Four centuries later appearance in a reality TV-show or a carefully orchestrated social media presence as an 'influencer' has exactly the same effect. It does not so much report a life as become it.

Without question, it is not terribly unusual for appearing in the press, even without having such ambitions for celebrity, to have unanticipated life-changing consequences. The Harm Principle clearly applies. There is no uncertainty about the causation of the change nor of the nature of it. The only caveat is that, on occasion, the intention is to harm. The degree to which this is ethically justified depends on the nature of the person being exposed: unmasking criminals or uncovering corruption, for instance, qualify the Harm Principle. Examples are easy to come by:

- In 1997, London police's failure to bring the racist killers of a young person of colour, Stephen Lawrence, to justice occasioned (it must be said, against the grain of the paper's usual prejudices), the headline '**MURDERERS**' and the following strap over pictures of the five suspects: '**The Mail Accuses These Men of Killing. If we are wrong let them sue us**'[30] [emphasis in the original].
- In 2002, Spotlight, the investigative team at *The Boston Globe*, revealed: '**Church allowed abuse by priest for years**', opening a can of worms which eventually infected the Papacy itself[31] [emphasis in the original].

However, the New Journalism of the 19th century introduced techniques of press intrusion which greatly increased the possibility of ethical transgressions. The press borrowed the legal concept of public interest to justify, for example, going through private garbage or, later, hacking phones, but it did not effectively argue away the clear ethical failings that are prima facie involved in so doing. It reached for the legal concept of a public interest but acted on it as meaning nothing more than what interested the public. And glib amorality has flourished, fueled by and fuelling sensationalism. 'If it bleeds it leads' is, supposedly, a guiding light for the tabloid press, and it speaks to a journalism neglecting its ethical responsibilities.

Rupert Murdoch's *News of the World*, a paper which from its foundation in 1843 had always been most obedient to the other populist journalistic injunction that 'sex sells', made much of its early 21st news-gathering synonymous with illegal phone-hacking. The most egregious example of the activity – which was eventually to cost Murdoch millions in compensation, prison sentences for journalist and private-eye perpetrators, and the closure of the title (although many other papers were also at it) – involved hacking and tampering with the mobile of a murdered child in 2002. It was done to suggest, for the sake of a headline, that she was alive days after her killing.[32] But the element of fakery renders this one example exceptional.

For the most part, the UK hacking scandal of the century's first decade involved the illegal acquisition of actual data, which is (or can be) a species of press misbehavior, but not of fake news. The failure to follow ethical procedures when on the one-way street reflected not mendacity, but rather a disregard of the fundamental ethical injunction and the advisories of professional bodies regulating behavior. The undercutting of the press's better practices on the two-way street – which can be convincingly claimed as a norm for most (mainstream, comparatively sober) titles and outlets – did more than sap its ability to defend itself in the coming fakery storm. It also highlighted that the protocols of philosophy, even when in some respects they amount to no more than the ethical principles conventionally called common decency, are no more essential to journalism-as-practiced than are those of science or law.

And this, then, is the bottom line. Our argument is that journalism has moved over the last century. Instead of a claim of truth as a species of brand – a slogan – it morphed so that, now glossed as objectivity, it has increasingly been claimed as the essence of the project and the measure of the press's quality. Objective journalism is (still), simply, taken as good. But the claim when so glossed gives hostages to fortune as we have tried to highlight in this section of the book, with a comparison of practices of science, law, and philosophy on the one hand, and on the other those of the press.

In a context where much beglamoured and panicked attention is paid to the press's supposed influences (while its actual critical importance as a political player is taken more or less as a given) these hostages become ever more debilitating. They are the taproot of fakery's main source of nourishment. And it is on this basis that we object to 'objective journalism'.

There is another way.

Notes

1 Schudson, Michael (1978). *Discovering the News: A Social History of American Newspapers.* New York, Basic, p. 8.

2 Katz, Elihu & Paul Lazarsfeld (1955). *Personal Influence*. New York: The Free Press.
3 Klapper, Joseph (1960). *The Effects of Communications*. New York: The Free Press.
4 Katz, Elihu, Jay G. Blumler, & Michael Gurevitch (1973–1974). 'Uses and gratifications research', *Public Opinion Quartely*, 4, ser. 37, pp. 509–523.
5 Gerbner, George *et al.* (1986). 'Living with television: The dynamics of the cultivation process' in *Perspectives on Media Effects* (Jennings Bryant & Dorf Zillman, eds.). Hillsdale, NJ: Lawrence, pp. 12–40.
6 Livingstone, Sonia (1996). 'On the continuing problems of media effects research' in *Mass Media and Society* (J. Curran & Michael Gurevitch, eds.). London: Edward Arnold. http://eprints.lse.ac.uk/21503/1/On_the_continuing_problems_of_media_effects_research(LSERO).pdf [accessed 19 November 2014].
7 Anon (OFCOM) (2017). 'Children and parents: Media use and attitudes report', 29 November, p. 122.
8 The effect named for the eponymous hero of Johann Wolfgang von Goethe's 1774 novel, *Der Leiden der jungen Werthers / The Sorrow of Young Werther*, who kills himself for unrequited love.
9 Anon (Samaritans) (n/d). *Samaritans Media Guidelines*. www.samaritans.org/about-samaritans/media-guidelines/Aon [accessed 6 November 2019].
10 Etzersdorfer, Elmar & Sonneck Gernot (1998) 'Preventing suicide by mass media reporting: The Viennese experience 1980–1986', *Archives of Suicide Research*, 4, pp. 67–74.
11 Pfefferbaum, Betty., Pascal Nitiema & Elana Newman (2019). 'Is viewing mass trauma television coverage associated with trauma reactions in adults and youth? A meta-analytic review', *Journal of Traumatic Stress*, 32:2, pp. 175–185; Tappenden, Peter (2019). 'Distress from the screen: The impact of the media on PTSD Symptoms', *Stress Points*, November. https://onlinelibrary.wiley.com/journal/15736598 [accessed 6 November 2019].
12 Ahern, Jennifer *et al.* (2002). 'Television images and psychological symptoms after the September 11 terrorist attacks', *Psychiatry Interpersonal & Biological Processes*, 65:4, pp. 289–300.
13 Ben-Zhur, Hasida., Sharon Gil & Yinon Shamshins (2012). 'The relationship between exposure to terror through the media, coping strategies and resources, and distress and secondary traumatization', *International Journal of Stress Management*, 19:2, pp. 132–150.
14 Goodwin, Robin *et al.* (2013). 'In the eye of the storm or the bullseye of the media: Social media during Hurricane Sandy as a predictor of post-traumatic stress', *Journal of Psychiatric Research*, 47, pp. 1099–1100.
15 Anon (WHO) (2019). *Measles and Rubella Survellience Data*. www.who.int/immunization/monitoring_surveillance/burden/vpd/surveillance_type/active/measles_monthlydata/en/index1.html [accessed 8 December 2019].
16 Boseley, Sarah (2019). 'The rising toll of measles: Nearly 10m cases and 142,000 deaths', *The Guardian*, 6 December, p. 1.
17 Noar, Seth (2006). 'A 10-year retrospective of research in health mass media campaigns: Where do we go from here?', *Journal of Health Communications*, 11:1, pp. 21–42; Leavy, Justine, Fiona Bull, Michael Rosenberg & Adrian Bauman (2011). 'Physical activity mass media campaigns and their evaluation: A systematic review of the literature 2003–2010', *Health Education Research*, 26:6, December; Foerster, Susan & Gregson Hudes (1994). *California Dietary Practices Survey*. Sacramento, CA: Californian Department of Health Services and California Public Health Foundation.
18 Guttman, A (2019). 'Global advertising spending from 2010 to 2019, *Statistica*, 9 August. www.statista.com/statistics/236943/global-advertising-spending/ [accessed 7 December 2019].
19 McQuail, Denis (1977). 'The influence and effects of mass media' in *Mass Communication and Society* (James Curran *et al*, eds.). London: Edward Arnold, p. 76; cf. Nash, Kate &

John Corner (2016), 'Strategic impact documentary: Contexts of production and social intervention', *European Journal of Communication*, 31:3, pp. 227–242.
20 Ignatidou, Sophia (2019). *EU–US Cooperation on Tackling Disinformation*. London: Chatham House, p. 39.
21 Kalla, Joshua & David Brookman (2018). 'The minimal pesuasive effects of campaign contact in general elections: Evidence from 49 field experiments', *American Political Science Review*, 112, pp. 148–166.
22 Philo, Greg (1990). *Seeing and Believing: The Influence of Television*. London: Routledge, p. 5.
23 Philo, Greg (1990). *Seeing and Believing: The Influence of Television*. London: Routledge.
24 Lamb, Jonathon (2009). *The Evolution of Sympathy in the Long Eighteenth Century*. London: Pickering and Chatto.
25 Feinberg, Joel (1983/1985). *Harm to Others* (vol 1)/ *Offense to Others* (vol 2): *The Moral Limits of the Criminal Law*. New York: Oxford University Press.
26 Jonson, Ben (1625). *The Staple of News*: Act V.
27 Levinas, Emmanuel (1981): 141,166; (1998): 174,195–6; Levinas, Emmanuel (1969). *Totality and Infinity: An Essay on Exteriority* (Alphonso Lingis, trans.). Pittsburgh, PA: Duquesne University Press, p. 150.
28 Shakespeare, William (1609). *Hamlet* Act III, Scene II.
29 Kemp, William (1600). *Kemps nine dais vvonder*. London: Nicholas Ling.
30 (1997). 'Murderers', *The Daily Mail*, 14 February, p. 1.
31 (2002). 'Church allowed abuse by priest for years'. *Boston Sunday Globe*, 6 January, p. 1.
32 Leigh, David (2012). 'Police files expose *NOW interference* and harassment in the Milly Dowler case', *The Guardian*, 24 January.

The fourth estate

13

SHOUTING FIRE ON A CROWDED WEBSITE

> 'Don't confuse me with the facts. I've got a closed mind'
> *Earl Landgrebe (1916–1986)*
> *Republican congressperson*

So, finally, fake news:

Veles is a city in the Republic of North Macedonia with a population of around 44,000, and if we are going to talk about fake news and the internet, it's a surprisingly good place to start. During the run-up to the 2016 US elections, a significant amount of popular fake news content, mostly pro-Trump, was traced to apolitical operators in Veles, posting this particular type of clickbait in order to gain ad revenue via online advertising services run through the likes of Facebook and Google.[1] In a fairly economically depressed town in Eastern Europe, the news that there was significant money to be made from duping gullible Americans is said to have spread like wildfire among young people with time and digital literacy, but relatively limited employment opportunities. It was claimed, though difficult to verify, that some fake news merchants were earning thousands of euros a day in a city where the average salary was around €350 a month. An anonymous teenager who claimed to have spent a month as a professional fake news merchant, albeit small-time, responded to a BBC reporter's question about feeling any guilt over perhaps unfairly influencing a foreign election by laughing and saying: 'Teenagers in our city don't care how Americans vote. They are only satisfied that they make money and can buy expensive clothes and drinks!'[2]

We might also talk about political consultancy Cambridge Analytica, who, via Facebook, used an app and a survey which was ostensibly 'for academic purposes', to harvest the personal data of millions of Facebook users (those who took the survey, and all those in their Facebook networks) in order to target political advertising, and thereby allegedly win elections for Ted Cruz and Donald Trump, and tip the Brexit referendum in the UK in favour of the Leave campaign. The scandal knocked $100 billion off the value of Facebook and forced Mark Zuckerberg to testify before the US Congress.[3]

Political activist Micah Sifry suggests that it is far too easy to read far too much into these scandals, and the many others like them, past, present, and yet to come. The short version of why the impact of such things should not be overestimated is the fact that there's no proof, or even significant evidence, that this stuff actually works:

> If the weaponization of misinformation was such a powerful tool for changing hearts and minds, why did the left win recent elections in Mexico and Istanbul? Why did Democrats retake the House in 2018? We aren't losing the war for the future because of some new media masterminds. If we're losing, it's because our message – and messengers – aren't connecting.[4]

It is as Chatham House reported: 'Regrettably, clear and verifiable links between cause and effect are still lacking'. The improper influencing of elections via new technology is an example of what Stanley Cohen classically described as a 'moral panic'.

A moral panic occurs when '[a] condition, episode, person or group of persons emerges to become defined as a threat to societal values and interests [and] its nature is presented in a stylized and stereotypical fashion by the mass media'.[5] The point of Cohen's construction of the concept is that the threat is more a creation of the media (albeit generally with some modicum of truth and/or motivating incident at its heart, as is the case here) than it is a response to actual jeopardy. In this instance, there is evidence to suggest the impact of the media on voting patterns is in any case overstated. For example, Joshua Kalla and David Broockman, in an article with the charmingly straightforward title 'The Minimal Persuasive Effects of Campaign Contact in General Elections: Evidence from 49 Field Experiments', presented the findings of a meta-analysis of 40 existing field experiments, plus the results of nine new field experiments of their own, finding an average effect of zero in both cases. While they do not conclude that political mass-persuasion is impossible, they do go so far as to say that:

> The circumstances in which citizens' political choices appear manipulable appear to be exceedingly rare in the elections that matter most ... our consistent finding of null effects suggests that non-experimental studies of campaign communication or studies conducted outside of active campaign contexts that claim to find large campaign effects in general elections should be viewed with healthy skepticism.[6]

While, of course, a victim of media manipulation may be unaware, or even embarrassed to have been duped, it is still perhaps worth pondering the fact that nobody seems to be able to locate users claiming to have been successfully politically manipulated via online social media, any more than there were people admitting to having panicked at the imminent arrival of fictional Martian invaders. In both instances, as is so often the case with such things, this is a terrifying effect that the media has on somebody else (presumably not as sophisticated and intelligent as we are). But, does any intelligent person really believe that there are large numbers of people out there making their way to polling booths and casting their votes on the basis of clickbait? That is to say, intelligent persons other than journalists. Rather like naïf positivist media sociologists, the press seem to need to believe in the impact of new media – otherwise how can it argue for its own impact?

It was *The* [London] *Observer* which primarily tore down, during a yearlong investigation, Cambridge Analytica's 'vizards and vailes and disguises' and illuminated Facebook's dubious ways with the data it holds on us. The headlines kept coming:

- **Revealed: 50 million Facebook profiles harvested for Cambridge Analytica in major data breach**
- **Cambridge Analytica boasts of dirty tricks to swing elections**
- **Cambridge Analytica: links to Moscow oil firm and St Petersburg university**
- **Facebook's week of shame: the Cambridge Analytica fallout**
- **Investigators complete seven-hour Cambridge Analytica HQ search**[7]

The lead journalist involved in this exemplary investigative exercise, Carole Cadwalladr, quite properly won nine press prizes and a Pulitzer nomination for the diligence and significance of her work. And there can be no question of its value as compelling evidence of the misuses of the internet's 'panopticon' affordances and the difficulties of effectively policing political campaign spending rules and the like. But of direct evidence of any actual corruption at the ballot there was nothing.

It is vital to remember, here, that the media has never been convincingly demonstrated to have direct effects on its audience, with a uniform input causing similar actions in a mass of viewers/readers. It is arguably somewhat strange that this even needs saying but the simple fact is that there is no conclusive proof that Macedonian clickbait-merchants, or British big-data hustlers, or, for that matter, much-feared Russian troll-farms, can actually impact an election, let alone swing one. (Perhaps, just perhaps, people targeted by lies about Hillary Clinton, for example, ready to click on some wild story about her wanting to confiscate all guns, or ritualistically murder children in a pizza-place, or whatever, were probably already going to vote for Trump?) Videogames do not cause people to be violent, radio dramatisations of sci-fi classics don't cause mass-panics, social media platforms do not catalyse otherwise dormant revolutions, and social media manipulations, as far as we know, do not swing elections.

As Marshall McLuhan, commenting on a 1950s media panic about violent comics, pointed out, even '[t]he dimmest-witted convict learned to moan, "it wuz comic books done this to me"'.[8]

When thinking about the fake news panic, it is essential not to overemphasise the role the net plays, of course. Fake news, as we have been insisting, isn't new. Not its existence, not its nature, not its features, not its impact, not its supposed power. There are arguments to be made that the ways in which it is created, and the ways in which it spreads, have been changed by the internet, just as they were changed by the printing press, photography, radio, television, etc., but again this is not the same as a fundamental change. The internet didn't create fake news, and the internet can't fix it. Which is not to say that attention should not be paid to how the internet is involved in the problem, but rather that it is vital that we do not scapegoat the internet, and/or the affordances of Web 2.0, as the sole cause of present ills. This line of reasoning can lead us to giving up, since we mistakenly assume the internet to be impervious to regulation or reform, or it can have us clamouring for radical changes to the internet in order to solve this 'crisis' (though they will do no such thing). Any position built on the misconception that this is essentially a problem with the internet will, by definition, never get to grips with the heart of the matter.

But if the rise of Web 2.0 is simply not, in and of itself, that significant, what is? Let us begin with the assertion that human beings are not rational, or more precisely, we are not as rational as we like to think that we are. As is hopefully clear by this point, the problems we are discussing are not solely caused by deliberate manipulation and mendacity – ignorance, stupidity, and various kinds of irrationality all have their roles to play as well. When it comes to considering how people end up believing that all evidence that the Earth isn't flat has been faked, or that chemtrails are doing whatever it is people are worried that chemtrails are doing, it is important to remember Hanlon's Razor – 'Never attribute to malice that which is adequately explained by stupidity'.

It is also important to remember that what might uncharitably be called 'stupidity' takes on many forms, and nobody's mind is free of all of them. Whether it's absurd slippery slopes (e.g. 'If you legalise gay marriage, next you'll legalise incestuous polygamy with minors'), the just-world fallacy (e.g. 'Education being underfunded doesn't matter – I know all it takes to succeed is hard work, because that's what worked for me'), appeals to ignorance (e.g. 'If they don't know what causes autism, how can they be so sure it isn't vaccines?'), the bandwagon effect (e.g. 'Everybody knows that playing videogames is bad for kids'), or any number of other types of failure of reasoning, in a very meaningful sense, we are all stupid about something. One aspect of this which is particularly relevant to the phenomenon under discussion is the question of how such thinking can relate to the popularity of that peculiar category of fake news, known as the conspiracy theory.

For example, let's consider one of the many theories peddled by the 9/11 'truther' community. 7 World Trade Center, a building next to the Twin Towers, collapsed hours after the towers fell on 9/11, but its proximity to a literally earth-shaking event, and its bombardment with fire-igniting debris, are not acknowledged at all by some fake news addicts as the causes of its collapse. For them, it is more likely (by which we mean more intellectually satisfying) to insist, that the building was destroyed by a bomb. After all, these people know what controlled demolitions look like and to them this looked very much like a controlled demolition.[9]

Who, then, planted the bomb(s)? Well – take your pick: the Israelis, the US military, President Bush …. And, whoever planted them, since that building was bombed, it follows that the Towers' collapse cannot have been because jet liners unexpectedly ploughed into them either. So they too were surely demolished by bombs. The planes were just theatre. Ergo, thinking things through, who detonated these bombs? The Israelis, the US military, President Bush …. (Don't forget that all the Jews who worked in the World Trade Center were warned not to go to work on 9/11!) Al Qaeda? Don't be ridiculous. 'Wake up, sheeple!'

Here, people are taking details of a complex event, confusing their own 'common sense' (at best, and their bigotries at worst) for expertise, and extrapolating wildly, while, via the internet, reinforcing each other's nonsensical ideas. It is easy to sneer, but it is important to remember that, as we asserted above, we are all of us guilty of such illogical thought processes, to some extent, some of the time. Coincidence becomes a rich source of evidence of what must really be going on. Sticking with considering people's ideas about 9/11, there are many more examples. For some, the fact of unusual trading in American Airlines and United Airlines stocks in the days before 9/11 is, obviously, clear evidence of forewarning of the attack, which in turn substantiates the bomb theory (or other 'inside job' theories, if the bombs aren't your poison, so to speak).[10] After all, these were the two airlines involved, so those in the know had the opportunity to make a killing (as it were). Triangulated (that is, actual) evidence reveals that one investor moving from United Airlines to American Airlines, and an investors' newsletter recommending the switch to others, account for the coincidence.[11] But for the alt-fact consumer, correlation, or even coincidence, can often look too much like causation to be distinguishable from it. People anyway don't tend to be very willing to accept information that contradicts their opinions, their worldviews, or their 'common sense'.

This, incidentally, is not a cognitive phenomenon that we as a species just figured out recently and now commonly refer to as confirmation bias. Four centuries ago, Francis Bacon suggested that:

> The human understanding when it has once adopted an opinion (either as being the received opinion or as being agreeable to itself) draws all things else to support and agree with it. And though there be a greater number and weight of instances to be found on the other side, yet these it either neglects and despises, or else by some distinction sets aside and rejects, in order that by this great and pernicious predetermination the authority of its former conclusions may remain inviolate.[12]

Many of Bacon's ideas have not withstood the test of time very well, but modern psychology, neuroscience, and the political/social sciences, more or less agree that in this instance he was bang on the money.

In terms of the effect of this phenomenon on conspiracy theorists, as well as on any and all other consumers of news media, there is more going on here than just closed-mindedness and/or rejecting news stories you don't like. When coincidence confirms prejudice, it readily becomes causation – what is insignificant to a doubter will be recognised as 'the smoking gun' by anybody who was, consciously or unconsciously, already looking for one. Spurious correlation is not just an alt-facts business, and it is also not the only type of illogical reasoning relevant to this discussion.

While conspiracy theorists and other species of subscribers to sets of alternative facts, whatever their nature, may seem to be different in kind from 'the rest of us', this is illusory. Clinging to every anomaly and/or coincidence in order to formulate and support a supposedly superior alternative to the 'official story' is only one aspect, one type of example, of how a person 'neglects and despises, or else by some distinction sets aside and rejects'[13] a pile of evidence which does not support their views – a type of error we all make in some form or another, from time to time. Anytime we see a headline and think some form of 'That can't be right', from a certain perspective we are not so different from more militant forms of 'truthers'. Charging news coverage with in fact being a 'cover-up' is, after all, ultimately just an extreme form of calling the news 'biased'. And so, just as a central question about conspiracy theories as a category is that of how people come to believe in them, obviously a central question of press bias, considered from the readers' side of things, is that of how people look at news coverage and perceive bias.

Cornelia Mothes' work relating to confirmation bias and objective journalism in Germany, was an attempt, using the usual protocols of media sociology, to reconcile the suggestion that both journalists and other citizens valued objectivity in their news content, with research which seems to suggest that both groups actually favour content which agrees with their own beliefs and opinions. She asked two sample groups – one of more than 400 journalists and one of more than 400 non-journalists – all with opinions, for or against, about the extension of the life of German nuclear power plants (a highly controversial issue in Germany at the time).

Mothes exposed them to a short 'expert statement' which either supported or decried the practice (same length, each with three arguments one way, undercut by six arguments the other way), and asked her test subjects, in effect, to gauge both the text's factuality (facts as opposed to opinion, i.e. a key component of objectivity) and its information value. To oversimplify, a lot, the findings indicated that people found objectivity to increase information value, fairly unsurprisingly … but the findings also indicated that people would tend to consider an article which agreed with their preconceptions to be more objective than one that did not. And this was true both for the German journalists and for the ordinary German citizens. In other words, this study suggested that both journalists and non-journalists valued arguments presented to them more highly if they found them to be objective …

AND considered them to be more objective if they told them what they wanted to hear:

> By believing that messages supporting one's own worldviews were more objective than opinion-challenging information, objectivity becomes a function of subjective beliefs.[14]

Even when (or if …) we do care about the journalism we see being objective, the difference between what we consider to be objective journalism and what we consider to be not objective journalism is, unfortunately, not entirely unlike, say, the difference between our ideas of 'good music' and 'bad music', in the sense that we confuse what we like with what is 'good', and what we don't like with what is 'bad'. This instinct can be strong in us even when it regards something we know to be in some sense a matter of taste – how much stronger when, as is often the case with the news, it is about something we consider to be tied directly to right and wrong.

The problem here does not just lie with our journalism. The imperfections in our minds' logical, rational reasoning are the larger and more fundamental problem. Even if every reporter woke up every morning desperate to be honest and unbiased and objective (and there's reason to believe that a lot more of them do that than you might think) it wouldn't get us away from the fundamental problems of the bias, and the subjectivity, of reception. They really are fundamental, inescapable aspects of how human beings think. Even if Galbert were a sacred example – the patron saint of good reporting – universally revered and emulated, we would still have found our way to the mess we're currently in, not least because, as Mothes points out:

> If journalists and citizens equally fail to recognize that opinion-challenging arguments are as vital as attitude-reinforcing arguments for ensuring an objective approach to reality, public discourse in contemporary high-choice media environments may become increasingly susceptible to severe misperceptions about political reality and an onward political polarization of social groups.[15]

She notes also that this is, of course, 'troubling for democracy'.

This is the core of how media consumers can find themselves in the so-called 'echo chambers' which reinforce their personal beliefs, and edit out anything that might challenge the foundations of how they see the world. The algorithms of online social media, showing you what you'll want to see and never exposing you to what you won't want to see, are simply not of the essence. Your brain will do a pretty good job with or without Facebook, in assessing 'objectivity' and 'bias' and simple questions like, 'Is this worth reading or looking at?' and 'Do I want to give this piece of news-reporting my attention, and my trust?' Perhaps, and this idea may be shocking to some, in some respects it doesn't actually make much difference if we aren't shown different perspectives we would in any case have more or less dismissed out of hand, because we have already made up our minds. As Nixon partisan, Congressperson Earl Landgrebe, famously said the day before his man resigned in disgrace: 'Don't confuse me with the facts. I've got a closed mind'.[16] It was, is, and ever shall be, perfectly possible pre-emptively to reject alternative points of view, without any help from online social media.

And speaking of such made-up minds, a central issue, here and elsewhere within the effort to understand fake news, is what we usually call partisan opinions, and of course the partisans who adhere to them. On any given issue, as well as in more general questions of 'camps' of broader political opinion, partisans matter, often above and beyond the weight of their numbers, in that:

> Their viewpoints can powerfully influence public opinion and public policy; They are the ones who campaign and lobby, who demonstrate, parade, and picket, who promote their viewpoints in countless ways, and when they feel marginalized or alienated, may resort to extreme or antisocial actions.[17]

In the public sphere, the people who are the most invested in their opinions, and in their certainty regarding them, are the ones who make the most noise. They are the ones who speak, and they are the ones who act. We wouldn't go so far as to say unequivocally that they are the ones who affect (or prevent) change, but fairly straightforwardly an opinion that gets you to write or call your elected representatives, to sign petitions, or even to take to the street in protest, is an opinion that will have more effect on the world than an opinion which you hold in private and don't even think about, let alone talk about, that much. And partisans have consistently been found to perceive bias against their causes in mainstream media coverage of the issues which are dear to their hearts As Kathleen Schmitt, Albert Gunther and Janice Liebhart point out, there are three main theoretical explanations as to how this perception of bias may operate at a cognitive level.[18] Firstly, there is the idea that a partisan, seeing a balanced news report on their issue, will pay more attention to the parts of the report which contradict or undercut their beliefs, thinking about them more and recalling them more prominently. This theory is termed 'selective recall'. Secondly, a partisan may view more of the content of such a report as hostile to their views, in that neutral and/or ambiguous content will still be perceived as not supporting 'the truth'. This is called 'selective categorisation'. And thirdly, perhaps a partisan will view the inclusion of any opinions or approaches to the issue other than their own not as a matter of balance, but as biased, since opposing viewpoints are not considered valid or worthwhile. This idea is given the shorthand 'different standards'.

It seems probable that all of these things happen some of the time, with some people. It is not necessary here to wade too much farther into the murky waters of research into the cognitive processing of information, but it is important to note that even when a journalist writes objective journalism (inasmuch as that is possible – a point we do not concede), that does not mean that it will be what the readers encounter when they read it. The positivist Uses and Gratifications school of media theory posits that people select media texts to suit their purposes, and turn them to whatever use they intend, from escapism to entertainment to facilitating social integration. Dennis McQuail, Jay Bulmer, Elihu Katz and their colleagues, originators of the theory,[19] argued that one of these purposes was education/information, but it is worth noting that, as anybody who has ever watched somebody yell at a news broadcast can attest, to say that 'People consume the news to get information' is a considerable oversimplification. There is a surprisingly wide gulf between the desire to be informed and the desire to *feel* informed, particularly when either or both are subordinated to the desire to know that you're right.

Fake news is tailor-made for the strange ways in which people process the news. Irrational subjectivity and the problems represented by conspiracy theories, and by political polarisation and partisanship, are essential to its diffusion, credibility, and popularity. How then does it work? To attempt to answer that, we will consider a by-now classic example: 'Pizzagate'.

As far as we can tell, Pizzagate began as a coincidence that somebody made a joke about. On the dark web, 'cheese pizza' is allegedly used as a code-phrase for child pornography, because it is an innocuous term with the same acronym, 'CP'. Whether or not paedophiles actually use this phrase is not, however, directly relevant here. What is of concern is how in the somewhat chaotic media/public response to a scandal surrounding presidential candidate Hillary Clinton's having used a private e-mail server while Secretary of State, this belief led to some truly bizarre results, including, eventually, a man entering a popular pizza-place called Comet Ping Pong ('CP' again), armed with an AR-15 and intent on discovering the secret dungeon where, he believed, the Satanic child abuse was happening. When the gunman was sentenced to four years in prison, James Alefantis, owner of the establishment, said that he hoped that:

> one day in a more truthful world, every single one of us will remember this day as an aberration, a symptom of a time of sickness when some parts of our world went mad, when news was fake and lies were seen as real, and our social fabric frayed.[20]

The authors share this hope, but would advise Mr. Alefantis not to hold his breath.

What happened, in a nutshell, is that the world got a chance to have a look at some e-mails to and from Hillary Clinton, as well as to and from her campaign chairman, John Podesta. Suffice to say, that some e-mails talked about events which took place at Comet Ping Pong. It was not uncommon for it to be used as a venue for some political and quasi-political events. There was no mention of child abuse or Satanic rituals, however there was, understandably, some mention of pizza. It is not clear when the first connection was made between the pizza being mentioned in the e-mails, and the possible dark web meaning of cheese pizza, nor is it clear who made it, or whether they were, as seems likely, making a joke. But if it was a joke, it was a joke that very quickly got out of hand. On 30 October, two days after the then FBI Director James Comey informed Congress that he was reopening the investigation into Clinton's e-mail server, somebody on Twitter (using the handle @DavidGoldbergNY, which of course tells us nothing) referred to rumours that the new e-mails found on former Congressman Anthony Weiner's computer, which had prompted Comey's actions, pointed to a paedophile ring with Hillary Clinton 'at the center'.[21] This was retweeted more than 6,000 times, which, granted, isn't all that much activity in terms of the modern internet, but things were just getting started. These baseless rumours picked up steam as they migrated across social media, including 4chan and Reddit.

And then along came Alex Jones, of *InfoWars*. If you are unfamiliar with his work, it is difficult, or at least complicated, to describe exactly what Alex Jones says and does. He is, by profession, a controversial commentator, who paints himself as a purveyor of truths kept hidden by the mainstream media, and opinions excluded from mainstream politics. *The Washington Post* coverage which we have been citing above refers to his website as 'far-right', but this seems somewhat inaccurate, in a sense. The far-right and Alex Jones share many evil beliefs, but in many ways Alex Jones far outpaces the typical fascist in sheer insanity. Alex Jones has claimed that Bill Gates is part of a eugenicist conspiracy, that the US government controls the weather and causes natural disasters, and that 9/11 and the Boston Marathon bombing were inside jobs, while the mass-shooting at Sandy Hook Elementary School was a hoax.[22] He is a master of getting attention (and money) out of truly crazy conspiracy theories, and on this occasion he repeatedly accused Clinton and Podesta of involvement in the paedophile ring and Satanic rituals which were, clearly, the truth that the powers that be were struggling to hide from the public. In a YouTube video he posted early in November, viewed hundreds of thousands of times, he said:

> When I think about all the children Hillary Clinton has personally murdered and chopped up and raped, I have zero fear standing up against her. Yeah, you heard me right. Hillary Clinton has personally murdered children.[23]

Jones called on his audience to investigate for themselves, and one man did so with a gun. A lot more happened, and a lot more wild conspiracies were circulated (apparently there were hidden code-words, and Satanic symbols on the pizza place's sign, or something …), but this brief account should give you a rough idea of what Pizzagate was.

But for all this represents the stupidity (and indeed evil) that would seem to be part of the price of the untrammeled 21st century notion of 'free speech', it perhaps also illustrates our contention as to the persistence, if not inevitability, of such malfeasance, when placed in the context of another 'news' report with an unsettling degree of similarity with the strange tale of Pizzagate. This story, however, became a popular conspiracy theory and news phenomenon slightly under 900 years earlier than the spread of the bizarre notion that Hillary Clinton and other Democrats were ritually raping, torturing, and murdering children in secret dungeons underneath a popular pizza parlour, about three and a half centuries before *Dracule Wajda* was printed. In examining the nature of fake news, there is value in comparing the story of Pizzagate with the story of the murder of William of Norwich, more commonly referred to, particularly by medievalists (and students of the history of antisemitism), as the Blood Libel.

A young boy was found, murdered, in a wood, and a monk named Thomas of Monmouth waged a PR campaign to convince people that the boy had been ritually slaughtered by a secret international cabal of Jews who, every year, selected a country in which to murder a Christian child via torture and crucifixion, to celebrate Passover.[24] This was not the origin of the perennial myth that Jews secretly murder children, but it did firmly fix the idea, and set its parameters, in the western mind, from which it has never been entirely dislodged. Even today, the Blood Libel itself is still occasionally referenced as fact, not unlike the utterly discredited *Protocols of the Elders of Zion*, which supposedly outlines the secret Jewish plan for world domination. To give a recent example, the Blood Libel was referenced in a story in the Egyptian newspaper *At Taliya News* in the spring of 2014.[25] Specifically, the article alleged that a classified but leaked CIA report confirmed that Jews use the blood of their (or, really, 'our' – both the authors of this book are Jewish) murder victims in the baking of matzot for Passover.[26]

Other people have noticed the unsettling similarities between the Blood Libel and Pizzagate. David Perry's article in *The Pacific Standard* (cited above), referred to Pizzagate as 'the new Blood Libel'. But, despite discernible and fascinating thematic and mythical links to that reiterated accusation, we are not primarily concerned here with antisemitism and its seemingly endlessly repeating patterns. The monstrous 'other', lurking amongst us, usually made up of members of some group we already mistrust, will perhaps always be a good way to grab people's attention and manipulate their emotions, particularly if you throw in some gory details and make the victim(s) as innocent and sympathetic as possible. This is true whether you want their political support, or you just want to sell them a story. (Thomas of Monmouth and Alex Jones both had their own ways of profiting from their fear-mongering, of course.)

This particular type of fake news is perhaps as old as recorded history, if not older. It is not difficult to imagine some member of a hunter-gatherer tribe of early humans, yet to develop written language, already reinforcing his leadership by telling tales of the atrocities and abominations that were regularly committed by the strange and terrifying people of a different, neighbouring tribe. As Benedict Anderson forcefully establishes, fear of outsiders is one of the simplest psychological/social forces through which to unify, and energise, a group of people. It would seem that communities (e.g. nations) seem to need to identify not just neighbouring nations, but also the 'other' within, if they are to know themselves.[27]

Leaving Jews and elites and, in general, the targets of both tales out of this discussion for a moment, what do we notice here? Well, both stories involved convincing people that a terrifying secret cabal (of Jews, in the 12th century version, and of politicians in the 21st century) was abducting and murdering innocent children. Both played off existing fears and prejudices. Both caused hysteria. Both were utter nonsense. But both had their political uses for those who chose to tell, retell, publish, broadcast, or otherwise circulate them. To put it simply, there are reasons why medieval terms like 'witch hunt' and 'inquisition' are showing no signs of losing relevance. For all our rhetoric of progress in this area, Monmouth at least had an actual dead child on which to hang his story. The people who spread the story of Pizzagate just had some emails about a pizza place, which happened to mention pizza.

This is, to underline the point once again, not an aspect of sociology, or even of what comes to be called media, which is created by modern communications technology. The internet age may, to some extent, exacerbate the problem (though even this is historically questionable – Europe tortured, burned, and otherwise executed a great many suspected witches, for example, without the need for or influence of Facebook) but it does not significantly alter its underlying shape. People will tell, spread, and believe both questionable interpretations of facts (perhaps 'alternative facts' in its non-legal sense would be the right phrase to use here) and monstrous lies for many reasons and in many circumstances. The notion that it is possible to deal with the problems this causes by, in a sense, cutting off the supply of untruth, as by regulating and reforming and purging journalism until the news is nothing but pure truth, with which, then, all will agree, is in some ways a fantasy even more ridiculous and implausible than the grotesque image of Hillary Clinton murdering children in a secret dungeon.

Facts do not defeat fiction. It would be wonderful if they did, but they don't. Many still believe in Pizzagate, and consider all evidence that it is nonsense to be, perversely, confirmation of the reach of the cover-up. Many still believe that Jews murder children, amongst other victims, as part of the practice of the Jewish faith. Many still believe the moon landings were a hoax, or that the Earth is flat, or that Obama is an Islamist communist who was born in Kenya. If perfect journalism (which, as we've said, we emphatically insist is not in fact possible anyway) were going to be able to fix everything, then surely the journalism we already have would have been good enough to clear up these hoaxes, misunderstandings, and self-serving lies. But it has not. It cannot. That is, quite simply, not how these things work.

Worryingly, this might seem to be an argument in favour of a free-for-all, almost nihilist approach, i.e. why should 'the honest common People' not 'ha' their pleasure [i]n the believing Lyes'.[28] To be clear, this is not, however, the point being made. Just because we can't remove such ideas from public discourses and/or by any other means eliminate them from people's beliefs, does not mean that nothing can be done. People can never be persuaded that the facts are the facts, truly, but that doesn't mean we can't make a better stab at understanding that our opinions are our opinions.

Much has been said about the problems that have supposedly been caused by journalism's blurring of the line between fact and opinion. But we contend that the real roots of our troubles are in fact entangled with our ever having pretended there was a line there in the first place. It might be widely held that our culture has a 'biased journalism' problem, but we have a 'believing there's such a thing as unbiased journalism' problem. Solving this would make our perceived 'fake news all over the internet' problem, if not itself soluble, then at least manageable.

The 'journalism question' (if we can put it like that) in fact has a relatively straightforward solution.

Notes

1 Kirby, Emma Jane (2016). 'City getting rich from fake news', *BBC News,* 6 December. www.bbc.co.uk/news/magazine-38168281 [accessed 26 October 2019].
2 Ibid. Television reports from Veles, it can be noted, contained no visual evidence of wealth. Street interviews revealed scuffed sneakers and worn jeans rather than designer T-shirts and Harley Davidsons.
3 *The New York Times* (2018). 'Mark Zuckerberg's Testimony: Senators question Facebook's commitment to privacy', 10 April. www.nytimes.com/2018/04/10/us/politics/mark-zuckerberg-testimony.htm.
4 Sifry, Micah (2019). 'What Netflix's "Great Hack" gets wrong about Cambridge Analytica' *The Nation,* 6 August. www.thenation.com/article/archive/cambridge-analytica-facebook-hack/ [accessed 31 January 2020].
5 Cohen, Stanley (1972). *Folk Devils and Moral Panics: The creation of the Mods and Rockers.* London: Routledge, p. 10.
6 Kalla, Joshua & David Broockman (2018). 'The minimal persuasive effects of campaign contact in general elections: Evidence from 49 field experiments', *American Political Science Review,* 112:1, p. 14.
7 Cadwalladr, Carroll *et al* (2018/9). 'The Cambridge Analytica file', *The Observer.* www.theguardian.com/news/series/cambridge-analytica-files\ [accessed 26 October 2019].
8 Mcluhan, Marshal (1964). *Understanding Media.* Toronto: McGraw Hill, p. 1648.
9 Gage, Richard, Gregg Roberts & David Chandler (2014) 'Conspiracy theory or hidden truth....' *Architecture News.* www.worldarchitecturenews.com/index.php?fuseaction=wanappln.commentview&comment_id=158 [unavailable].
10 Gage, Richard, Gregg Roberts & David Chandler (2014) 'Conspiracy theory or hidden truth...', *Architecture News.* www.worldarchitecturenews.com/index.php?fuseaction=wanappln.commentview&comment_id=158 [unavailable].
11 McDermott, Hugh (2011). '9/11 terrorists made millions on the stock market', *Independent Australia,* 10 November. https://truthout.org/articles/911-terrorists-made-millions-on-the-stock-market/ [accessed 26 October 2019]; Anon (n/d) *9/11Research* <http://911research.wtc7.net/cache/sept11/londontimes_insidertrading.html> cites (without title, etc.) James Doran writing in *The* [London] *Times* on 'INSIDER TRADING APPARENTLY BASED ON FOREKNOWLEDGE OF 9/11 ATTACKS' [accessed 26 October 2019].
12 Bacon, Francis (1826 [1620]). *Novum Organum (The Works of Francis Bacon),* Vol VIII. London: C&J Rivington *et al,* XLVI.
13 Ibid, §46.
14 Mothes, Cornelia (2017). 'Biased objectivity: An experiment on information preferences of journalists and citizens', *Journalism & Mass Communication Quarterly,* 94:4, p. 1081.
15 Mothes, Cornelia (2017). 'Biased objectivity: An experiment on information preferences of journalists and citizens', *Journalism & Mass Communication Quarterly* 94:4, p. 1081.

16 Pearson, Richard (1986). 'Obituaries', *The Washington Post,* 1 July. www.washingtonpost.com/archive/local/1986/07/01/obituaries/1a979939-0198-4aaf-9945-71e239df1e36/ [accessed 20 November 2019].
17 Schmitt, Kathleen, Albert Gunther & Janice Liebhart (2004). 'Why partisans see mass media as biased', *Communications Research,* 31:6.
18 Schmitt, Kathleen, Albert Gunther & Janice Liebhart, (2004). 'Why Partisans See Mass Media as Biased', *Communications Research,* 31:6, p. 624.
19 Blumler, Jay & Dennis McQuail (1969). *Television in Politics: Its Uses and Influence.* Chicago, IL: University of Chicago Press; Katz, Elihu, Jay Blumler & Michael Gurevitch (1973). 'Uses and gratifications research', *The Public Opinion Quarterly,* 37:4, pp. 509–523.
20 Merlan, Anna (2019). *Republic of Lies: American Conspiracy Theorists and Their Surprising Rise to Power.* New York: Metropolitan Books.
21 Fisher, Mark, John Woodrow Cox & Peter Herman (2016). 'Pizzagate: From rumor, to hashtag, to gunfire in D.C', *The Washington Post,* 6 December. www.washingtonpost.com/local/pizzagate-from-rumor-to-hashtag-to-gunfire-in-dc/2016/12/06/4c7def50-bbd4-11e6-94ac-3d324840106c_story.html [accessed 27 October 2019].
22 Killelea, Alex (2017). 'Alex Jones' Mis-InfoWars: 7 bat-sh*t conspiracy theories' *Rolling Stone,* 21 February. www.rollingstone.com/culture/culture-lists/alex-jones-mis-infowars-7-bat-sht-conspiracy-theories-195468/hillary-clinton-is-running-a-child-sex-ring-out-of-a-d-c-area-pizza-restaurant-118803/ [accessed 27 October 2019].
23 Killelea, Alex (2017) 'Alex Jones' Mis-Infowars: 7 bat-sh*t conspiracy theories' *Rolling Stone,* 21 February. www.rollingstone.com/culture/culture-lists/alex-jones-mis-infowars-7-bat-sht-conspiracy-theories-195468/hillary-clinton-is-running-a-child-sex-ring-out-of-a-d-c-area-pizza-restaurant-118803/ [accessed 27 October 2019].
24 Perry, David (2018). 'The New Blood Libel: The tragic history – and scary future – of fake news and anti-Semitism, *Pacific Standard,* 31 October. https://psmag.com/news/the-new-blood-libel [accessed 27 October 2019].
25 Levitt, Joshua (2014). 'Egyptian newspaper ascribes proof of "Blood Libel" myth to classified CIA report', *The Algemeiner Journal,* 28 April [citing report by Ghada Abd El Moneim in *Al Talyia News* (Egypt)]. www.algemeiner.com/ [accessed 5 February 2020].
26 By way of a side-note, it is perhaps tempting to wonder if in a hundred years, or more, there may still be occasional, vestigial references to pizza restaurants in whatever hysterical fake news tales of terrifying cabals the future successors to Thomas of Monmouth and Alex Jones will be throwing around. The authors hope not, but we have our doubts.
27 Anderson, Benedict (1983). *Imagined Communities. Reflections on the Origin and Spread of Nationalism.* London: Verso.
28 Jonson, Ben (1625). *The Staple of News,* Act 1, Sc 5. http://hollowaypages.com/Jonson1692news.htm [accessed 13 March 2012].

14

SPEAKING TRUTH TO POWER

'[M]ore important far than they all'
Edmund Burke (1729–1797)
Philosopher, statesman, parliamentarian

For George Washington's Revolutionary Army, the days before Christmas, 1776, were dark. As they were being slowly pushed back from Fort Lee, New Jersey, towards Trenton, by the British and their Hessian mercenary allies, with them was a journalist, Tom Paine. Paine was filing reports – legend has it by 'scribbling at night by the light of camp-fires … with wooden pen on a drum head' – back to *The Pennsylvania Journal* in Philadelphia, detailing the skirmishes and the Americans' failing morale.[1] He was, though, no proto-objective 'travelling gentleman' in, say, the fashion of *The Times*'s Crimean War correspondent, William Russell. Paine was a committed revolutionary; an aide-de-camp to one of Washington's generals, as well as a war reporter. At Trenton, he left the troops, walked 33 miles to Philadelphia, whence the revolutionary Congress had already fled to Baltimore, and there penned a response to what he had being seeing. It was an editorial for independence:

> **THESE** are the times that try men's souls. The summer soldier and the sunshine patriot will, in this crisis, shrink from the service of their country; but he that stands it now, deserves the love and thanks of man and woman. Tyranny, like hell, is not easily conquered; yet we have this consolation with us, that the harder the conflict, the more glorious the triumph. What we obtain too cheap, we esteem too lightly: it is dearness only that gives every thing its value. Heaven knows how to put a proper price upon its goods; and it would be strange indeed if so celestial an article as **FREEDOM** should not be highly rated.[2]

It was published first in *The Pennsylvania Journal* and then, on 19 December, 1776, issued as an eight-page pamphlet – *The American Crisis* – printed by Melchior Steiner and Carl Cist in an initial run of 18,000 copies.[3] Eventually, pirated up and down the 13 'Revolted Colonies', perhaps as many as 200,000 copies of it and of the follow-ups Paine wrote, were in circulation – one for every dozen settlers. Paine wrote in the first person but he was no lying propagandist: 'I dwell not upon the vapours of imagination. I bring reason to your ears and, in language as plain as A, B, C, hold up truth to your eyes'.[4] He was partisan and subjective, but in terms of what we might call the pre-objective press, his announced position was seen as perfectly legitimate.

The American Crisis, written to be read aloud, was heard by Washington's troops in their camp at Trenton on Christmas Day, 1776. That night he crossed the Delaware and on the morning of the 26th his army held together and dispersed the Hessians, capturing two-thirds of them. The tide of war slowly began to turn.

Obviously, the victory needed more than Paine's eloquence. Inspiring speeches alone do not tend to turn the tide of wars (or, indeed, even of football games), except in movies, but it is important to remember that stories such as this are a part of how the press came to be embedded in the mythic history of America, and deservedly so. Such journalism, and also the journalistic ideology which underpinned it, has much to recommend it. We have already referenced the partisan 18th-century American press, but let us now propose it as a model.

To put it in simple terms, this is how things used to be done – and not just in the US – and it functioned, there and elsewhere, arguably, at least in some respects, better than our current journalistic ideology of objectivity embedded in professionalism. That front page of *The Pennsylvania Journal* is an historical example of an alternative approach which might prompt the question (if further prompting is required): What if we determined we did not need a balanced, neutral, impartial, unbiased, objective (etc.) press – nor even, say it softly, a truthful press? None of that can ever be guaranteed, after all (and, as we've argued, in the context of journalism that last term – 'truthful' – can't even really be *defined*), but what if journalism's functions were seen as achievable without making these ambitions essential? We do not accept the implication that Tom Paine should have included the views of the British ('King George III was contacted but declined to comment …'), in the name of making his journalism more 'balanced' and 'professional'. On the contrary, our assertion here is that what we need, in order to sustain journalism's positive social functions, is a press that ceases to aim at the impossible, but instead unashamedly nails its colours to the mast.

After all, it was during this period that, according to Thomas Carlyle, Edmund Burke, speaking in the British Parliament, characterised the press as being, in addition to the three Estates (the Lords Spiritual, the Lords Temporal, and the Commons), 'a *Fourth Estate* more important far than they all'. Carlyle adds: 'It is not a figure of speech, or witty saying; it is a literal fact – very momentous to us in these times'.[5] This is still received opinion.

The ideology of objective journalism reinforces this vision and now it is so entrenched, naturalised, and hegemonic, as to make this seem an extremely radical proposal, and perhaps it is. But we do live, supposedly, in a post-truth world where facts are not what they used to be and neither is authority – a world where fiction is easily presented as news by any digitally literate fantasist, empowered by the billion-dollar platforms that are the engines of Web 2.0. But more than that: it is a world where the implicit claim of truth enhances the strength of lies, when those lies ape news presentational norms, disguising and downplaying bias, aka subjectivity. The dwindling credibility of the mainstream press is damaged, just a little more, each and every time another example of the news's failures to meet its own high standards becomes visible to the public. The initial, foundational claim of truth, therefore, does more for *InfoWars* than it does for *The New York Times*, for without it the mendacities of the former lose force, while the trustworthiness of the latter might well – however paradoxically – be enhanced.

Moreover, it does not help that highfaluting affirmations made on the mainstream press's behalf can be seen (and not only by Hunter S. Thompson) to be nothing more than pretentious pomposities. Changing all this is indeed a big ask, but there are some signs of (long overdue) movement in the right direction. The stridency of the claim of objectivity, for example, is becoming increasingly muted, at least in some circles, and there remain, here and there in the background, echoes of this historic pre-objectivity model for an effective democratic press.

As we have pointed out, in the 1990s, as Jay Rosen claimed objectivity to be American journalism's gift to the world, he also had to acknowledge that '[o]f course, no one can be really objective'.[6] And, well before that, Gaye Tuchman had already noticed (as we have also mentioned previously) that in journalism, objectivity may be seen as:

> a strategic ritual protecting newspapermen from the risks of their trade… Attacked for a controversial representation of "facts", newspapermen invoke their objectivity almost the way a Mediterranean peasant might wear a clove of garlic around his neck to ward off evil spirits.[7]

Over the last few decades, Tuchman's 'garlic' of objectivity has (as it were) been losing a little of its potency, and it has slowly become more fashionable among those concerned with press theory and practices to declare that we are moving beyond objectivity (see p. 160). Eulogies for the concept are often to be found in the editorial/opinion sections of the same news publications that elsewhere habitually reference it as the hegemonic standard, without a trace of criticality, as you may have noticed if you Googled the term when we suggested it (see p. 6). Yet: '[i]t's Time to Say Goodbye' announced John McManus in 2009 in the very journal, *Neiman Reports,* that had so insisted on objective truth a mere eight years earlier. He was not having much of that rhetoric: 'As a standard to separate news from nonsense and a guide to ethical reporting, objectivity is about as reliable as judging character by the firmness of a handshake.'[8] We couldn't have put it better ourselves.

Given that objectivity is, according to its ideological construction, in a state of binary opposition with subjectivity, it necessarily follows that if objectivity is abandoned, journalism would perform its functions by owning its subjectivity, its biases, and contextualising the information which it presented openly, according to its own clearly and explicitly defined perspectives, political and otherwise. The clarity and logical consistency of this context would condition the credibility of what is reported. And such a change of understanding is not unthinkable.

As one of the authors of this book has discussed elsewhere,[9] there was a (fairly long) period in the history of American journalism during which the news was openly biased, and, to oversimplify quite a bit, it still worked just fine. It can be argued, as we said at the beginning of this chapter, that this press earned a role for itself in the founding myth(s) of the American republic which conditions, to this day, the high claims made for its journalism. The arrow flies straight from Tom Paine's time to John Carey now, hitting the bullseye and allowing Carey boldly to assert that 'journalism is usefully understood as another name for democracy'.[10] But for much of this arrow's flight – how much is a matter of debate – objectivity was not just irrelevant, but unheard of.

As another eminent US media scholar, Robert McChesney, observed:

> During the first two or three generations of the republic such notions for the press would have been nonsensical, even unthinkable. The point of journalism was to persuade as well as inform, and the press tended to be highly partisan.[11]

Gerald Baldasty, in discussing the 'opinionated, politically biased, one-sided, argumentative and frequently strident'[12] newspapers of the Jacksonian era, which were also publicly subsidised, privately patronised, and openly partisan, noted that in the early 1800s, it was in fact a *failure* to adopt and espouse clearly defined political positions that was taboo. This was not because of a lack of professionalism, or of a lack of respect for the importance of newspapers in the functioning of a democracy, but rather because journalism was viewed differently. Neutrality, thought Horace Greely, was a gag.

In essence, as Baldasty notes, a newspaper's failing to express a clear opinion would have been viewed as evidence, not of fairness, detachment, etc., but that either the editor did not have an opinion, or did not have the courage to express it. Neither was acceptable. Baldasty says, 'Evenhandedness or objectivity was not so much bad as inappropriate.'[13] While some might view the move from such an ideological position towards professionalism and objectivity as an example of progress, from the primitive to the sophisticated, and from worse to better, we, obviously, do not see it in this way. This admittedly now unfamiliar ideology seems to us far from incomprehensible or obviously inferior, given the nature and importance of lively public debate, informed not just by facts, but by popular understanding of the context(s) and meaning(s) of the news.

Conscious that some may reply that much of the news is already openly politically-slanted, a note of clarification: though within the (admittedly fuzzy) borders of the mainstream press, there are of course news outlets of various kinds which might conventionally be considered as highly partisan (e.g. *The Daily Mail*, but also the likes of *The Guardian*), even their rhetoric is grounded, invariably, in presenting news/truth, with the only bias ever explicitly acknowledged being the national/common interest. The rhetoric of the spectacularly partisan Fox News network, which until relatively recently had the phrase 'fair and balanced' trademarked, exemplifies this point. Since admitting to your bias is no admission at all if you define it as a bias in favour of being right, this type of stance, still ultimately grounded in the ideology of objectivity, must not be confused with the honest, explicit partisanship from which we are suggesting the press should never have departed, and to which it should return.

The word 'objectivity' comes into the language in 1803 but it is not immediately applied to the press. Nevertheless, according to Dan Schiller, selling what amounted to objectivity had, by the 1830s, become a shrewd commercial move for newspaper publishers.[14] He grounds his case for its de facto adoption in the press of that era in terms of a response to the growing scepticism of the age of industrialisation and urbanisation – a new world of trains and electricity, of probabilistics and increasingly democratic modes of government.

Objectivity at this point can in fact perhaps best be understood as a hustle, designed to obscure the exercise of power within the realm of news. Schiller describes how the con was pitched:

> With its universalistic intent, its concern for public rationality based on equal access to the facts, objectivity harbored a profoundly democratic promise. From the 1830s the informational system was not to be the exclusive preserve of a king, a baron, a president or a class but rather, as it seemed, of the political nation itself.[15]

He also observes that this was, of course, a falsehood. These 1c papers were the forerunners of our tabloids, sensationalist (as well as being, as we have seen, mendacious, see p. 51) with an overwhelming focus on human-interest material. That they were not primarily focused on the politics of the day helped their aura of neutrality, though this aura was patchy, even then. As Schiller notes, they were also willing to speak truth to power, following the line of the small, radical 'Labor Press' then publishing – also scarcely exhibiting the weak, 'grubby neutrality' of which Horace Greeley complained. On balance, it is in their acting as a de facto uncommitted forum for public debate that Schiller sees the reflection of a new commitment to objectivity (though one that others deny).

As the techniques of the press developed after the 1830s – from the emergence of the interview, for example, to the 'stunts' and stings that characterised the New Journalism/Yellow Press of the period – subjectivities, such as those of Gordon Bennett Sn, say, or Nellie Bly, were as significant as any claim of being an objective 'blind observer'. Nevertheless, a technicist explanation can be made for the de facto presence of objectivity in advance of the overt use of the term. It rests on the emergence of the wire services in the later 19th century. Here the argument is that, as the news agencies sought to service multiple client publications, they needed not to be biased against the predilections of any of their subscribing titles.[16] The term 'objectivity', though, did not figure among their selling points. Be that as it may, whether consciously or unconsciously, the American press, for whatever underlying reason, began to operate under assumptions of objectivity and professionalism.

As the century turned, this became a newly dominant journalistic ideology, but it was not, historically speaking, itself a politically neutral change. By the start of the Second World War, at least in the Anglophone world, objectivity had triumphed as the essential mark of serious, 'good' journalism. And it was in place then to be denied by isolated voices such as Tuchman's and, in effect, eventually by the highly subjective reporting of the second New Journalism, which did not think much of objectivity either: 'a pompous contradiction in terms'.[17]

Clearly, to be seized with post-modern doubts as to the possibility of ever knowing reality objectively was fatal to any claim of objectivity. The New Journalism argument was that its subjective reports were paradoxically more honest and revealing of doings in the world, exactly because they swapped the always spurious presentation of non-involvement for the honesty of their self-reflexivity. In short, they told a story, and in the telling revealed how they had come to it. They did not pretend to any sort of objectivity. In journalism, it 'had been regarded as an antidote to bias, but now it came to be looked on as the most insidious bias of all'.[18]

And this, in essence, is why the authors of this book assert that the 200-year-old ideology of partisan, subjective journalism, described above, makes a lot more sense than the 100+-year-old ideology of objective journalism which replaced it. There lies, we think, the answer to the journalism problem. But arguing against objectivity has become in some respects like arguing against freedom, or honesty (or neoliberal capitalism …). To many, objective journalism is so obviously superior to all conceivable alternatives, that it is like advocating evil itself to suggest that actually, biased journalism (even of the open and in that sense *honest* kind which came before) is what is now all but unthinkable – not that this past journalistic mode is generally remembered at all. To quote Schiller again:

> Disagreement over the substantive character of objectivity itself, however, has tended to be sharply limited. Instead, social conflicts have been disguised, contained, and displaced through the imposition of news objectivity, a framework legitimating the exercise of social power over the interpretation of reality. Those without institutionalized resources have, time and again, found themselves pilloried and marginalized in the press, while crucial issues have been amplified in such a way as to lead the general public to accept institutional control.[19]

In addition to the theoretical and practical issues which we have raised with objectivity, for these reasons (and others) it is a nightmare politically speaking, and it always has been.

To reiterate and summarise what we learn from such illumination, and from the rest of this exercise: good journalism is still biased journalism, because biased is just the word we use for 'subjective' when we intend to show disapproval, and all journalism is, as we have argued, subjective. But, uncoupled from objectivity, good journalism would not label itself as unbiased. It would no longer cling to the imaginary protection of objectivity. It would own its subjectivity, its biases, and contextualise the information which it presented openly, according to its own clearly and explicitly defined perspectives, political and otherwise.

To dispute the ideology of objective journalism seems radical, not a little because the alternative is mostly unknown outside the world of scholars of media history. Nevertheless to put it in simple terms, this is how things used to be done and, we say again: it could be argued it worked better than does our current approach.

The alternative, previous ideology of journalism, in which different parties, and parts of the political spectrum, are openly and explicitly represented by different news outlets, informing, contextualising, persuading, and mobilising a democracy's citizenry, is better suited to the actual nature of the news's audience. Objectivity presupposes both an impossibly objective journalist and an impossibly objective reader, while the ideas of journalism of the early 19th century make neither error. In this sense, we would argue, it is both better for a modern democracy and more ethical, in both the pragmatic and the theoretical senses, though we will leave an attempt to elucidate the latter fully to the philosophers.

So, although proposing a detailed plan for reforming journalism is not our mission, as we've said, let us take a moment here, more or less at the end of our argument, in order briefly to provide some additional support for our idea of an honest, subjective, biased foundation on which journalism may be rebuilt. To that end, a return to Schudson, and the six core functions of journalism.

To provide information about what is not generally known

This function will, at worst, not be fulfilled any worse in our proposed system. To the charge that inconvenient facts will be removed or just de-emphasised in the name of bias, we would answer that that happens already. It is, we insist, better that people understand this aspect of news than that its existence be denied. Removing bias entirely is, fundamentally, not an available option.

To investigate as guardians those who should be the guardians of public welfare

This function will, at worst, not be fulfilled any worse in our proposed system. To the charge that only those who are considered part of 'the other side' will be so investigated, in the name of bias, we would answer that that happens already. This function can, in fact, be much more effectively carried out if biases/perspectives are clear and explicit, meaning that debate over what is uncovered can be more easily extricated from debate over who is on whose side. (Which is to say that claiming a medium is biased against the politician or other person being depicted in a bad light would be, perhaps, a given, rather than an effective argument with which to dismiss their allegations.)

To be a public forum for the expression of ideas and opinions

This function will, self-evidently, be fulfilled far better in our proposed system. Without the requirement to pretend to an impossible, 'gagging' neutrality, different perspectives will be able to be explored, and to contend with one another, openly, and without the value quixotically assigned to 'objectivity', etc., distorting the nature of the discourse.

To analyse the context in which events occur

This function will be fulfilled far better in our proposed system, for much the same reasons which will lead to a superior public forum and marketplace of ideas. Context is, as we've discussed, always subjective. It can be illustrated far more effectively when journalists aren't having to twist themselves into knots attempting to maintain the ever-deteriorating illusion that this is not the case.

To encourage 'social empathy' better to understand 'how the other half lives'[20]

This function will be fulfilled far better in our proposed system. Again, freeing the news to discuss and consider different viewpoints and perspectives and biases (if we must call them that) will facilitate a far greater level of understanding, if only because the other person's point of view can be considered as it should be considered, as the other person's point of view, rather than simply as ... well, fake news.

To mobilise, in the name of partisanship, like-minded groups of the citizenry[21]

This function will be fulfilled far better in our proposed system, since it will be embraced as a fundamental function of journalism, rather than an incidental side-effect. The news will explicitly address, as it once did, the audience as a political body. And to the charge that this will produce tribalism and antipathy, we reply that the news does this already, but again, how can the situation not be improved by the understanding that different groups have different opinions, as opposed to the currently dominant idea that 'our side', whatever it may be, is objectively right, while the other side is lying and biased and not listening to 'the facts'?

This proposed alternative ideology also relates directly to our discussions of the internet. The myth of objective journalism is what creates the space for the worst mainstream-media offenders, when it comes to faking, twisting, distorting the news. It allows them to present themselves (with *sotto voce* disclaimers when challenged) as 100% unbiased and truthful – when without such an ideology, the absurd idea that such a thing is possible would be, if not non-existent, certainly nowhere near as potent as it has become. It's the claim which powers, even more than the actual technology, the internet's capacities to amplify the problem. Whether the 'news' and/or journalism is a physical newspaper, TV report, YouTube video, forwarded blog-post, clickbait article, and/or whatever media form is to come next, the idea of dealing with 'fake news' by somehow trying to make sure that no 'bad' journalism circulates in our media ecology is, as we've said, simply ridiculous, both theoretically and practically. The only way to cut the head off the dragon is to move society's understanding of news past the myth of objectivity, to the point where pointing at any item of news coverage and saying 'This is an example of unbiased journalism' is generally, and correctly, understood to be ridiculous.

The internet, then, may empower and exacerbate our misunderstandings, but it is nonetheless the misunderstandings themselves which are the real problem. That is where the true causes of the 'fake news' panic are to be found. Neither the internet nor bad journalism created our problems. The situation is what it is because the nature, and limits, of what the news is and is not, can and can't do, should, and shouldn't be are not understood. It is our society's understanding itself which is the heart of the matter. It is our fundamental idea of journalism which is broken. That is what needs to be fixed.

If there is a 'crisis' – a 'journalism question' – it is not around fake news, alt facts, post-truth. It is not around a communication technology which has been left to its own (too often malodorous) devices. Rather, the current lack of confidence is grounded, history clearly shows, in the centuries of claims to be providing that which cannot be delivered; claims to be honoured and respected which cannot be sustained. This is what threatens the press's ability to perform its crucial roles.

These are (indeed) times that try our souls, but the seemingly all but insurmountable problems which journalism faces can be overcome, once they are properly understood.

Notes

1 Keane, John (2009). *Tom Paine: A Political Life*. London: Bloomsbury, pp 141–145.
2 Paine, Thomas (1776). 'The author of *Common Sense*', *The American Crisis I*. Philadelphia, PA: Steiner & Cist, p. 1.
3 Ibid.
4 Ibid.
5 Carlyle, Thomas (1840). *On Heroes, Hero Worship and the Heroic in History* (reprinted: *Collected Works*). London: Robson & Sons, p. 194.
6 Rosen, Jay (1993). 'Beyond objectivity', *Nieman Reports*, 47, Winter, p. 48.
7 Tuchman, Gaye (1972). 'Objectivity as strategic ritual: An examination of newsmen's notions of objectivity', *American Journal of Sociology*, 77:4, January, pp. 660. No offence is intended by the authors in the deployment of this stereotype. We are merely quoting. Moreover, it could also be argued, were one so inclined, that such actions are an entirely rational response to the alienation of the modern world. See: de Martino, Ernesto (2015 [1959]). *Magic: A Theory from the South*. Chicago, IL: HAU, University of Chicago Press.
8 McManus, John (2009). 'Objectivity: It's time to say goodbye', *Neiman Reports*, Summer. https://niemanreports.org/articles/objectivity-its-time-to-say-goodbye/ [accessed 10 October 2019].
9 Winston, Matthew (2014). *The Gonzo Text: Disentangling Meaning in Hunter S. Thompson's Journalism*. New York: Peter Lang, pp. 67–80.

10 Carey, James (1997). 'Afterword: The culture in question' in *James Carey: A Critical Reader* (Eve Stryker Munson & Catherine Warren, eds.). Minneapolis, MN: University of Minnesota Press, p. 332.
11 McChesney, Robert (2003). 'The problem of journalism', *Journalism Studies,* 4:3, p. 300.
12 Baldesty, Gerald (2011). *'American political parties and the press'* in *The American Journalism History Reader* (Bonnie Brennen & Hanno Hardt, eds.). New York: Routledge, p. 278.
13 Baldesty, Gerald (2011). 'American political parties and the press' in *The American Journalism History Reader* (Bonnie Brennen & Hanno Hardt, eds.). New York: Routledge, p. 283.
14 Schiller, Daniel (1981). *Objectivity and the News: The Public and the Rise of Commercial Journalism.* Philadelphia, PA: University of Pennsylvania Press, p. 36.
15 Schiller, Daniel (2011). 'Democracy and the news' in *The American Journalism History Reader* (Bonnie Brennen & Hanno Hardt, eds.). New York: Routledge, p. 427.
16 Carey, John (1989). *Communication as Culture: Essays on Media and Society.* Boston: Unwin Hyman, p. 210.
17 Thompson, Hunter S. (1983). *Fear and Loathing: On the Campaign Trail '72.* New York: Warner Books, p. 48.
18 Schudson, Michael (1978). *Discovering the News: A Social History of American Newspapers.* New York, Basic, p. 160.
19 Schiller, Daniel (2011). 'Democracy and the news' in *The American Journalism History Reader* (Bonnie Brennen & Hanno Hardt, eds.). New York: Routledge, p. 438.
20 Riis, Jacob A. (2011[1890]). 'Introduction: Framing the poor – The irresistibility of how the other half lives', in *How the Other Half Lives: Studies Among the Tenements of New York.* Boston, MA: Bedford/St.Martin's.
21 Schudson, Michael (2007). *Why Democracies Need an Unloved Press.* Malden, MA: Polity, p. 12.

INDEX

4chan 188
9/11 182–183, 188

ABC (American Broadcasting Company) 99
abcnews.com.co 99
abcnews.go.com 99
abuse 173
academic journalism 5
Accounts 23, 35
Acres, Bert 61
actualités 62
Addison, Joseph 42
Adolphus, Gustavus 39
Advanced Research Project Agency *see* ARPA (Advanced Research Project Agency)
Advises 35
Affaires of the Court 41
Against Henry King of the English 24
Albert, Edward 126–127
Alefantis, James 187
Amazon 87
American Airlines 183
American Crisis, The 194
American films 140, 146
American journalism 5, 140, 159, 196
American newspapers 7, 8–9; fake news 51–52, 80–81
American press 4, 162, 193–194, 197–198
American radio 71–72, 73–74, 75, 76; *The War of the Worlds* 69, 70–71, 75, 167
American Revolution 45

American television 79–80
Analytical Engine calculator 113
Anderson, Benedict 189
animal behaviour 113, 115
anthropology 121–122, 123, 124–125
anti-slavery 45
Antwerp, siege of 35
Arab Spring 90
Arago, François 58
Archer, Thomas 37–38
ARPA (Advanced Research Project Agency) 84–85
ARPAnet 84, 85
Asch, Timothy 123
Assange, Julian 94
assassination of 'Good' Count Charles of Flanders 28
Assertion of the Seven Sacraments, The 24
Attenborough, David 115
Auden, W. H. 119
Australia 152
avvisi 23, 24, 35
Ax Fight, The 123–124

Babbage, Charles 113
Bacon, Francis 110–111, 129, 183–184
Baldasty, Gerald 196
Bandura, Albert 115–117
Barlow, John Perry 86, 88, 149
Barthes, Roland 60, 62
Battle of Santiago Bay, The 62
BBC (British Broadcasting Corporation) 76–77, 78–79, 80, 160–161

BBCo (British Broadcasting Company Ltd) 76
BEF (British Expeditionary Force) 63
behaviourism 113
Beheim, Michael 19, 25, 29, 34
Behind Asylum Bars 56–57
Bell, Tom 77
Bell company 85
Bentham, Jeremy 89, 122, 133–134, 135
Berkenhead, John 40–41, 42, 43
Beveridge, John 78
bias 6–7, 183, 184–186, 196–197, 199
Bible, The 22
Biograph company 62
Blackstone, William 140, 141, 145
blasphemy 138, 139
Blood Libel 189–190
Bly, Nellie 56–57, 93, 197
Bobo Doll experiment 115–117
Bonaparte, Napoleon 46
Bornet, Françoise 59
Boston Globe 173
Boston Marathon bombing 149, 188
Bourne, Nathaniel 38–39, 40
Boxer Rebellion, China 61
Brant, Sebastian 20
Braudel, Fernand 36
Brexit 171, 180
Briggs, Asa 77
British Admiralty 64
British Board of Film Censors 64
British Broadcasting Company Ltd *see* BBCo (British Broadcasting Company Ltd)
British Broadcasting Corporation *see* BBC (British Broadcasting Corporation)
British Expeditionary Force *see* BEF (British Expeditionary Force)
British Movietone News 63
British Muslims 100
British television *see* BBC (British Broadcasting Corporation)
broadcasting 7, 64, 71–72, 73, 74–76, 146
broadsheets 18, 20–21, 23, 25, 26, 34, 35
Broockman, David 180
Bulmer, Jay 187
Bureau of Investigative Reporting 127
Burke, Edmond 45, 194
Butter, Nathaniel 38–39, 40
BuzzFeed News 97, 98, 100

Cadwalladr, Carole 181
Cambridge Analytica 179–180, 181
canard 25

Capa, Robert 61
captioning 60, 62, 63, 123–124
Carey, James 101, 102
Carey, John 196
Carlyle, Thomas 45, 194
Carolus, Johann 34, 35, 37
Categorical Imperative 157
CBS Radio Network 69, 70
CDA (Communications Decency Act, 1996) 150
censorship 21, 24, 36, 37, 50; films 151; internet 151; newsreels 64; radio 71, 76; theatre 139, 146
Cerf, Vint 84, 86
Chagnon, Napoleon 123, 124
Chancellor of the Exchequer 76
Charles I 33–34, 40, 41, 42, 43, 93
Charles V 21
Chartist movement 45, 126
Chatham House 171, 180
Chesterfield, Earl of 139
China 61, 89, 151
church texts 18, 22
Cist, Carl 194
citizen journalists 92
Civil War, England 39, 40
Clinton, Hillary 99, 181, 187, 188, 190
Cochrane, Elizabeth *see* Bly, Nellie
cognitive dissonance 60, 86, 90, 122, 151
Cohen, Stanley 180
coherence theory 156
Columbus Dispatch 91
Comet Ping Pong 187
Comey, James 187–188
commentary 63, 123, 124
common carrier 100, 147–148, 150
common law 133–134, 135–136, 138, 145, 147
Communications Decency Act *see* CDA (Communications Decency Act, 1996)
CompuServe 148
computers 84–86, 87, 113
confirmation bias 183, 184
conspiracy theories 182–184, 187
Cooke, Janet 80–81
Coos Bay World 6
copycatting 168–169, 170
copyright 147
Corante, or, news from Italy, Germany, Hungarie, Spaine and France 38
corantos 36, 37–40
correspondence theory 156
Courante uyt Italien, Duytslandt, &c. 37
Cox, Chris 149, 150

Index

Crimean War 59
Cromwell, Oliver 44
cross-examinations 135–136
Cruz, Ted 179
crying Murther, The 25
Cubby, Inc. v. CompuServe Inc. 148
Cultivation Process 167
cyberfreedom 149

Daesh jihadi attacks 100
Daguerre, Louis 58
Daily Mail 52–53, 197
Daily Telegraph 56, 98
data harvesting, official 125–126
@DavidGoldbergNY 188
dead-letter law 138–139
Declaration of the Independence of Cyberspace 86, 149
Deep Play: Notes on the Balinese Cockfight 121–122
defamation 132, 137, 138, 142, 150
Defence of the Realm Act 77
Defenestration of Prague 37
Defleur, Melvin L. 128
De multro ... on the murder etc. of the glorious Charles 28, 29
Derby 61
desuetude 138–139
digital communications 86–90
digital image manipulations 60–61
digital news 91, 92–93
Dilburn, Samuel 35
Discworld 156–157
Disney 99
Disputation on the Power of Indulgences – the 95 Theses 18
distortions 52–53, 63, 100, 124, 161
Diurnals 33–34, 37, 41, 97
Doisneau, Robert 59
DPP-516 85
Dracula 19, 20, 21
Dracule Wajda 20, 21, 23, 25
Dunkirk 63
Durkheim, Émile 128

Easter Uprising 72
East India Company 27
ECHR (European Charter on Human Rights) 146, 147
Edelman, Bernard 147
Eden, Anthony 63
Edinburgh Courant 51
Edinburgh Journal of Science 51
EEGs (electroencephalograms) 114

Egyptian revolution 90
Eisenhower, Dwight 161
election campaign (US, 2016) 99–100, 179
electoral politics 171, 179–180, 181
electric telegraph 63–64
electroencephalograms *see* EEGs (electroencephalograms)
Ellesberg, Daniel 93
Enlightenment 158
ethics 102, 157–158, 166–167, 172–174
EU (European Union) 152
European Charter on Human Rights *see* ECHR (European Charter on Human Rights)
European Court of Justice 152
EU–US Cooperation on Tackling Disinformation 171
experiments 109, 110–111

fabrication 11–12, 51–53; *The Great Moon Hoax* 51–52; Zinoviev Letter 52–53, 80
Facebook 86, 100, 142, 152, 153, 179–180, 181, 185, 190
fake news 10–13, 17, 19, 25–27, 39, 44, 71, 84, 97–103, 172, 182–184, 186, 200–201; Blood Libel 189–190; *The Great Moon Hoax* 51–52; Hussein story 10; internet 97–98, 99–100, 145, 152, 179–181, 182; Jimmy's World 80–81; Pizzagate 187–188, 189–190; spaghetti harvest 80; Zinoviev Letter 52–53, 80
Falklands War 10
Faques, Richard 23
FCC (Federal Communication Commission) 70, 73, 74, 76, 99, 135
Fenton, Roger 59
Ferdinand II 37
Fierce People, A 123
films 61–63, 91, 151
First Amendment (US Constitution) 71, 73, 74, 76, 79, 139, 140, 146, 150
First Draft of a Report on the EDVAC, The 113
First World War 53, 113, 146
fMRI (functional magnetic resonance imaging) 114
Fox News network 197
France 18, 19, 20, 23, 40, 125, 147
Frankel, Max 94
Frankfurter, Felix 74
freedom of expression 50, 74, 132, 136–137, 139, 140, 141, 145, 146, 149, 167
freedom of the press 3, 50, 75, 76, 132, 137, 145, 147, 151

freedom to broadcast 74–75
free speech 50–51, 137–138, 139–140
French Revolution 45
Freud, Sigmund 119, 120
Frightening and Truly Extraordinary Story 20
Fugger, Jacob 22
functional magnetic resonance imaging *see* fMRI (functional magnetic resonance imaging)

Gaitskill, Hugh 78
Galbert of Bruges 27–28, 29, 34
Garcia, Federico Borrell 61
gatekeepers 7
Gates, Bill 188
gazeta dele novita 23
gazzete 23
Geertz, Clifford 121–122, 125
General Post Office 76
General Strike 77
George II 139
Germany 25–26, 63, 74, 90, 184–185
Gionali 35
Goebbels, Joseph 63, 74
good journalism 5, 6, 199
Google 5–6, 87, 179, 195
Gordon, John 50
Gordon Bennett Jr, James 56, 135
Gordon Bennett Sn, James 51, 54, 55, 136, 197
Gort, Lord 63
gossip 4
Grade, Lord 161
Great Moon Hoax, The 51–52, 70, 80
Great War 72, 73
Greco-Turkish war 61
Greeley, Horace 162, 197
Grosseteste, Robert 111
Guardian 197
Gunther, Albert 186
Gutenberg, Johannes 17, 18, 19, 22, 29, 36

Hall, Lord 161
Hamilton, Alexander 139, 140
Hamlet 113, 173
Hanlon's Razor 182
Harm Principle 150, 158, 173
Harvard Protesters: Objective Journalism Is "Endangering Undocumented Students" 6
Hearst, William Randolph 57–58
Henry VIII 23, 24
hereafter ensue the trewe encountre of Batayle 23
Hershel, John 52

Hevy Newes of an Horryble Earthquake 20
Hill, Lord 79
Hindenburg disaster 75
Hitler, Adolf 12, 74
holy texts 18, 22
Honeywell 85
human behaviour 115–117, 121
human cognition 114
humanity 87, 112–114, 149, 150
Human Rights Act (UK, 1998) 27
Hurricane Sandy 169
Hussein, Saddam 10, 98
Hutchinson, Frances 158

IBM 85
incitement 141–142
Independent Press Standards Organisation 100
India 89
Indigenous villages, South America 122–124
InfoWars 188, 195
intellectual property rights 147
interactivity 91–92, 97, 168
internet 86–91, 92, 93–94, 142, 145, 185, 189, 190, 195, 200, 201; censorship 151; fake news 97–98, 99–100, 145, 152, 179–181, 182; law 147, 148–153
Internet Exchange Points 87
internet service providers 148–150
interventions 57–58, 59–62
interviews 54, 55, 122, 127, 135, 136
investigative journalism 127–128
Iran 89
Irish Republican Army 80
irrelevancy hypothesis 186
Iwo Jima, Battle of 59

Jefferson, Thomas 75, 132, 138, 139, 146
Jerusalem Post 6
Jewitt murder 54
Jews 189, 190
Jimmy's World 80–81
Johnson, Boris 98
Johnson, Samuel 3, 20, 41–42
Jones, Alex 188, 189
Jonson, Ben 11, 27, 39, 41–42, 172
Journal 35
journalism 3–5, 11–13, 27–28, 42–45, 50, 53–54, 101–103, 110–112, 120–121, 127–129, 155–159, 190–191, 194–201; good 5, 6, 199; investigative 127–128; law 132–133, 134, 136, 138; objective 5–8, 9, 11, 174, 184–185, 194, 195, 198, 199,

200; sober 9, 20, 28, 55, 65; subjective 198, 199
Journalism industry falters 6
Journalist 57
Journalist Creed 101
journalistic objectivity *see* objective journalism
journalists 81, 92, 111, 117, 122, 129, 145
Junius 45
juries 133–134

Kalla, Joshua 180
Katz, Elihu 187
Kelner, Bill 94
Kempe, William 173
Kemps nine dais wonder 173
Kennedy, John 45
Kinetoscope 61
King of Hungary 20
King Solomon's Ring 115
Kinomatograph 62
Knowlton, Stephen 159–160, 161
Kovach, Bill 156, 158–159
Kuhn, Thomas 112, 117
Kurtze Beschreibung 35

Landgrebe, Earl 186
Latour, Bruno 109
l'autre 172–173
law 132–139, 140–142, 145–146, 147–153
Lawrence, Stephen 173
Leach, Edmund 123
legal testimony 54–55
La Gazette de France 40
Leipzig, East Germany 90
le Journal des sçavans 51
Levant, Oscar 64
Levinas, Emmanuel 172
Lévi-Strauss, Claude 122–123
Le Vrai Portrait Comme Les Rebelles 35
Levy, Joseph 56
Lewinsky, Monica 8
L'homme Machine 113
libel 138, 142, 148
licences 71, 72, 73, 74, 76, 80, 146
Liebhart, Janice 186
Liebling, A. J. 151
Life 59
Lippmann, Walter 4, 158, 159
Livingstone, Sonia 167
Locke, John 145–146, 150
Logical Positivism 157
London Gazette 45
London Labour and the London Poor 128

London Metropolitan Obscene Publications Squad 141
Long Parliament 40
Lorenz, Konrad 115
Louis XIII 40, 52
Ludovico III Gonzaga 21
Luther, Martin 18, 24, 37, 50

McChesney, Robert 196
Macdonald, Ramsey 52–53, 80
McLuhan, Marshall 36, 86, 182
McManus, John 195
McQuail, Dennis 187
Maiden Tribute of Modern Babylon, The 58
manipulation 59–61, 62, 180–181
manuscripts 18, 22
Marston Moor, Battle of 43
Marx, Karl 156
Mayhew, Henry 126–128
measles 170
mechanemorphism 113
media 3, 114
media effects 167–174, 179–181
media sociology 7, 70, 90, 141, 169, 171, 181, 184
Méliès, Georges 61
Mercurius Aulicus 40–41, 42–43, 44–45
Mercurius Britannicus 42, 43, 44
Mercurius Civicus 43
Mercurius Fumigosus 45
Mercurius Gallobelgicus 35
Mercurius Politicus 44
Mercurius Pragmaticus 44
Messerelation 35
MI5 78, 79
Michael ab Isset 35
Microsoft 87
Middle East 89
Mill, John Stuart 158
Milton, John 37, 44, 50
Minimal Persuasive Effects of Campaign Contact in General Elections: Evidence from 49; Field Experiments, The 180
Minot, Laurence 19
minstrels 19, 22
misquotations 98–99
misrepresentations 53, 100–101
MMR vaccination 170
Modi, Narendra 89
Money Talk 148
Moore, G. E. 156
morality 167
moral panic 180

Moral Philosophy 158
Morning Chronicle 126
Morrison, Herbert 75
mosque attack, New Zealand 152
Mothes, Cornelia 184–185
Munchetty, Naga 160–161
Murdoch, Rupert 60, 100, 102, 173
Mussolini, Benito 74

Naseby, Battle of 42, 43, 93
National Geographic 60
National Review 6
National Union of Journalists (UK) 160
Nazi Germany 63, 74
Nazi resistance 45
NBC Blue Network 99
Needham, Marchmont 40, 42–44, 53, 55, 93
Neiman Foundation for Journalism 155
Neiman Reports 195
Netherlands 75
Networks of Outrage and Hope 91
network working group *see* NWG (network working group)
Neuer Zeitung 23
newes 11, 25, 33, 81
Newes and Strange Newes of a tempestuous spirit 25
New Journalism 57, 58, 128, 163, 173, 197, 198
news 4, 9–13, 18–19
News 23
news 28–29, 35–36, 39, 44–46, 51–53, 91–92, 102, 196–197
newsbooks 18–19, 20, 21, 25–27, 35
news film *see* newsreels
newsletters 22–23, 25
News of the World 173
newspapers 7–8, 24, 25, 34, 35, 45, 63–64, 71, 91, 93, 100–101, 151, 197; English Civil War 40–44; Thirty Years' War 37, 38–39
news photography *see* photographic images
news platforms 4, 91, 92, 102
news publications 23–24, 40, 45
newsreels 61–63, 64, 71
news selection 7, 8–9
New tidings from Speyer About the acts of the Prince 20
New Tidings from the Japanese Island 20–21
New York Journal 57–58
New York Morning Herald 51, 54, 56
New York Sun 51–52, 53, 54
New York Times 6, 10, 94, 98, 195

New-York Tribune 162
New York World 56–57
Nichols, Bill 4
Nietzche, Friedrich 156
Nocturnals 97
nuclear power plants 184
Null Effects Hypothesis 167
NWG (network working group) 86

Obama, Barack 8, 99, 190
obituaries 23
objective journalism 5–8, 9, 11, 174, 184–185, 194, 195, 198, 199, 200
objectivity 159–162, 163, 195–196, 197–198, 199, 201
obscenity 76, 137, 141
Observer 181
obstinate dissenters 109, 110, 111, 124
occasionnels 18, 23
OED 12, 111
Offray de La Mettrie, Julien 113
Omni libri et scriptae 24
online pornography 150
operant conditioning 113
opinions 186–187, 196–197
Orwell, George 78
over-verification 56, 112, 135, 166

Pacific Standard 189
Paine, Tom 193–194, 196
Pall Mall Gazette 55, 58
pamphlets 24
Panorama 79, 80
par l'intercession de la vierge 25
partisan opinions 186–187
party newspapers 41
Pathé 62
Pathé-faits divers 62
Pathé Journal 62
Pavlov, Ivan 113
Peace of Augsburg 36–37
Pecke, Samuel 33–34, 37, 42
Peirce, Charles 12, 59
Pennsylvania Journal 193, 194
Pentagon Papers, The 80, 94
Perfect Diurnal of Some Passages in Parliament 33–34, 37, 41
Perry, David 189
pestblätter 18
PET (positron emission tomography) 114
Peucer, Tobis 36
Philo, Greg 172
Philosophical Proceedings of The Royal Society 51

phone hacking 174
photographic images 59–61, 71, 147
Photoshop 60
Pilate, Pontius 166
Pizzagate 187–188, 189–190
placards 24
plague-sheets 18
PMG (Post Master General) 76
Podesta, John 187, 188
Pope Backs Trump – <WTOE5> 99–100
Popper, Karl 111–112, 120
populism 12
positivism 128
Post Master General *see* PMG (Post Master General)
post-traumatic stress disorder *see* PTSD (post-traumatic stress disorder)
pragmatism 156
Pratchett, Terry 156–157
press 3–4, 45–46, 50, 102–103, 145–146, 194
press freedom *see* freedom of the press
Press Gazette 60
Prince of Wales Investiture 78–79
printed texts 17–19, 22, 24, 36; *see also* broadsheets; newsbooks; newspapers
printers 22, 36
Prodigy 148–149
Protocols of the Elders of Zion 189
psychoanalysis 119–120
psychology 119–120
PTSD (post-traumatic stress disorder) 169
Pulitzer, Joseph 56, 57
Pulitzer prize 80–81, 127
Punch 126
Purkiss, Diana 11

Quételet, Adolphe 125

Race Rocks Marine Ecological Reserve 114–115
radio 64, 69–74, 75, 146; regulation 70, 71, 72, 73, 74–76, 146; UK 76–78, 79, 91
Rain-am-Lech, Battle of 39
Raising of the Stars and Stripes on Mount Surabachi, The 59
Readick, Frank 75
Reconstitution of the Coronation of Edward VII 61
reconstitutions 71
Reddit 149, 188
Re-enforcement Theory 167
Reformation 24, 36, 37

regulation 146–147; radio 70, 71, 72, 73, 74–76, 146; television 79, 80
Reith, John 77–78
Relatio Historica 35
Relation 21
Relation aller Fürnemmen und gedenckw ü rdigen Historian 34, 35
Relationen 35
Remington, Frederic 58
Renaissance 24
Renaudot, Théophraste 40, 52
repeatability 109, 110, 111–112
reportisto 23
Restoration 45
Revolutionary Army 193, 194
riots 91, 141–142
Rosen, Jay 101, 103, 110, 127, 159, 160, 163, 195
Rosenstiel, Tom 156, 158–159
Rosenthal, Joe 59
Rothermere, Lord 53
Rouch, Jean 123
royal proclamations 23
Rudolph, Emperor 37
Rules of Sociological Method, The 128
Rushdie, Salman 139
Russell, Bertrand 156
Russell, William 193
Russo-Japanese war 61
Ryle, Gilbert 103, 121

Salute to Fair and Objective Journalism, A. 6
Sandy Hook Elementary School 188
San Francisco earthquake 62
San Francisco Examiner 58
Satanic Verses, The 139
Schiller, Daniel 162, 197, 198
Schmitt, Kathleen 186
Schöffer, Peter 17
Schudson, Michael 102, 103, 110, 128, 162, 163
Scitex 60
Scrips, E. W. 64
Seattle Times 6
Second World War 7, 59, 63, 75, 78, 79, 84, 198
secrecy 22–23, 36, 89, 91, 93, 94, 97
Section 230 (CDA) 150, 153
sedition 137–138, 139, 140, 141
selective recall 186
Shakespeare, William 113, 173
Sifry, Micah 180
Skinner, B. F. 113

Sky Sports Channel 98
slander 138, 142
sober journalism 9, 20, 28, 55, 65
social media 90, 91, 181; *see also* internet
Sorenson, Richard 124
Soviet Union 90
spaghetti harvest 80
Spanish-American war 57–58, 61, 62
Spanish Civil War 61
Spectator 42
spin 53, 57, 60, 63, 100
Spotlight 173
stage plays 139, 146
Stalin, Joseph 60
Stanley/Livingstone meeting 55–56
Stanton, Frank 70
Staple of News, The 27, 39
Star Chamber 37, 39, 40
Stationers' Company 37, 38, 40
Station WLS, Chicago 75
statistics 125–126
Statue of Liberty plinth 57
Stead, W. T. 55, 58
Steiner, Melchoir 194
Sterling, Raheem 98
strange newes 11, 25–26, 81
Strange newes from Lancaster 26
Strange Signes 25–26
Stratton Oakmont, Inc. v. Prodigy Services, Inc. 148–149
structuralism 122–123
stunts 55–57, 71, 128, 173
subjective journalism 198, 199
subjectivity 162–163, 196
Suez invasion 78
suicides 168–169
Sun 10, 60, 100, 171
Supreme Court, US 74, 148, 150, 153
Surrender of Tournavos, The 61
susceptibility hypothesis 169

Taliya News, At 189
technology 36, 54, 63–64, 92, 147, 171
Technology Rules, OK hypothesis 186
Telecommunications Act (US, 1996) 150
Telefonico Hirondel, Budapest 65, 72
telephones 64
television 78–80, 91; regulation 79, 80
Thames Television 80
theatre 139, 146
The Hill 6
The Onion 97
thick description 121, 125, 127
Thirty Years' War 36–37, 38–39

Thomas of Monmouth 189, 190
Thompson, Hunter S. 11, 195
Thurber, James 91
Tidings 21, 23, 35
Times 193
Times Newes 39
Tinbergen, Nikolaas 115
To the Christian Nobility of the German Nation 24
Trakle Waida (devil prince) 19
Treaty of Versailles 76
Trenchard, Thomas 50
Trethowan, Ian 79
troubadours 19
Troubles 79, 80
True and frightening new tidings 21
True And Wonderfull 26–27
Trump, Donald J. 46, 160, 161; fake news 12, 98, 99
Trump Shuttle 98
truth 3–4, 5, 7, 10, 11, 13, 50, 51, 156–157, 158–159, 166–167, 174, 195
Truthful News of Conquest of Placentz and Parma 21
Tserclaes, Johannes 39
Tuchman, Gaye 5, 195, 198
Tunisian revolution 90
Turkish Pyracies, The 39
Twinning, William 134
Twin Towers 182–183, 188
Twitter 89
Two-Step Flow 167

Ufa-Tonwoche newsreel 63
UK (United Kingdom) 137–138, 139, 140–142, 146; radio 76–78, 79, 91; riots 91, 141–142; television 78–79, 80; theatre 139, 146
Umma 90
United Airlines 183
Universal Declaration of Human Rights (UN, 1948) 136, 146, 167
University J-Schools 166
US (United States) 65, 139, 140, 146
Uses and Gratifications model 167, 186–187
Utilitarian Ethics 158

van Buren, Martin 55
van der Keer, Peter 37, 38
Veles, Macedonia 179
Verhoeven, Abraham 35
Veseler, George 37, 38
videogames 181, 182

Vietnam war 93
Villiers, Frederick 61
Vitagraph 62
Vlad the Impaler 19–20; *see also* Dracula
von Aitzing, Michael 35
von Fisch, Karl 115
voting influences 52–53, 99–100, 171, 179–180, 181

Walpole, Robert 139
War of Independence, US 193, 194
War of the Worlds, The 69, 70–71, 75, 167
Washington, George 166, 193, 194
Washington Post 80–81, 101, 152, 188
Watson, John 113
Web 2.0 84, 151, 152, 182, 195
Weiner, Anthony 188
Welles, Orson 70, 71, 75, 167
Wellington, Duke of 140
Werther Effect 168–170
Westboro Baptist Church 99
White Mountain, Battle of the 38
WHO (World Health Organization) 170
Wikileaks 80, 93–94, 99, 127
Wikipedia 88
William of Norwich 189–190
Williams, Walter 101
wireless telephony 72
Wonderful and strange newes 25
woodcuts 20, 25, 35
World Health Organization *see* WHO (World Health Organization)
World Trade Center 182–183, 188
World Wide Web 147, 148
Wyden, Ron 149, 150

Yellow Press 56, 128, 197
Yeo, Eileen 127
YouTube videos 188

Zeitung 35
Zeyttungg 21, 35
Zinoviev, Grigori 52
Zinoviev Letter 52–53, 80
Žižek, Slavoj 93
Zuckerberg, Mark 150, 152–153, 180